AMERICAN FILM CYCLES

AMERICAN
FILM
CYCLES

REFRAMING
GENRES,
SCREENING
SOCIAL
PROBLEMS,
& DEFINING
SUBCULTURES

AMANDA
ANN
KLEIN

University of
Texas Press

AUSTIN

An earlier version of Chapter 3, titled "From Greaser to Gangsta: The Changing Face of the Filmic Juvenile Delinquent," appeared in the anthology *Media(ted) Deviance and Social Otherness: Interrogating Influential Representations*, edited by Kylo-Patrick Hart (Cambridge: Cambridge Scholars Press, 2007). Published with the permission of Cambridge Scholars Publishing.

Requests for permission to reproduce material from this work should be sent to:
   Permissions
   University of Texas Press
   P.O. Box 7819
   Austin, TX 78713-7819
   www.utexas.edu/utpress/about/bpermission.html

♾ The paper used in this book meets the minimum requirements of ANSI/NISO Z39.48-1992 (R1997) (Permanence of Paper).

LIBRARY OF CONGRESS CATALOGING-IN-PUBLICATION DATA
Klein, Amanda Ann, 1976–
   American film cycles : reframing genres, screening social problems, and defining subcultures / Amanda Ann Klein. — 1st ed.
      p. cm.
   Includes bibliographical references and index.
   ISBN 978-0-292-72680-2 (cloth : alk. paper) —
ISBN 978-0-292-73541-5 (e-book)
   1. Film genres—United States.   2. Motion pictures—Social aspects—United States.   I. Title.
   PN1993.5.U6K525   2011
   302.23'43—dc23
                                        2011021427

For Zach, Maisy, and Jude

ACKNOWLEDGMENTS

The successful completion of this project would not have been possible without the financial support of the English Department of the University of Pittsburgh and the intellectual support of its faculty and students. In particular, I would like to extend my gratitude to the members of my dissertation committee, including Lucy Fischer, Jane Feuer, Neepa Majumdar, and Paula Massood, for their encouragement, suggestions, and feedback. This book was conceived and nurtured through exposure to their teaching and professional work and through individual meetings and discussions. I feel extremely fortunate to have worked with such a brilliant and supportive group of scholars. I especially want to thank Lucy Fischer, my dissertation chair, for investing her time, energy, and care in my academic career in general and in this project in particular.

I am also indebted to the friends, colleagues, and professors I met during my graduate work at the University of Pittsburgh. These individuals read countless drafts of these chapters in various stages: Kara Andersen, Amy Borden, Molly Brown, Christine Feldman, Brenda Glascott, Tara Lockhart, Moya Luckett, and Kirsten Strayer. I am thankful for their intellectual support, which aided me in the completion of my degree, and their friendship, which helped me survive the completion of my degree.

I extend my gratitude to my writing group at East Carolina University, the fabulous "Femidemics": Anna Froula, Marame Gueye, Su-ching Huang, Anne Mallory, and Marianne Montgomery. Their thoughtful suggestions and critiques helped me to chisel my unwieldy dissertation into a coherent book. I am also eternally grateful to the English department at East Carolina University for providing me with the time, support, and encouragement to pursue my ambitious research agenda.

My appreciation goes also to the editorial staff at the University of Texas Press, in particular Jim Burr, for believing in this project and guiding it to publication. Jim's diligence and willingness to answer my questions at any hour of the day made my first experience with publishing a book a true pleasure. I also thank Kip Keller, copy editor, for his diligent editing and Lynne F. Chapman, manuscript editor, for cheerfully leading me through the final steps of the publication process. I am grateful to my outside readers, Rick Altman and Tim Shary. Not only has their work served as an inspiration throughout the writing of this book, but their insightful comments were also invaluable to the revision process.

I thank my family, Sally, Joseph, and Adam Klein, for their support of my career path, interest in my work, and pride in my accomplishments.

I thank my husband, Zach Woodmansee, for his love, patience, and willingness to let me fill our Netflix queue with titles like *Leprechaun 5: Leprechaun in the Hood* (2000, Rob Spera). For more than a decade, he has fostered the stable and nurturing environment in which my ambitions could come to fruition. I cannot thank him enough for his support. Lastly, I thank my children, Maisy and Jude, who always give me a good reason to turn off my computer and go play.

AMERICAN FILM CYCLES

LOVE AT FIRST SIGHT

The *John C. Rice–May Irwin Kiss* (1896, William Heise), later known simply as *The Kiss*, is believed to be the first sex act captured by the cinema (Linda Williams, *Screening Sex*, 27). For most of the film's brief running time, the famous actors build anticipation for the embrace promised by the film's simple title.[1] They press their cheeks together lovingly and utter what appear to be "sweet nothings." Then, in the final seconds of the film, Rice pulls away from Irwin, twiddles his mustache, grabs her face as she turns toward him, and kisses her on the mouth.[2] *The Kiss* is hardly an erotic spectacle; indeed, its stars seem to be more amused than amorous as they cuddle and then kiss. But the film was unprecedented in offering audiences an opportunity not just to see a man and a woman kiss, but also to see this act in a medium close-up, a viewing position that would have been improper in real life. *The Kiss*'s strategic use of the medium close-up allowed for what Linda Williams has described as the "anatomization" of the sex act; the film provided voyeurs with a socially acceptable venue for examining the previously intimate, hidden act of kissing (*Screening Sex*, 27). It should not be surprising then that *The Kiss* was one of the earliest films to generate calls for censorship of the medium (Lewis, *American Film*, 24); one Chicago journalist, Herbert Stone, described the film as "absolutely disgusting" and demanded "police interference" (quoted in Dave Thompson, *Black and White*, 21). The moral outcry over the film is also one of the reasons why *The Kiss* was the most popular film produced by Thomas Edison's company that year (Auerbach, "Valentine Day's Feature").

The success of *The Kiss* spawned a series of imitators, each offering its own unique variation on the subject of kissing, including *The Soldier's Courtship* (1896, Alfred Moul and Robert W. Paul), *The Am-*

The Kiss (1896) offered audiences the first opportunity to see a sex act up close.

orous Guardsman (1898, British Mutoscope and Biograph Company), and *Tommy Atkins in the Park* (1898, Robert W. Paul). Once the financial viability of films depicting kissing was proved, early filmmakers capitalized on this successful subject by finding more creative ways to stage on-screen kisses; *The Kiss* is merely the image of a man and a woman kissing, while *Hanging Out the Clothes* (1897, G. A. Smith) stages the same events among drying garments. The proliferation of these kissing films highlights how the representation and display of sexuality was an important aspect of early cinema and its appeal (Linda Williams, *Screening Sex*, 27). In addition to kissing films, early cinema audiences also enjoyed short films that captured the movement of trains entering and exiting the film frame, such as *Arrival of the Train at La Ciotat* (1895, Auguste and Louis Lumiére). Filmmakers also mounted cameras onto the sides of moving trains in order to capture the movement of locomotives through space. These "phantom rides," as they were called, placed the viewer in the perspective of a passenger on a train. Films depicting trains and train movement brought together two emblems of modernity—mass transportation and the cinema. These symbols of modernity—like the city itself—were simultaneously frightening and fascinating to audiences of the time.[3]

Nervy Nat Kisses the Bride (1904) provided another variation on the "kissing on a train" film.

Given the success of on-screen kisses and phantom train rides as subjects in early cinema, it is not surprising that in 1899, the British filmmaker G. A. Smith decided to unite these two very popular, though seemingly unrelated, short film subjects in *The Kiss in the Tunnel*. In this brief film, a man takes advantage of the darkness created when the train enters a tunnel in order to kiss his female companion. *The Kiss in the Tunnel* established a viable new formula in early cinema, with imitators like *The Kiss in the Tunnel* (1899, James Banforth), *Love in a Railroad Train* (1902, S. Lubin), and *What Happened in the Tunnel* (1903, Edwin S. Porter) released in response. This new formula was so successful that one British film distributor, the Warwick Trading Company, offered film exhibitors the brief shot of a couple kissing inside a train car, which could be spliced into footage they had already purchased of trains exiting and entering tunnels (Gray, "*The Kiss in the Tunnel*," 57). By adding one new shot to their existing reels, exhibitors could update an overworked formula and generate more revenue with little financial or creative investment.

This brief history of the kissing film and its later iterations reveals that just a few years after the invention of moving pictures, filmmakers had already developed a production strategy resembling the modern film cycle. Like film genres, film cycles are a series of films associated with each other through shared images, characters, settings, plots, or themes. However, while film genres are primarily defined by the repetition of key images (their semantics) and themes (their syntax), film cycles are primarily defined by how they are used (their pragmatics). In other words, the formation and longevity of film cycles are a direct result of their immediate financial viability as well as the public discourses circulating around them, including film reviews, director interviews, studio-issued press kits, movie posters, theatrical trailers, and media coverage. Because they are so dependent on audience desires, film cycles are also subject to defined time constraints: most film cycles are financially viable for only five to ten years. After that point, a cycle must be updated or altered in order to continue to turn a profit.

A film cycle will form only if its originary film—the film that establishes the images, plot formulas, and themes for the entire cycle—is financially or critically successful. That is, the originary film must either draw a large audience or become a subject of discussion in the media. The buzz (financial or critical) surrounding the originary film convinces other filmmakers to make films that replicate the successful elements of that film, thus forming a cycle. The "kissing cycle" of the 1890s was formed because producers identified the most successful element of *The Kiss*—the chance to ogle two people kissing—and repeated or updated that formula in other films. The kissing cycle continued to grow as producers combined the successful kissing formula with other audience-pleasing formulas (such as phantom rides). These later films exploited contemporary interests in train movement, images of illicit behavior, and the burgeoning language of the multishot film. These subjects were chosen based on the desires (and anxieties) of the moviegoing audience rather than on the filmmakers' desire for artistic expression. Therefore, even in these early years of cinematic experimentation, when distributors like Edison Motion Pictures and the Warwick Trading Company were still determining how best to exploit the new invention of cinema, a basic truism of the industry was established: if audiences enjoy a film, it is wise to copy all or part of that film in another release.

This brief case study also indicates that film cycles predate film genres, the cycle's more established, better-understood relative. Indeed, there are countless books, articles, and college courses devoted to genre theory and film genres—taking approaches from the psychoanalytic to the anthropological to the ideological—but nothing substantial has been written or theorized about the nature and function of film cycles. It seems that film cycles receive critical attention only after they "grow up" to become stable genres. In this book, I argue that film cycles are not subgenres, minigenres, or nascent film genres; they are their own entity and a subject worthy of their own study. The study of cycles offers an important complement to traditional genre studies by questioning how generic structures have been researched, defined, and understood. Cycle studies' focus on cinema's use value—the way that filmmakers, audiences, film reviewers, advertisements, and cultural discourses interact with and affect the film text—offers a more pragmatic, localized approach to genre history. The various case studies in this book also illustrate the utility of the film cycle in broadening our understanding of established film genres, articulating and building upon beliefs about contemporary social problems, shaping and disseminating deviant subcultures, and exploiting and reflecting upon racial and political upheaval.

THE ABSENT CYCLE

The film cycle is a relatively unexplored topic of study. Although the term "cycle" appears in books devoted to film genres, it is generally referenced as an afterthought; a particular cycle of films might be mentioned, or "cycle" might be used interchangeably with "genre." Many film scholars have conducted in-depth studies of select film cycles, including blaxploitation films, biker films, and gross-out comedies, but only a few books discuss (however briefly) what the film cycle is, how it functions, and how it is different from the film genre.[4] For example, in *Genre and Hollywood*, Steve Neale offers a concrete definition of film cycles as "groups of films made within a specific and limited time-span, and founded, for the most part, on the characteristics of individual commercial success" (9). But this definition represents the extent of Neale's engagement with the film cycle and its function. The editors of *Mob Culture: Hidden Histories of the American Gangster Film* define cycles in their introduction as "small, nuanced groupings of films that are not transhistorical and often only operate within one or two seasons of production, whereas trends are broad and inclusive categories made up of interconnected cycles" (Grieveson, Sonnet, and Stanfield, 3–4). The volume goes on to analyze the gangster genre through the lens of its production cycles, but does not engage in any further definition of film cycles. In *Film/Genre*, Rick Altman offers the most detailed account of the film cycle. He defines the film cycle as a group of films that are associated with a single studio and that contain similar, easily exploitable features (61).[5] According to Altman, genres develop out of cycles only when they are able to establish a "balance" between a stable syntax and a stable semantics. He adds that film cycles serve as "adjectives" to the genre's "nouns": "Just as Kleenex tissues were soon referred to simply as *Kleenex*, and eventually reduced to the 'generic' term *kleenex*, so *musical comedy* became the *musical*" (62). Here and elsewhere, cycles are generally understood as messy structures in flux, poised either to become stable genres or to disappear quickly. As a result, film cycles have proved to be a difficult object of study. Nevertheless, film cycles are fascinating precisely because they resist neat categorizations and have the potential to disrupt or complicate the discrete categories frequently generated by genre studies.

Another reason film cycles have not been studied is because they are so transparently associated with commercialism and artlessness. Arthur Asa Berger has suggested that works of narrative art form a continuum: at one end of this continuum are works of "absolute originality and uniqueness," and at the other end are works of "slavish repetition" (*Popular Culture Genres*, 46). He adds, "Genre works tend to be conventional; works of elite art are often closer to the inventive pole" (47). Indeed, filmmakers who associate their craft with high art avoid making films that simply repeat the plots, characters, and themes of previously successful films, or that appear to pander to the audience's every whim. Unlike works of elite art, the film cycles discussed in this book are all examples of "slavish repetition." They were not created for the purposes of elevating public taste but, rather, to provide audiences with versions of the same images, characters, and plots that they enjoyed in previous films. Because the motives of the film cycle are so seemingly transparent—to cater to audience desires in order to turn a profit—they are rarely subject to critical analysis. Film cycles are simply cultural ephemera cranked out to capitalize on current events, trends, fads, and the success of other films.

Film cycles have also been marginalized in critical, popular, and academic discourses because of their often-deviant subject matter. The creators of film cycles lure moviegoers into the theaters by exploiting their interest in licentious, sensational, or even dangerous imagery. Indeed, most film cycles can be categorized as exploitation films. Eric Schaefer argues that classic exploitation films, which developed alongside but separate from classical Hollywood cinema (c. 1929–1960), depicted "unacceptable topics" and images, such as the spread of venereal disease, the creation of leper colonies, or the banishment of unwed mothers to convents. These images, which were normally invisible or covered over within mainstream cinema, were made visible and central in the exploitation film. Audiences went to

Advertisements for exploitation films like *Because of Eve* (1948) promised an experience they did not necessarily deliver.

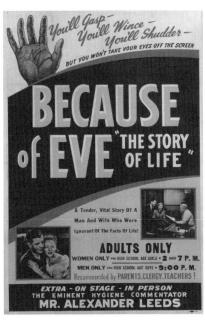

see these films not for their stars or their high-profile story properties, but because they showcased the spectacle of the unknown and the forbidden ("Of Hygiene and Hollywood," 34). This focus on a forbidden spectacle serves as the classic exploitation film's "organizing sensibility—at the expense of others" (Schaefer, *Bold! Daring! Shocking!*, 4–6). Several of the cycles discussed in this book—including the juvenile-delinquent-themed teenpic and the ghetto action cycle—likewise base their appeal on the showcasing of forbidden or sensational imagery.

Another defining feature of the exploitation film is its reliance on ballyhoo as a promotional strategy. Eric Schaefer defines "ballyhoo" as "that noisy, vulgar spiel that drew audiences to circuses and sideshows . . . a hyperbolic excess of words and images that sparked the imagination" (*Bold! Daring! Shocking!*, 103). Ballyhoo promises its audiences something—an image, an experience, or reaction—that it does not necessarily fulfill. The unfulfilled promises of ballyhoo are one of the more striking aspects of exploitation advertising: images and slogans are often an exaggeration—and occasionally, a complete misrepresentation—of what occurs in the film itself. Schaefer explains, "A[n exploitation] film could be completely misrepresented by the advertising and could disappoint spectators, yet the ballyhoo that preceded it was part of the overall entertainment experience, a fact the audience evidently recognized and appreciated and in which they were complicit" (111). Many of the film cycles discussed in this book, particularly the juvenile-delinquent-themed teenpic and the ghetto action cycle, were advertised based on the promise of providing an experience they did not always fulfill. For example, the promotional trailers and theatrical posters for ghetto action films like *Boyz N the Hood* (1991, John Singleton) and *Juice* (1992, Ernest R. Dickerson) implied that these films were violent and antisocial. However, both films promoted strong antiviolence messages and condemned the very mentality that their advertising copy promoted.

Like the classic exploitation film, which posed a threat to the mainstream film industry because it was diametrically opposed to "the definition of what constituted a 'better film'" (Schaefer, *Bold! Daring! Shocking!*, 156), the majority of the films discussed in this book stand in opposition to what is commonly thought of as "quality cinema." According to Eric Schaefer, the Production Code Administration was formed in 1934 to "reinforce the conception of Hollywood film as something morally unobjectionable, narratively coherent, plausible, realistic and noneducational" (156). The case studies discussed in this book violate this ideal view of the classic Hollywood film in that they are often morally objectionable, narratively incoherent, or unrealistic. Furthermore, all the cycles I discuss in this book aim to educate their audiences in some way—about the corrupting power of city living (melodramatic gangster films), the plight of the post-Depression street urchin (Dead End Kids films), the power of rock 'n' roll and fast cars to corrupt today's youth (teenpics), and the temptations of gang life for African American youth living in the nation's postindustrial ghettos (the ghetto action cycle).

The film cycle is a commodity to be assembled, packaged, and sold as quickly as possible, not a timeless piece of art. Thus, the contemporaneity of the cycle has also contributed to its marginalized status in the field of film studies. Genre films were once saddled with a similar stigma; up until the 1960s and 1970s, most American audiences and critics dismissed American genre films as cookie-cutter products on a studio production line.[6] But with the development of auteur theory and the application of structuralism to the study of American genre films, film genres took on a greater cultural significance, effectively breaking down "the artificial distinctions between art and entertainment" (Schatz, *Hollywood Genres*, 8). Genre studies of the 1970s argued that genre films tapped into timeless cultural mythologies, performed the function of mass rituals, or offered their audiences a necessary form of psychological release.[7] As Rick Altman points out: "Likening genre to myth provides clear gains for genre theorists. This strategy provides an organizing principle for genre study, transmuting what might have been a hollow commercial formula into a culturally functional category, and thus lending the prestigious support of cultural anthropology to the heretofore lowly study of popular genres" (*Film/Genre*, 20). The study of film genres gained cultural capital once they were associated with timelessness—or what audiences are interested in watching for decades to come. Film cycles, by contrast, value timeliness—or what audiences are interested in watching right now.

Although its timeliness links the film cycle with "low culture" and the masses, it is precisely this quality that makes film cycles useful social documents. Because cycles form within a shorter frame of time than film genres do, it is easier to make conclusive statements about their use and function. For example, the melodramatic gangster cycle I examine in Chapter 1 is an intrageneric cycle. That is, it is one of several smaller film cycles that exist within the larger gangster genre. Breaking a large genre, like the gangster film, into its smaller, intrageneric cycles can facilitate a more detailed, nuanced understanding of that genre.[8] While the study of genres reveals the stories that audiences are drawn to over a period of decades, its intrageneric cycles can serve as a cross-section of one specific moment in time, accurately revealing the state of contemporary politics, prevalent social ideologies, aesthetic trends, and popular desires and anxieties. The same can be said of the intergeneric cycles discussed in Chapters 2 through 4. Intergeneric cycles begin their existence as independent entities rather than as part of a larger film genre (though many individual entries within these cycles could also be categorized as belonging to a specific genre).[9] Like intrageneric cycles, intergeneric cycles are able to capitalize on a sentiment or trend, thus offering film historians a time capsule of the cultural moment.

Finally, the accessibility of the cycle—its ability to give audiences exactly what they want—is yet another factor that has marginalized film cycles, since it further separates these films from the world of elite art. The pleasures to be gained from elite art are not instantly accessible—they require work, even years of study, on the part of the art lover. Pierre Bourdieu argues that "the encounter with a work of art is not 'love at first sight' as is generally supposed, and the act of empathy *Einfühlung*, which is the art-lover's pleasure, presupposes an act of cognition, a decoding operation, which implies the implementation of a cognitive acquirement, a cultural code" (*Distinction*, 3). This opposition between "love at first sight" and acquired cultural capital necessarily implies a class bias, since only select members of the moviegoing audience have the resources to obtain this cultural capital. Bourdieu argues that the lower and working classes are not predisposed to view art objects with detachment, since their livelihoods depend on a constant, active engagement with the material world. By contrast, "the denial of lower, coarse, vulgar, venal, servile . . . enjoyment, which constitutes the sacred sphere of culture, implies an affirmation of the superiority of those who can be satisfied with the sublimated, refined, disinterested, gratuitous, distinguished pleasures forever closed to the profane" (7). Bourdieu concludes that cultural consumption fulfills the social function of legitimating social differences, famously claiming that "taste classifies, and it classifies the classifier" (6). Designations of taste also work to keep certain ideas, images, and texts in "their place."

Bourdieu's work has two important implications for the films and cycles discussed in this book. First, "bad" or maligned art objects are most frequently those whose pleasures are easily accessed and immediately apparent. Special knowledge or training is not required in order to enjoy the slapstick interactions between Huntz Hall and Leo Gorcey in an East Side Kids comedy like *Clancy Street Boys* (1943, William Beaudine). This film seeks to provide an immediate pleasure to the audience by replicating the images, plots, and conventions of previous East Side Kids films in order to generate a quick laugh or an easy scare. Of course, all films seek to gratify their audiences in some way. Even those films that attempt to deny the audience certain filmic pleasures—such as a coherent narrative or competent acting—nevertheless gratify those viewers who seek out precisely this kind of viewing experience.[10] However, the desire to please and to fulfill audience expectations defines the East Side Kids cycle above all else. These films were made only because producers believed that replicating a previous formula would fill theater seats; they were not concerned with garnering positive reviews or Academy Award nominations. Film cycles exist to please their audiences, and as soon as they are unable to fulfill that function, they must adapt.

Bourdieu's work also highlights how audiences become "classified"—as uneducated, as lower class, or as an Other—by choosing to watch certain films. For example, fans of 1950s juvenile-delinquent-themed teenpics were, more often than not, teenagers. These generational Others, whose tastes were newly acquired and thus ripe for exploitation by producers, were a source of concern for contemporary adults and moral entrepreneurs. Similarly, public discourses surrounding the 1990s ghetto action cycle characterized it as a cycle that attracted dangerous, gun- and knife-wielding Others into safe, suburban movie theaters. This cycle threatened to turn otherwise calm, nonviolent viewers into that dangerous entity. Audiences of the ghetto action cycle were, consequently, subjected to preemptive discussions of the films' controversial content (and occasionally, heightened security measures) in order to contain the (alleged) threat of violence that lurked in the images on screen. In the case of all four cycles examined in this book, these questions of taste are what ultimately contributed to their marginalization in film history or to the limited ways in which they have been documented and analyzed.

CYCLE VERSUS GENRE

If the relationship between audiences and genre films can be described as a long-term commitment with a protracted history and a deep sense of familiarity, then audiences' relationship with the film cycle is analogous to "love at first sight." There is an instant attraction—represented in concrete terms by box-office dollars, media buzz, or, less frequently, critical success—that leads to the creation of a cycle. But what prompts an audience to fall in love with a particular film or group of films? Usually, the originary film that launches a cycle taps into a subject of contemporary relevance, something in which the audience is already emotional invested. In the 1890s, audiences were titillated by the possibilities of the cinematic medium and its ability to depict an intimate sexual moment, so it makes sense that kissing films would be successful (Linda Williams, *Screening Sex*, 27). But it is important to keep in mind that not every successful film has the ability to start a film cycle. The originary film must have a set of images that are recognizable enough to be easily duplicated in several more films. *Forrest Gump* (1994, Robert Zemeckis), to name one prominent counterexample, was a critical and financial hit at the time of its release. *Forrest Gump* was the top-grossing film of 1994 and won six Academy Awards, including those for Best Picture, Best Actor, and Best Screenplay. The film also generated several catch phrases ("Life is like a box of chocolates . . . you never know what you're going to get") that became a fixture of popular culture. However, *Forrest Gump*'s most successful elements—its folksy, handicapped protagonist and its historical vignettes—could not be easily duplicated in a series of films. Consequently, this successful film did not lead to the establishment of a film cycle.

In order to form, film cycles need a successful originary film with easily reproducible elements. Films within the successful slasher cycle of the 1970s and 1980s, including *The Texas Chainsaw Massacre*

(1974, Tobe Hooper), *Halloween* (1978, John Carpenter), and *A Nightmare on Elm Street* (1984, Wes Craven), replicate scenes of teenage slaughter and sexual dalliances. Similarly, Judd Apatow's comedies of the 2000s, such as *The 40 Year Old Virgin* (2005) and *Knocked Up* (2007), focus on schlemiel protagonists who end up winning over audiences as well as the girl of their dreams. Audiences who regularly seek out these films are paying to see these particular elements replicated in film after film. Of course, early entries in a film cycle are not always created to capitalize upon the success of the originary film. Occasionally, the similarities between early films in a cycle are the result of some sociocultural cue—a new artistic trend, a social problem, a political movement, or a defining world event—that several filmmakers decide to address independently of one another. For instance, although the popularity of *Rebel without a Cause* (1955, Nicholas Ray) and *Blackboard Jungle* (1955, Richard Brooks) led to the formation of the 1950s juvenile-delinquent-themed teenpic cycle, the films were not released in response to each other or with the explicit aim of creating a film cycle aimed at teenagers.[11] Rather, both films were marketed to adult audiences as social problem films about youth running wild. As I discuss in Chapter 3, these two films unintentionally tapped into the teen zeitgeist at a time when the teenage moviegoing audience was becoming increasingly important to studios. The films' success with teenagers was a happy accident. Once their success with teenage audiences had been proved, however, the iconography, formulas, conventions, and themes of these juvenile-delinquent-themed teenpics were purposely repeated in new films in an attempt to hold on to the lucrative youth demographic.

Steve Neale labels this process "systemization," or the repetition and exploitation of a film's most marketable elements (*Genre*, 51). Rick Altman has another name for this process: the "Producer's Game":

1. From box-office information, identify a successful film.
2. Analyse the film in order to discover what made it successful.
3. Make another film stressing the assumed formula for success.
4. Check box-office information on the new film and reassess the success formula accordingly.
5. Use the revised formula as a basis for another film.
6. Continue the process indefinitely. (*Film/Genre* 38)

Both Neale's and Altman's models are descriptions of how film genres form. However, these models are also appropriate for describing cycle formation, since both structures are dependent on the desires, interests, and belief systems of the audience. So if cycles and genres appear to form in the same way and for the same reasons, how are they different?

Cycles differ from genres when it comes to their topicality; a film cycle needs to repeat the same images and plots over and over within a relatively short period of time. A cycle must capitalize on an audience's interest in a subject before it moves on to something else. For example, in 2004, the gory, serial-killer film *Saw* (James Wan) was a huge box-office hit.[12] Noting *Saw*'s overwhelming financial success, studios seized upon on the formula, releasing films that reused the most successful elements of the originary film: a killer with little plausible motivation for his killings, seemingly random victims, and, most importantly, extended, graphic scenes of torture and violence. These films, including titles like *Hostel* (2005, Eli Roth), *Wolf Creek* (2005, Greg McLean), *The Devil's Rejects* (2005, Rob Zombie), *Last House on the Left* (2009, Dennis Iliadis), and, of course, the various *Saw* sequels, were soon collectively referred to as "torture porn," a label highlighting the cycle's emphasis on gratuitous, fetishized violence (Cochrane, "For Your Entertainment").[13] This cycle formed for two reasons. First, the box-office numbers for these films were high. In 2004, *Saw* made $18 million its opening weekend, but its 2005 sequel made more than $31 million. The next three installments continued to pull in a $30 million opening weekend. Second, the torture-porn cycle garnered a lot of attention in the press, with critics attempting to pinpoint why audiences were so interested in these gruesome films.[14]

The torture-porn cycle demonstrates how film cycles are created to fit the contours of audience desires in precise ways, responding to audience needs at every turn. The success of this cycle in the 2000s is clearly linked to burgeoning American anxieties over the atrocities committed in, and as a result of, America's ongoing war in Iraq (2002–2010), but also to the availability of images of real-life torture and death, such as the recorded and widely circulated executions of Daniel Pearl in 2002 and Saddam Hussein in 2006, and the photographs of torture and humiliation leaked from Abu Ghraib in 2004. The filmmakers responsible for the early films in the torture-porn cycle might not have been aware of the timeliness of their products. However, as public discourses began to increasingly view this cycle as one addressing contemporary anxieties, such as the torture debate, filmmakers began to insert overt references to contemporary concerns. For example, *Saw VI* (Kevin Greutert), released in the fall of 2009, depicts the prolonged torture of the CEO of a health insurance company who routinely denies coverage to patients (including the Jigsaw Killer himself). This movie, in which the corrupt health insurance industry is made to suffer for its transgressions, was tailor made to coincide with the nation's heated debates over health care reform, which had been raging throughout 2009. Here we can see how entries in a film cycle both repeat key elements from previously successful films and alter certain elements in order to attract and maintain audience interest.

However, a film cycle can only court the audience for so long. Early entries in the *Saw* cycle averaged $30 million in their opening weekends, but *Saw VI* made just $14 million. So what happened? Between 2005 and 2009, filmmakers flooded the market with gruesome images of torture, and this rapid increase in torture-porn films over a short period of time led to a critical backlash. This backlash is best exemplified by the outcry over billboards advertising *Captivity* (2007, Roland Joffé), a film about the kidnapping and torture of a young woman (Elisha Cuthbert). The billboards, which were placed all over Los Angeles, featured graphic images of Cuthbert bound, nude, or comatose. Los Angeles residents, including members of the film and television community, expressed outrage over *Captivity*'s advertising campaign in a series of editorials.[15] One of the campaign's most prominent critics, Joss Whedon, published an open letter to the Motion Picture Association of America: "The ad campaign for 'Captivity' is not only a literal sign of the collapse of humanity, it's an assault. I've watched plenty of horror—in fact I've made my share. But the advent of torture-porn and the total dehumanizing not just of women (though they always come first) but of all human beings has made horror a largely unpalatable genre. This ad campaign is part of something dangerous and repulsive, and that act of aggression has to be answered" (quoted in Soloway, "Remove the Rating for *Captivity*"). Whedon's comments are reflective of most of the complaints directed at the torture-porn cycle as a whole. Audiences were likewise disgusted with its imagery, and by 2009, the formula had ceased to be financially viable. The production of torture-porn-style films slowed down the following year; in 2010, the producers of the *Saw* franchise announced that *Saw 3-D* (2010, Kevin Greutert) would be the last film in the series (Bowles, "Final Cut for Horror Franchise"). Audiences may fall in love with cycles quickly, but if those same audiences lose interest in a particular cycle, they may become annoyed or frustrated if it continues to be produced for too long.

This frustration with film cycles that overstay their welcome occasionally leads to the appearance of cycle parodies. According to S. Craig Watkins, the appearance of a film like *Don't Be a Menace to*

The controversial billboard for the torture-porn film *Captivity* (2007) enraged critics inside and outside the film industry.

South Central While Drinking Your Juice in the Hood (1996, Paris Barclay), a parody of the 1990s ghetto action cycle, "signaled both the popularity and waning appeal of one of the most intriguing film production trends of the 1990s . . . it suggested that the narrative strategies, conventions and formulae that made up the cycle had become predictable, worn and clichéd" ("Ghetto Reelness," 236). The appearance of a parody acknowledges that a particular film cycle's themes and images have lost their ability to communicate with the audience as they once did, even as they capitalize on and profit from the past success of the very films they are lampooning.[16] Both cycles and genres are subject to parody if their images and themes are repeated too often in a short period of time. However, compared with film cycles, film genres can better withstand these interludes of audience apathy, exhaustion, or annoyance. Westerns, to name one prominent example, enjoy periods of intense audience interest as well as more fallow periods, when audience interest wanes. This genre was extremely popular during the silent era. Tag Gallagher estimates that between 1909 and 1915, "there were probably more Westerns released *each* month than during the entire decade of the 1930s" ("Shoot Out," 265). But with the adoption of sound technology in the late 1920s and the audience's concomitant interest in films with urban themes, major Hollywood studios curtailed their production of westerns. Consequently, throughout the 1930s, the western genre appeared mostly in the form of low-budget, B-serial films or "singing cowboy" pictures. Then, starting in the late 1930s, with the success of films like *Stagecoach* (1939, John Ford) and *Destry Rides Again* (1939, George Marshall), the western returned to its former widespread popularity (Schatz, *Hollywood Genres*, 47). This rise-and-fall pattern has continued throughout the history of the western.

Film genres are equipped to weather such periods of audience uninterest for several reasons. First, film genres are founded on a large corpus of films that accumulates for decades. Westerns were well established, with a corpus of thousands of films, by the time audiences began to lose interest in the genre in the 1930s. Second, the basic syntax or themes of the most established genres—including the gangster film and the western—address a profound psychological need in their audiences. As Judith Hess Wright argues, "When we return to the complexities of the society in which we live, the same conflicts assert themselves, so we return to genre films for easy comfort and solace—hence their popularity" ("Genre Films," 43). For better or worse, film genres endure for decades at a time because they fulfill a need in their audiences. Thus, the marks of established genres are stability, longevity, and resilience. By contrast, the appeal of the film cycle is based less on its syntax and more on its semantics, including its plots, characters, and imagery. The semantics of the film cycle are crafted to reflect a facet of the contemporary moment—a popular film, a social problem, a cultural trend. Therefore, film cycles are far more bound to the whims of contemporary tastes than genres. Once interest in a particular set of semantic elements wanes, the corresponding film cycle will cease to make money at the box office. Studios will stop making films that replicate those semantic elements, and the film cycle appears to end altogether.[17]

Another difference between cycles and genres lies in the way they communicate with audiences. The longevity of film genres and the vastness of their corpora make them highly informative and allow viewers to formulate decisions about the films they choose to see; describing a film as a "western" provides the viewer with a wealth of information in an instant—about its basic iconography, its themes, and its likely narrative resolution—even if such preconceived notions do not ultimately play out in each individual western film (Kaminsky, *American Film Genres*, 2). A viewer sitting down to watch a revisionist western like *The Assassination of Jesse James by the Coward Robert Ford* (2007, Andrew Dominik) has decades of westerns with which to contextualize this new viewing experience. And even if a viewer has not seen a single western before seeing this film, popular culture itself is steeped in western mythology.

Cycles, by contrast, are unable to offer audiences the same kind of knowledge and viewing positions offered by established genres. Audiences approach film cycles with some knowledge of what to expect—

The semantic elements of a western like *Stagecoach* (1939) are instantly recognizable to fans of the genre.

based on their viewing of one or two previous films in the cycle or on public discourses surrounding the cycle—but these elements are not nearly as codified as they are in genre films. In hindsight, it is possible to study a film cycle and identify its visual and thematic elements (as I will be doing in this book), but at the time of their release, films early in a cycle are too new to provide audiences with the same class of information that is provided by film genres. Compared with film genres, film cycles are far less stable objects of study.

This leads to another difference between cycles and genres—their perceived "stability." Rick Altman best codified the concept of generic stability in his seminal essay "A Semantic/Syntactic Approach to Film Genre," which analyzes genre through both its semantics and its syntax. The semantics of the gangster film include the city setting, a minority protagonist, and the spectacular death of the gangster at the film's conclusion, while the gangster film's syntax is the opposition between the needs of the individual and the needs of society (Sobchack, "Genre Film," 110). The semantic approach to genre study creates a large, inclusive corpus for a genre, while the syntactic approach is more limiting, creating a more exclusive corpus. Altman argues that when defining a genre and its corpus of representative films, scholars should combine these two approaches in order to create the most accurate picture. Furthermore, a stable genre, according to Altman, is one that has struck a balance between its semantics and its syntax: "The Hollywood genres that have proven most durable are precisely those that have established the most coherent syntax (the Western, the musical); those that disappear the quickest depend on recurring semantic elements, never developing a stable syntax (reporter, catastrophe, and big-caper films to name a few" ("Semantic/Syntactic Approach," 39). For example, the Dead End Kids films of the 1930s and 1940s (which I discuss at length in Chapter 2) retain a coherent set of semantics (the same troupe of actors, an urban setting, and plots in which the boys cause trouble and get caught) but not a stable syntax (early films in the cycle were social problem films, while later examples ranged from comedies to horror films to westerns to war propaganda). Their lack of a stable syntax characterizes these films as a cycle rather than a genre.

However, Altman later complicated his model of genre study when he argued in favor of a "semantic/syntactic/pragmatic" approach. This revised approach moves beyond the study of a film's surface meanings and its deep structure in order to bring in a third factor, the uses or applications of a film or genre: "Like reception study, a semantic/syntactic/pragmatic approach refuses determinacy to textual structures taken alone, but in addition it acknowledges the difficulty of extracting those textual structures from the institutions and social habits that frame them and lend them the appearance of making meaning on their own. While pragmatic analysis sometimes destabilizes meaning by showing just how dependent it is on particular uses of a text or genre, at other times it succeeds in revealing the meaning-grounding institutions that make meaning seem to arise directly out of semantics and syntax" (*Film/Genre*, 211). Pragmatics, the "use factor" of genres, demands that we understand genre films not just as sets of images and themes, but as texts that are used—by audiences, producers, exhibitors, and even cultural agencies (Altman, *Film/Genre*, 210). Indeed, one of the most well-known models of genre criticism is "a triangle composed of artist/film/audience" (Ryall, "Teaching through Genre," 28). Ryall's model implies a give-and-take relationship among the film, those who create it, and those who consume it. He adds that unlike other critical models, genre criticism is useful in that it "conforms most closely to the way in which the popular audience actually views the films" (29). Cycle studies complements the approaches laid out by Altman and Ryall by offering an even more detailed look at the pragmatics of popular cinema. If film genres are a macro view of Ryall's triangle metaphor—providing a broad, generalized view of a culture over time—then film cycles are a micro view—providing small, detailed snapshots of that culture at a single moment in time. Cycles are capable of producing these detailed snapshots because they have such an intimate relationship with the culture that produces them.

As the title of this chapter states, the audience's relationship with a film cycle is one of love at first sight. Once audiences fall in love with the originary film, studios will scramble to replicate its most successful elements. Since cycles exist in order to capitalize upon the success of a particular cinematic formula, their raison d'être is their resemblance to, rather than their difference from, previous films. However, in their attempt to capitalize on audience desires before they cool down, film studios actually hasten the film cycle's demise. Like a lover who is too eager to please, the film cycle eventually bores or annoys the audience, which stops paying to see these films. And the moment that a film cycle begins to falter at the box office, film studios will either heavily revise the original formula or cease making the cycle altogether. Relationships forged in the passions of love at first sight often cool down quickly. Indeed, once the audience tires of a film cycle, they quickly move on to the next love object. Cycles, as microstructures with smaller, more fickle fan bases, are more strongly affected by their audience's whims and desires.

One final difference between film genres and film cycles lies in their functionality for the film historian. A general tendency when initiating a genre study has been to ignore texts that complicate a genre's accepted blueprint and act as exceptions to the rule. More often than not, a genre ends up being defined by a few central, or "classic," texts, or those texts that conform to one critic's definition of a particular genre. This traditional approach to genre is fundamentally ahistorical, marginalizing texts that could enrich, rather than detract from, our understanding of a genre, its context, its function, and even its aesthetics. Thus, rigidity and discrete categorizations mark the long history of genre studies, despite the fact that "genre is, tacitly, a loose assemblage of cultural forms shaped by social conflict and historical vicissitude" (Browne, *Refiguring Genres*, xiii). The more established a genre has become, the more that is written about it. And the more that is written and theorized about a genre, the more its history becomes obscured: "Most genre studies cover their traces, erasing all evidence of the constitution of a corpus, the choice of categories, and the development of terminology, thus leaving the reader methodologically where he/she started, able only to borrow other people's conclusions" (Altman, *American Film Musical*, 126).

However, recent books, like Rick Altman's *Film/Genre*, Steve Neale's *Genre and Hollywood*, and Nick Browne's collection *Refiguring American Film Genres: Theory and History* attempt to correct this problem by reinserting history into genre studies. These studies employ historical and archival evidence to question and complicate the way genres have traditionally been defined and used, and to recognize the fluidity and mutability of generic terminology and categories. Cycle studies extend the innovative work begun in these books by using the study of film cycles as a way to understand how culture, industry, and economics, that is, how history, affects how and why certain films are grouped and understood together.

Because the majority of the films discussed in this book were released quickly, with small budgets, they were better able to capitalize on the contemporary moment than films that took months or years to go from conception to theatrical release. We can therefore view film cycles as a mold placed over the zeitgeist, which, when pulled away, reveals the contours, fissures, and complicated patterns of the contemporary moment. By revisiting the sites of their release, promotion, and reception, we can not only understand how and why these films fell to the margins (and the ideology and politics behind their outlaw status), but also expand the way film studies documents and theorizes the history of cinema. These kinds of films are significant not so much because of what they are, but because of why they were made, why studios believed that they were a smart investment, why audiences went to see them, and why they eventually stopped being produced. Any film or film cycle, no matter its budget or subject matter, has the potential to reveal a wealth of information about the studio that made it and the audience that went to see it. This aspect of film history, which is so often ignored in traditional genre studies, is illuminated by cycle studies.

OUTLINE OF THE BOOK

American Film Cycles is a series of case studies of prominent film cycles: the melodramatic gangster film of the 1920s, the 1930s Dead End Kids cycle, the 1950s juvenile-delinquent-themed teenpic cycle, and the 1990s ghetto action cycle. Although some of these film cycles are more well known (ghetto action) than others (Dead End Kids), I have chosen these four cycles because were all made in reaction to a particular social anxiety, problem, or crisis, and such cycles resonate particularly strongly with their audiences. These films are tied to anxieties about urbanization, crime, and the slow creep of moral corruption from its presumed breeding ground in the nation's cities into the suburbs. Concerns over the supposed threat posed by the American city space date back to the early 1900s, and are also bound up with apprehension over the cinema and its corrupting influence on audiences. Both moviegoing and life in the congested modern city of the early 1900s were indicative of modernity and were thought to create "crowd consciousness," or a loss of individuality, characterized by an individual's inability to distinguish between reality and fantasy.[18] The cycles studied in this book illustrate this enduring fear of cinema's potential to alter its audience in some way. Their alleged corrupting potential explains why these cycles were able both to draw fans into theaters and to repel them. Furthermore, this book addresses not just the films themselves, but also their political, social, and aesthetic function in American culture, as well as their multiple, competing histories. To that end, this book situates these films in several historical trajectories: the Progressive movement of the 1910s, the beginnings of America's involvement in World War II, the emergence of an influential teenage consumer group in the 1950s, and the drug and gangbanger crises of the early 1990s. Traces of these events are immanent in these film cycles. Close readings, not just of the films but also of the films in the context of their cycles, offer new ways of understanding how the popular imagination interprets moments of social change, and how the film industry seeks to capitalize on these interpretations.

In Chapter 1, "Real Gangsters Do Cry: A Cyclical Approach to Film Genres," I build on the work of critics like Rick Altman and Tag Gallagher, who have argued that, as a critical and explanatory tool, the evolutionary model of generic change, based on a fetishization of the genre's so-called classic stage, is ahistorical, bending history to the needs of the interpretative frame being used and limiting our understanding of that genre. Once a genre, its corpus, and its recurrent characteristics are sketched out (a necessary first step in any genre study), we must step back from the "center" of a genre, where many genre studies begin and end, and instead venture out to the "borders" of its generic corpus, where the films that do not fully comply with the rules of the genre reside. Therefore, this chapter focuses on early gangster films with redemptive endings, including *Regeneration* (1915, Raoul Walsh) and *Underworld* (1927, Josef von Sternberg), which have been marginalized in studies of the genre due to their links with melodrama.

Melodrama has been viewed, historically, as a low-culture phenomenon, belonging to the "masses" and to women. Its visceral satisfactions, which seek to pull in rather than to distance the viewer, are often characterized as being antithetical to the more masculine, tragic structure of the classic gangster cycle. This chapter focuses on an intrageneric cycle in order to demonstrate the significance of cycle studies to the broader field of genre. I argue that the marginalized redemption cycle is actually quite significant within the larger gangster genre and offers an understanding of the many functions served by the cinematic gangster. Though consideration of these "border texts" complicates the traditional, neat generic map, this cyclical approach to genre, which confers as much generic weight on *Underworld* as it does on the "classic" gangster film *Scarface* (1932, Howard Hawks), has far more explanatory power than traditional studies. I argue that it is more illuminating to study a genre as a series of cycles rather than as a monolithic entity broken down into discrete stages of evolutionary development.

Though Chapter 1 abandons the concept of generic evolution, Chapter 2, "A Dying Serpent: Understanding How Film Cycles Change over Time," recuperates this model by theorizing what cycle evolution might look like. I argue that while generic evolution ultimately fails the test of history, we can accurately trace cycle evolution, since cycles are local, time-bound structures. I analyze the social problem film, looking at the Dead End Kids cycle (1937–1939) and its B-movie spin-offs in order to theorize how cycles originate, flourish, and change over time. The chapter takes a historical-materialist perspective on the film cycle—tracked primarily by how public discourses issued by the press, the studios, and critics reacted to each new entry in each cycle—in order to paint a picture of the social and cultural context on which a viewer's reading of these films is at least partially predicated. I discuss how the original Dead End Kids cycle successfully exploited real and media-generated concerns about the contemporary plight of urban youth. Over time, this cycle became less effective at generating sympathy for this pressing social problem, and the various spin-offs of the Dead End Kids films ultimately adopted the syntax of other genres, like the comedy and the horror film. Thus, the same images that had induced viewers to cry in the original Dead End Kids cycle generated laughter in later cycles. The chapter addresses how and why certain images or tropes, no matter how far they stray from their original context, never disappear from popular culture, despite the common use of the word "death" in genre studies.

While Chapter 2 investigates how and why cycles grow in reaction to the audience and contemporary politics, Chapter 3, "I Was a Teenage Film Cycle: The Relationship between Youth Subcultures and

Film Cycles," investigates a particular type of audience interaction—the synergistic relationship between subcultures and their parent cultures—and its manifestation in a film cycle: the 1950s juvenile-delinquent-themed teenpic. This successful cycle, which includes entries like *Teenage Doll* (1957, Roger Corman) and *I Was a Teenage Werewolf* (1957, Gene Fowler, Jr.), exploited fears about contemporary controversial topics, which eventually snowballed into widespread moral panics over the newly emerging concepts of the "teenager," "juvenile delinquency," and rock 'n' roll music. Building on the work of Dick Hebdige, Thomas Doherty, and Stuart Hall, among others, the chapter traces how deviant subcultural signifiers come to be exploited for profit and how they lose their subcultural appeal once they become too identified with the mainstream. While many models of subcultural theory—building on the work of the influential Birmingham school—argue that subcultures are intrinsically resistant to mainstream culture and that there is a definitive line between a subculture and its parent culture, film cycles confirm that there is a constant exchange of elements between the two. An analysis of teen-targeted magazines, advertising strategies, and the teenpic cycle reveals that the producers of these films were invested in maintaining, rather than dulling, each subculture's authenticity as a way to keep their exploitative hook sharp. Mainstream culture was therefore integral to the definition and formation of this deviant youth subculture, with the economic motivations of the former acting as a catalyst, rather than a deterrent, for the growth of the latter. The study of film cycles reveals another way that subcultures and so-called mainstream culture are highly dependent upon each other.

Chapter 4, "Not Only Screen but the Projector as Well: The Relationship between Race and Film Cycles," examines the fraught relationship between African Americans—on the screen, behind the camera, and in the audience—and American commercial cinema by looking at how race and contemporary fears over the relationship between race, urbanity, and violence led to the formation of a highly successful film cycle. Much has been written about the ghetto action cycle, so I focus on how these films were conceived, packaged, distributed, and recognized.[19] By understanding the motivations of the films' producers and the politics of the films' audiences, we can get a clear picture of the racial climate of the early 1990s. In particular, this chapter analyzes the highly publicized outbreaks of theater violence at the screenings of ghetto action films like *Boyz N the Hood* and *Juice*, as well as the studios' skill at incorporating the media's inflated coverage of this violence into their advertising campaigns. The

CHAPTER 1

REAL GANGSTERS DO CRY
A CYCLICAL APPROACH
TO FILM GENRES

Toward the end of *The Public Enemy* (1931), the tough-as-nails gangster hero, Tom Powers (James Cagney), avenges the murder of his
best friend, Matt Doyle (Edward Woods), by launching a surprise attack against Schemer Burns. Burns and at least eight members of his
gang are holed up in the Western Chemical Company warehouse, and
Tom is alone, armed with just two revolvers. The audience knows that
this is a suicide mission, but the gangster hero is so grief-stricken and
enraged by his friend's death that he does not realize, or care, that the
odds are against him. As Tom approaches the warehouse in the pour-
ing rain, he smiles before entering; he is going to enjoy this. However,
because of the restrictions on screen violence dictated by the newly
formed Production Code Administration (PCA), the audience is not
privy to the bloody action that takes place inside.[1] Instead, the camera remains outside of the warehouse. Within a few moments, we hear
a cacophony of gunshots and shouting, culminating with the sounds
of a man's dying howls. Tom soon emerges from the warehouse, and it
is clear that he has been seriously injured. The camera, which has so
far remained at a distance, cuts to a medium close-up of the gangster.
This new perspective allows the audience to see Tom cough and wince
in pain, just before he tumbles forward onto the sidewalk. Although
it appears that Tom is down for the count, he summons the strength
to pull himself up one more time in order to launch both of his pistols
through the windows of the warehouse. By now, the offscreen wails
of police sirens have become louder, spurring Tom to make his get-
away. Framed by a floor-level camera, he shambles along the street
gutters, an appropriate visual metaphor, since gangsters are often referred to as coming "from the gutter."[2] He is able to stand upright for
only a brief moment before falling to his knees. The camera cuts again

At the conclusion of *The Public Enemy* (1931), Tommy Powers (James Cagney) whimpers, "I'm not so tough."

to a medium close-up, focusing the viewer's attention on Tom's defeated face. He looks upward and says to no one in particular, "I ain't so tough," before collapsing to the ground. The screen fades to black.

Tom's final comment—an admission of weakness—seems out of place, given that he is a gangster hero, a "tough guy." As Martha Nochimson writes, "No one seeing this film for the first time expects a statement of vulnerability here; indeed, the timeless cultural spin on Cagney creates anticipation of pugnacity" (*Dying to Belong*, 34). The statement is also unexpected because the gangster hero is typically described by critics of the genre as being a "product of his harsh environment, violent, laconic and tough" (Baxter, "The Gangster Film," 29). The gangster is "no sickly, effeminate weakling," but instead "a tough guy whose position resulted from a commanding physical presence and exceptional prowess in the various arts of violence" (Ruth, *Inventing the Public Enemy*, 93). The gangster is also a man of action. He is a man who does things; things are not done to him.[3] But at this extreme moment of vulnerability, Tom admits that despite what we have seen in the first half of the film and despite the way the gangster is so often understood in American culture, he is not "so tough." His suffering is made visible through medium close-ups that highlight his agonized visage. He lost control of a situation he intended to master and became victim instead of victimizer. He is weak, flawed, and therefore pitiable. In other words, this scene paints the gangster hero as his seeming antithesis: the melodramatic hero. In this way, *The Public Enemy* violates the tough "masculine" tone so often associated with the gangster film, by injecting the comparatively soft, "feminine" mode of melodrama.

The melodramatic qualities of *The Public Enemy* are further amplified in the following scene, in which Tom is resting in a hospital bed, swathed in white bandages. Tom's mother (Beryl Mercer) enters the room and calls out softly, "Tom? Tommy boy? Do you know me?" As Tom slowly opens his eyes, it is clear that he is a changed man. His characteristic sneer has disappeared. He no longer looks like a menacing "public enemy." Instead, he looks like the chastened little boy his mother calls to mind when she repeatedly refers to him as her "baby." Mrs. Powers and Tom's older brother, Mike (Donald Cook), seat themselves on the edge of his bed, each clutching a hand. The contrite gangster then tells his distraught family, "I'm sorry." "Sorry for what?" Mike asks. "Just . . . sorry. You know." Tom's last-minute repentance—in which he apologizes to his family for leading a life of vice, corruption, and murder—redeems him in the nick of time. In the next scene, Tom's mother joyfully prepares for her son's return from the hospital. But Tom, who has been kidnapped by his enemies, returns home as a bullet-ridden corpse instead. We see his trussed-up body teeter over the doorframe, framed in a low angle, so that it seems to fall right on top of the viewer. Mrs. Powers's phonograph, which had been playing a happy song, "I'm Forever Blowing Bubbles," reaches the end of its tune. All we can hear is the sound of the phonograph needle on the record as Tom's brother solemnly moves out of the frame, presumably to break the bad news to his mother. Tom's in-the-nick-of-time redemption may have reconciled him with his family, but it came too late to save his life.

The Public Enemy is frequently described as a "classical" gangster film, that is, as one of the three films epitomizing the semantics and syntax of the entire gangster genre, along with *Scarface* (1932, Howard Hawks) and *Little Caesar* (1930, Mervyn LeRoy). According to the classical formula, the gangster dies unrepentant, still believing in his supremacy over others. The audience, which once identified with the gangster, is then encouraged to celebrate the reestablishment of law and order and the elimination of the gangster's antisocial drives. Despite the fact that *The Public Enemy* is viewed as a crystallization of the gangster film, as part of the classical cycle, its final scenes appear to defy the genre's central traits. Tom's death is not the result of the reestablishment of the social order. Schemer Burns's gang, not the police, kills Tom. Criminals, not society, exact justice. And although Tom's death can be viewed as a just payment for his immoral life, Burns's gang, painted as more ruthless and dangerous than the boys working for Paddy Ryan (Robert O'Connor), remains free. Such an ending—in which the hero suffers, repents for his sins, dies, and invokes the audience's empathy—seems more characteristic of the melodrama than the gangster film.

With its emphasis on emotion over action, and on the internal over the external, the melodrama is typically viewed as antithetical to the gangster film and other so-called masculine genres (Elsaesser, "Tales of Sound and Fury," 379–383). Viewers of tragedies know in advance that the hero will die or suffer. There are no surprising reversals or revelations, which allows for a certain emotional distance between viewer and narrative. But in the melodrama, the possibility of redemption, death, or both is always there, up until the film's final or penultimate scene. Audiences remain attached to the narrative, waiting to be carried emotionally from moment to moment. The melodrama's visceral satisfactions, which pull in rather than distance the viewer, are in opposition to the more highbrow, tragic structure of the classical gangster cycle. Christine Gledhill points out that "as drama [melodrama] represented debased or *failed tragedy* . . . in fiction it constituted a fall from the seriousness and maturity of the realist novel. . . . In this respect melodrama was at the beginning of the century constituted as the anti-value for the critical field in which tragedy and realism became cornerstones of 'high' cultural value" ("Melodramatic Field," 5; emphasis added). Thus, melodrama has historically been viewed as a low-culture phenomenon, belonging to the "masses" and to women (Merritt, "Melodrama," 25; Gledhill, "Melodramatic Field," 6). Consequently, gangster films that feature a suffering gangster's redemption, such as *Regeneration* (1915, Raoul Walsh) or *Underworld* (1927, Josef von Sternberg), are typically labeled as "preclassical" or "experimental," that is, as texts that are marginal to the basic gangster blueprint. The presence of melodrama in a gangster film precludes it from being considered central to the genre.

Rather than reading Tom Powers's redemption and melodramatic death as marginal to the genre, this chapter argues that the melodramatic conventions, thematics, and characters found in *The Public Enemy* as well as earlier gangster films like *Regeneration* and *Underworld* are central to the definition of the gangster genre as a whole. Analyzing the significance of such "border texts," or those that do not occupy a central place in a genre's corpus and do not wholly live up to the genre's most central criteria, activates a wider range of meanings within a genre. These meanings are normally discounted, marginalized, or glossed over in genre studies because they do not fit within the narrow parameters established by the classical cycle.[4] When we abandon this concept of a classical cycle, based on a linear, synchronic, evolutionary model of generic change, we are able to acknowledge the significance of all texts that contribute to the vast pool of generic elements composing the gangster genre. To that end, this chapter examines one particular production cycle within the larger gangster genre—the melodramatic redemption cycle of the gangster film. Although this intrageneric film cycle first appeared in the 1910s and continued to play a prominent role in the gangster genre up until the early 1930s, its significance to the genre as a whole has remained hidden in most critical accounts of the gangster genre. This chapter will uncover what an analysis of the melodramatic redemption cycle can add to our understanding of the gangster film's history and thematics.

GENERIC EVOLUTION AND THE CLASSICAL CYCLE

According to Henri Focillon's seminal work *The Life of Forms in Art*, there are four defined evolutionary stages in the life of an art form: "Experimental," "Classical," "Refinement," and "Baroque" (10). Focillon believes that these patterns of change move in a prescribed order—from straightforward interpretations of the form to increasingly self-conscious interpretations. Texts preceding the classical stage are considered undeveloped or experimental examples of the form, while texts following the classical stage are presumably more self-reflexive, stylized, or parodic (11–15). Prominent genre theorists like Thomas Schatz and John Cawelti have adopted Focillon's theories as a method for grappling with how genres grow and change over time. Cawelti applies Focillon's theories specifically to the final stage of a genre's evolution, the baroque stage, when a genre parodies itself. He argues that the appearance of a film parody acknowledges that a particular cultural product has fully saturated the audience. Cawelti explains that the presence of genre parody also signals "the tendency of genres to exhaust themselves, to our growing historical awareness of modern popular culture, and finally, to the decline of the underlying mythology on which traditional genres have been based" (*"Chinatown,"* 260). In his influential book *Hollywood Genres*, Schatz uses Focillon's categories as a useful way to describe "a genre's progression from transparency to opacity—from straightforward storytelling to self-conscious formalism," arguing that this evolution represents a genre's "effort to explain itself, to address and evaluate its very status as a popular form" (38).

According to these theories of generic evolution, a film genre that has reached its classical stage is defined by "stability, security, following upon experimental unrest" (Focillon, *Forms in Art*, 11). The classical stage is the moment when "the narrative formula and the film medium work together to transmit and reinforce that genre's social message . . . as directly as possible to the audience" (Schatz, *Hollywood Genres*, 38). While establishing and privileging a genre's classical stage is appealing, since it provides stable definitions and critical tidiness for an unwieldy body of heterogeneous texts, genre scholars like Tag Gallagher and Rick Altman have suggested that it is also inadequate for understanding how genres and their meanings grow, change, and proliferate in and through time. The classical stage—the point at which a genre and its meanings are supposed to be familiar to the audience, when its semantics and syntax are most identifiable, and when the genre in question is in its most transparent form—fixes and stabilizes a structure that is inherently mercurial.[5] Most problematically, as Altman has argued, an evolutionary model discounts the historicity of genre formations (*Film/Genre*, 22). The editors of *Mob Culture: Hidden Histories of the American Gangster Film* add: "In the formation of an idea of genre based on exclusionary principles, work on the gangster film falsifies the realities of Hollywood's production practices and the contexts in which films were received"; such scholarship serves "the need of the critic at the cost of historical record" (Grieveson, Sonnet, and Stanfield, 3). The fetishization of the classical cycle highlights the significant role that the film critic plays in shaping and defining genres, as well as the damage this process inflicts on film history.

Much like Andrew Tudor's "empiricist dilemma," which questions how it is possible to define a genre without first defining a corpus of representative films (and vice versa), the concept of the evolutionary model in genre studies frequently precedes the evidence of its existence.[6] In the case of the gangster genre, critics first focused on three primary texts (the classical cycle) and then placed the films that preceded and followed these texts—films made before 1930 and after 1932—into predetermined evolutionary stages. This approach to generic change is "entirely arbitrary, with the result that there is some disagreement about which pictures are 'classical' and which have evolved *astray*" (Gallagher, "Shoot Out," 264; emphasis added). The evolutionary model of generic change privileges certain films, making them central, while texts that drift from this model are placed on the margins of the genre.

Films in the gangster genre are usually discussed as being more or less faithful variations on the themes and images established in the classical cycle of *Little Caesar, The Public Enemy*, and *Scarface*. However, this privileging of the classical cycle discounts the almost seventy-five gangster or gangster-themed films that were released before *Little Caesar* (Rosow, *Born to Lose*, 395–396). With successful silent entries like *Regeneration, Underworld*, and *The Racket* (1928, Lewis Milestone), and talkies like *The Racketeer* (1929, Howard Higgin), *Lights of New York* (1928, Bryan Foy), and *The Doorway to Hell* (1930, Archie Mayo), why do so many critics contend that the gangster film did not reach maturity until the appearance of the classical cycle? Why are the same three texts used to define a genre that has existed since the early 1900s?[7]

Fran Mason's response to this question is that the privileging of the classical cycle is a catch-22; the classical cycle has come to define the gangster genre because genre scholars have decided that the classical cycle defines the gangster genre. Jonathan Munby adds: "These three films have probably selected themselves as 'classics' because of the way they *stand out* rather than fit into the bulk of gangster film production at the time"; with their overt depiction of class conflict and unrest, these three films were more violent and incendiary than the gangster films that preceded them (*Public Enemies*, 16). The consequent backlash from industry censors brought these films increased attention over the course of film history, further solidifying their outlaw status.

The valorization of the 1930s classical cycle is also tied to the general impression conjured up by this decade in film history. As Robert Sklar explains, "When talk of the movies turns ethereal—when words like *magic* and *myth*, *glamour* and *legend* crop up—it immediately evokes, for most people, images from 1930s Hollywood" (*History of the Medium*, 182). The star system had been fully developed by the 1930s, and vibrant performers like Fred Astaire, Ginger Rogers, Cary Grant, Clark Gable, and Katharine Hepburn became larger-than-life personalities for an American public in need of an upbeat worldview. Likewise, the stars of the classical cycle, Paul Muni, Edward G. Robinson, and James Cagney, were themselves highly charismatic movie stars cast in memorable roles. In particular, Cagney's "mannered performance of ethnic urbanity" in *The Public Enemy* "provided a model of behavior that was both easily imitated and immediately recognizable precisely because it was codified as a set of reiterable gestures"

(Maltby, "Why Boys Go Wrong," 56); most movie buffs can do an on-the-fly Cagney or Robinson impression. Given the convergence of these factors in the 1930s, as well as the introduction of sound and the general need for cheap entertainment during the Great Depression, it is not surprising that this trio of gangster films fixed themselves in the minds of critics and audiences as being indicative of the genre.

Fran Mason also believes that because the genre's seminal critical text, Robert Warshow's "The Gangster as Tragic Hero," focused primarily on *Scarface* and *Little Caesar*, "many critics have followed Warshow in identifying common themes within this period which have come to be seen as timeless dominants of the entire genre" (*American Gangster Cinema*, 7). So what are these timeless dominants described by Warshow? Perhaps the most prominent semantic element of the genre is its urban setting: "The gangster is the man of the city, with the city's language and knowledge, with its queer and dishonest skills and its terrible daring. . . . For the gangster there is only the city; he must inhabit it in order to personify it: not the real city, but that dangerous and sad city of the imagination which is so much more important, which is the modern world" ("Gangster as Tragic Hero," 131). In the world of the gangster film, the city is, like the gangster's marginal status, inextricably linked to criminality. Being a product of the city, the gangster also knows how to use it to his advantage. For instance, the opening sequence of *The Public Enemy* emphasizes the facility with which the two young boys (who will eventually grow up to be gangsters) navigate their urban terrain when chased by the police (Mason, *American Gangster Cinema*, 17). By depicting the boys' ability to move through a complex and dangerous urban space in unconventional ways (they slide down the escalator's rails to escape the pursuing police), the film foreshadows how the city can both protect its inhabitants and corrupt them. The city of the gangster film is also synonymous with modernity. The tools of the gangster's trade—the telephone, the automobile, and, most importantly, the tommy gun—are all products of modernity and the city (McArthur, *Underworld USA*, 28).

Warshow also argues that "the typical gangster film presents a steady upward progress followed by a very precipitate fall" ("Gangster as Tragic Hero," 132). Many critics consider this "rise and fall" narrative, in which the gangster is gunned down or arrested at the height of his success, to be central to the gangster genre in general and to the classical cycle in particular.[8] The rise and fall of *Little Caesar*'s Rico Bandello (Edward G. Robinson), for example, is marked vi-

Automobiles and other examples of modern technology become weapons in gangster films like *Scarface* (1932).

sually by the urban locations he inhabits throughout the film. In the film's opening scene, Rico is eating a plate of spaghetti at the counter of a small country diner. At the height of his career, his cohorts toast him at a flower-strewn banquet table at the Palermo Club. And we know that Rico has hit rock bottom when he checks into a flophouse advertising "Clean Beds 15¢." Given his precipitous fall, it is not surprising that Rico is gunned down in the next scene by his righteous nemesis, Detective Flaherty (Thomas E. Jackson). Likewise, in *Scarface*, Tony Camonte (Paul Muni) is killed only after reaching his nadir. In fact, Warshow attributes the gangster's demise *to* his success: "The very conditions of success make it impossible not to be alone, for success is always the establishment of an individual pre-eminence that must be imposed on others, in whom it automatically arouses hatred" (133). Tony dies shortly after his sister, Cesca (Ann Dvorak), the only person who still loves him, is fatally wounded. In the classical gangster film, to be alone is to die.

Finally, Warshow bases much of his argument in "The Gangster as Tragic Hero" on the belief that the genre's basic conflict is the individual versus society. He argues that the gangster's disenchantment with the opportunities that America offers to the uneducated immigrant (usually, mind-numbing wage labor) serves as a critique of the

American Dream and the idea that anyone who works hard enough can climb the ladder of social and financial success. In the gangster narrative, working a socially acceptable, nine-to-five job is equated with a kind of living death. In *Wiseguy: Life in a Mafia Family*, which was later adapted for the screen as *Goodfellas* (1990, Martin Scorsese), Nicholas Pileggi writes, "Anyone who stood waiting his turn on the American pay line was beneath [the wiseguy's] contempt. . . . They were the timid, law-abiding, pension-plan creatures neutered by compliance and waiting their turn to die. To wiseguys 'working guys' were already dead" (36–37). The gangster's antisocial reaction to the long-revered American values of hard work, sacrifice, obedience to authority, and deferred gratification is, according to Warshow, central to the character's appeal ("Gangster as Tragic Hero," 130). In his rejection of social expectations, the classical gangster hero "speaks for us," living out the audience's generalized fantasies of rejecting compliance and authority. The gangster, Warshow tells us, "is what we want to be and what we are afraid we may become" (131).

In addition to his antiestablishment behaviors, the gangster is an attractive figure because there is a part of the audience that also fears and despises him. As a result, whether he dies or goes to jail, "we gain the double satisfaction of participating vicariously in the gangster's sadism and then seeing it turned against the gangster himself" (Warshow, "Gangster as Tragic Hero," 131–132). The classical gangster film revels in the prolonged, painful death of its protagonist: *Scarface*'s Tony Camonte is gunned down by multiple policemen when he "turns yellow" (just as Guarino predicted), and Rico Bandello is shot down like a dog, hiding in a dark back alley, at the conclusion of *Little Caesar*. The bloody resolutions of classical gangster films also serve an ideological function, acting as warnings to the audience that transgressing the moral and social order will inevitably be punished. If the gangster is allowed to remain unpunished at the film's conclusion, then society might begin to question the appeal of obeying the law. Richard Maltby adds that in the 1930s, "the gangster pictures contributed to [the] scapegoating of an ethnic stereotype of criminality," making the gangster "an embodiment of guilt to be expiated" ("Spectacle of Criminality," 141). It was thus a mark of Hollywood's own ideological confusion in the early 1930s that characters like Tony, Rico, and Tom could simultaneously be both glorified heroes and stereotypes reinforcing the xenophobic beliefs of numerous Americans (Munby, *Public Enemies*, 63).

A major problem with defining the gangster film by the "dominant traits" I have just outlined is that this privileging serves to shut down other, competing meanings found in the genre. The films of the classical cycle are not definitive of the entire gangster genre; they merely represent the defining moment of one particular cycle of the gangster film. Furthermore, even among the three films of the classical cycle, there remain significant differences. For example, one of the most well-documented conventions of this cycle, its rise-and-fall narrative structure, is not found in *The Public Enemy*. Tom Powers, while he accumulates more wealth and power over the course of the film's narrative than he began with, never reaches a position of power placing him "alone at the top." When Tom is murdered at the film's climax, it is not because he has reached the peak of his success (and therefore needs to be eliminated), but because he foolishly attempted to avenge the death of his best friend, Matt. Steve Neale points out that by ignoring the significance of the gangster films released before the classical cycle, critics "are led to view films like *The Musketeers of Pig Alley* (1912, D. W. Griffith) and *Underworld* as isolated examples rather than as participants in distinct generic trends, and to underestimate the extent to which gangsters and gangster films had existed in various well-established forms prior to the advent of *Little Caesar*" (*Genre and Hollywood*, 79). Esther Sonnet adds: "Even a small sample of films produced during the 1929–1931 season indicates that *Little Caesar* and *The Public Enemy* were *atypical* in their concentration on the individual life history of the ambitious loner gangster" ("Ladies Love Brutes," 93).

Rather than a series of discrete developmental stages moving along a linear track, the gangster genre is more accurately described as a series of cycles, that is, as smaller groupings of films that appear at particular historical moments, thrive for a period of time, and then cease to be produced when interest in a subject wanes. A cyclical view of genres not only bolsters the arguments proffered by critics like Altman, Neale, and Gallagher, who discount the idea of a classical stage and generic evolution, but also provides a more nuanced account of the social, historical, and industrial factors behind the creation of genre films (Grieveson, Sonnet, and Stanfield, *Mob Culture*, 3). The contributions that so-called preclassical films like *Underworld* and *Regeneration* made to the gangster genre have been devalued because they are not indicative of the classical cycle. As I will demonstrate, this melodramatic-redemption cycle is central and significant to the gangster genre and continues to exert an influence on more recent gangster films and television programs, such as *Menace II Soci-*

ety (1993, Allen and Albert Hughes), *Casino* (1995, Martin Scorsese), *Road to Perdition* (2002, Sam Mendes), and *The Sopranos* (1999–2007), among others.

THE IMPORTANCE OF MELODRAMA IN THE GANGSTER FILM

Thomas Schatz opens his chapter on the gangster film in *Hollywood Genres* with the following statements: "The gangster genre has had a peculiar history. The narrative formula seemed to *spring from nowhere* in the early 1930s, when its conventions were isolated and refined in a series of immensely popular films" (81; emphasis added). Schatz's analysis of the gangster film is well researched and has been influential in the field, but his privileging of the classical cycle does damage to genre history; clearly, the genre's narrative formulas sprang from somewhere. Focusing on the classic cycle ignores variations and anomalies in order to create continuity and stability in a genre's definition. Likewise, in his seminal study of the gangster film, *Underworld USA*, Colin McArthur states, "There had, of course, been crime films before *Little Caesar* (1930), but they cannot, iconographically or thematically, be called gangster films" (34). McArthur's explanation for why a film like *Underworld* is not a true gangster film is that it lacks the plot formulas associated with the classical cycle: the film's protagonist, Bull Weed (George Bancroft), is a thief rather than a bootlegger and the plot lacks a discernible rise-and-fall structure.[9] But this justification for privileging the classical cycle is circular: films released before *Little Caesar* cannot be considered gangster films because they are not like *Little Caesar*.

McArthur also excludes *Underworld* from a central place within the gangster genre because it is a silent film. The introduction of sound, in 1927, is thought to have brought the gangster film to generic maturity because it signaled a new cinematic realism (Clarens, *Crime Movies*, 34): "The addition of sound is key in the development of the genre because the diegetic sounds of gangster language, gunshots, and the screeching of tyres, as well as the background noises of the city environment, more fully evoked the modern world that the gangster inhabited than the dark backstreet slums of the silent gangster film" (Mason, *American Gangster Cinema*, 4). Thomas Schatz adds that Hollywood's conversion to sound, combined with "America's desperate social and economic climate," was the primary catalyst in the formation of the gangster film's classical cycle, encouraging directors to "develop a fast-paced narrative and editing style" (*Hollywood Genres*, 83). Similarly, Eugene Rosow explains: "By 1930, the sound of gang-

ster films had established a realistic tone as one of the genre's qualities" (*Born to Lose*, 133). Jack Shadoian believes that "the addition of
sound gave the gangster film a true potency" (*Dreams and Dead Ends*,
33), while Martha Nochimson writes that "silent American gangster
films lack that sense of modern discontinuity that characterizes what
we recognize as the American gangster's experience of his world" (*Dying to Belong*, 110). But even if we accept the premise that sound enabled filmmakers to generate a more realistic, modern, urban milieu
and encouraged the snappy dialogue characteristic of city-based films
from the 1930s (particularly those scripts written by former journalist Ben Hecht), there is no clear indication why a realistic milieu or
fast-paced dialogue should be considered essential ingredients of the
gangster film.[10] The critic's explanation for the significance of sound
to the development of the gangster film is invariably solipsistic.

One reason why silent gangster films are considered "preclassical," and thus marginal to the gangster genre, is the association of
silent films with the oft-maligned category of "melodrama." Russell
Merritt has argued that the silent melodrama is considered "old fashioned" and antithetical to the realistic look, sound, and subject matter of "modern" sound films ("Melodrama," 29). Indeed, when discussing silent gangster films, including texts like *Regeneration*, *The Penalty*
(1920, Wallace Worsley), and *Underworld*, Mason puts them in the category of "old fashioned melodrama" (*American Gangster Cinema*, 1).
Mason acknowledges that these silent gangster films did have an impact on sound gangster films, but he clarifies that these films had an
impact on the genre in spite of the fact that they were "strongly based
in melodrama" (3). Thomas Schatz adds: "*Underworld* appears rather
rudimentary because of its lack of sound effects and dialogue, as well
as its dependence upon the conventions of silent melodrama" (*Hollywood Genres*, 85). Even early sound films like *The Doorway to Hell* are
excluded from the center of the genre's corpus because of their tendency "to reiterate the melodramatic form and ideology of the silent
gangster film" (Mason, *American Gangster Cinema*, 5). Here we can see
how films that are labeled "preclassical" are most often those texts
that can be aligned with melodrama.

Before attending to why melodrama is, in fact, integral to the gangster genre, we need to parse just what is meant by the term "melodrama" when the aforementioned scholars use it in their criticisms.
This broad term, with roots in literature, theater, film, and academic
criticism, has a long and disputed history, carrying different meanings depending on when, in what context, and by whom it is used. In
fact, it has been argued that because of melodrama's numerous defi-

nitions, both broad (melodrama is the opposite of realism) and narrow (melodramas are Technicolor films made in the 1950s, centering on issues of domestic strife, and directed by German expatriates), "it is difficult to escape the impression that one of the principle uses of melodrama is that of a dumping ground to enforce a spurious kind of critical tidiness" (Merritt, "Melodrama," 26). The varying uses of this term points to the difficulty of applying generalized labels to a large group of films, particularly when those labels have a history of shifting meanings (Altman, *Film/Genre*, 70). So what definition of melodrama is being invoked in the aforementioned histories of the gangster film?

In the 1970s, film scholars like Laura Mulvey began to take melodrama seriously, narrowing the definition of this otherwise broad term to a very specific type of film: 1940s and 1950s tearjerkers centering on women and conflicts generated within a domestic space (Neale, *Genre and Hollywood*, 181–184; Altman, *Film/Genre*, 77). Thomas Elsaesser's influential article "Tales of Sound and Fury" was instrumental in establishing this link between the category of melodrama and the depiction of roiling emotions in a domestic space (Neale, *Genre and Hollywood*, 181). According to Elsaesser's conception, the protagonists of the melodrama are tortured by the status quo but repeatedly fail to act in a way that might alter it or provide them with a particular object of desire. These characters are unable to get what they want through direct action. In fact, "their behavior is often pathetically at variance with the real objectives they want to achieve" ("Tales of Sound and Fury," 381). Although the melodrama ultimately valorizes the ideals of sacrifice and moderation, it is populated with characters that suffer because of their excessive natures: they drink too much, love too much, and work too much. As a result, we tend to think of melodrama as being emotionally manipulative, over the top, feminine, and unrealistic. Merritt adds: "It is a term generally applied to any machine-made entertainment marked by verbal extravagance, implausible motivation, contrived sensation or spurious pathos" ("Melodrama," 25). Similarly, Linda Williams points out that "the word melodrama seems to name an anarchic form—what vulgar, naïve audiences of yesteryear thrilled to, not what we sophisticated realists and moderns (and postmoderns) enjoy today" (*Playing the Race Card*, 12).

The term "melodrama" has become interchangeable with terms like "soap opera," "tearjerker," and "woman's film" (Merritt, "Melodrama," 25), implying that these are films dealing with the domestic, the intimate, and heightened emotions rather than with the public, the exterior, and actions. Melodrama is therefore characterized as being in-compatible with the hard, masculine, action-oriented modes of the western and the gangster film.[11] According to this binary, characters in gangster films act, while characters in melodrama are acted upon. Christine Gledhill argues: "The 'classical' genres were constructed by recourse to masculine cultural values—gangster as 'tragic hero'; the 'epic of the West'; 'adult' realism—while 'melodrama' was acknowl-edged only in those denigrated reaches of the juvenile and the pop-ular, the feminised spheres of the women's weepie, the romance or family melodrama" ("Melodramatic Field," 34).

This opposition between action and emotion, male and female, realism and fantasy, gangster film and melodrama, is also taken up by Thomas Schatz, who divides six major genres into two categories: "genres of order" and "genres of integration." The latter grouping of films, which includes the musical, screwball comedy, and domestic melodrama, has a "doubled hero" (almost always the heterosexual couple) and "trace[s] the integration of the central characters into the community" (*Hollywood Genres*, 34). This integration is made possible because the protagonists yield to the needs of the community, and because the film internalizes conflicts and translates them into emo-tional terms. These "genres of integration" usually conclude with the union of the heterosexual couple, who, throughout the film, repre-sent opposing worldviews. By contrast, in "genres of order," like west-erns, gangster films, and detective films, an individual hero questions the contradictions of his milieu: "Conflicts within these genres are externalized, translated into violence, and usually resolved through the elimination of some threat to the social order" (34). In the gang-ster film, this threat to the social order is the gangster himself. Ac-cording to this rubric, the melodrama and the gangster film are oppo-sites in every way.

Despite the fact that melodramas are often disparaged for being unrealistic or detached from real-world concerns, most melodramas seek to uncover some ostensible truth about a social ill and to explain its existence and consequences to the audience. In fact, melodrama has historically been deployed as a means for grappling with moral questions during times of moral uncertainty (Peter Brooks, *Melodra-matic Imagination*, 15); Charles Dickens's *Oliver Twist* (1838) and Har-riet Beecher Stowe's *Uncle Tom's Cabin* (1852), both hallmarks of liter-ary melodrama, were produced during periods of social crisis. Literary melodrama's emphasis on corruption and injustice as the primary sources of conflict encourages readers to empathize or engage with the plight of its innocent, powerless victims (slaves, orphans). These

The public display of mourning by Sarah Jane (Susan Kohner) for her dead mother comes "too late" in *Imitation of Life* (1959).

victims suffer in order to make the reader aware of the truth of their oppression.

Linda Williams adds that the revelation of truth in a melodrama is often marked through a visual tableau—a moment in which it is either "in the nick of time" or "too late" for a character with whom the audience has been encouraged to identify ("Melodrama Revised," 69). This truth may be the revelation that a character is repentant for a past transgression, such as the public apology by Sarah Jane (Susan Kohner) and her acceptance of her dead mother at the conclusion of *Imitation of Life* (1959, Douglas Sirk). The melodrama may also stage the revelation of a formerly hidden identity, such as Bob Merrick (Rock Hudson) admitting to Helen Phillips (Jane Wyman) that he caused her husband's death and her blindness in *Magnificent Obsession* (1954, Douglas Sirk). These truths come when it is either "too late" to make a difference or "in the nick of time." Endings in the mode of "too late" are intended to generate tears in the viewer because "crying is a demand for satisfaction that can never be satisfied" (Linda Williams, "Melodrama Revised," 70). Our crying is an act of mourning for lost time, for a past that can never be recovered or altered. When the truth arrives "in the nick of time," the viewer is still brought to tears. According to Neale, we cry in these situations because throughout the film, we have desired this outcome and watched, powerless, as this outcome was continually frustrated: "And the longer there is delay, the more likely we are to cry, because the powerlessness of our position will be intensified, whatever the outcome of events" ("Melodrama and Tears," 12). We cry with relief, and we also mourn our own powerlessness.

By revisiting the most commonly understood definitions and connotations of the term "melodrama," we can gain a better understanding of what prominent genre critics like Mason, McArthur, Munby, Schatz, and others are referring to when they argue that melodrama defines the preclassical gangster film or those films existing on the borders of the gangster genre. They invoke the term to refer to films populated with excessive protagonists, besieged victims, heightened emotions, and narratives of sacrifice, regeneration, or redemption. In these films there is dialectic between resolutions occurring "in the nick of time" or "too late." Finally, melodramas conclude with a definitive feeling of loss, which often drives the viewer to tears (Linda Williams, "Melodrama Revised," 42). These critics view such melodramatic elements as being antithetical to the gangster genre. However, these melodramatic conventions—in particular, the narrative of redemption—are quite central to the gangster genre as a whole.

The gangster film's melodramatic-redemption narrative plays out in two basic ways: through the love-triangle narrative and the reforming-mentor narrative.[12] In the love-triangle narrative the gangster falls for a woman who makes him into a cuckold or rejects him for a more stable, law-abiding citizen. Another variation on the love-triangle narrative involves having the gangster's right-hand man or best friend reject a life of crime (and by extension, the gangster himself) for the love of a woman on the straight and narrow. The rejection of the gangster by someone he loves is explicitly tied to his role as gangster hero; even if the girlfriend or friend loves the gangster, she or he knows the relationship is doomed to fail because of the gangster's excessive, criminal nature. If the gangster is unreformed at the film's conclusion, the love triangle drives him to destroy himself. If, however, this experience with rejection provides the gangster with an opportunity for self-reflection, the love triangle can also motivate him to commit an act of personal sacrifice and, as a result, gain redemption.

In the reforming-mentor narrative, the gangster hero is initially hardened and unrepentant, selfishly exerting his will on those around him. He eventually meets a reforming figure—in the form of a lover, an educator, or even a stranger—who convinces him to turn away from his criminal lifestyle. Yet making this choice almost always proves to be a case of too late, since the gangster either dies or loses someone close to him as a result of his past misdeeds. Occasionally, the gangster is able to reform in the nick of time in order to help someone he loves, but he ultimately suffers for his past transgressions. In this case, redemption comes both in the nick of time and too late. In both the reforming-mentor and love-triangle narratives, the audience is compelled to feel sympathy for the gangster hero and his suffering, and consequently mourns his death or empathizes with the pain he experiences over someone else's death. Because these redemption narratives are characterized by their last-minute reversals, performed either too late or in the nick of time, we are never sure who will be dying or suffering, or when. And this element of surprise, "the moment when agnition reduces the tension between desire and reality," is what causes us to cry (Linda Williams, "Melodrama Revised," 69). Consequently, another central convention of the melodrama, a profound sense of loss (70), is also quite central to the melodramatic-redemption cycle.

Critics characterize the classical gangster hero as a character who is unable to fully reflect upon the devastation he has caused. If he is mournful at the end of the film, it is because he is mourning his own death. For example, at the conclusion of *Little Caesar*, Rico Bandello laments, "Mother of Mercy, is this the end of Rico?" as he dies of a gunshot wound. Rico expresses no regret for the life he lived or the people he killed. He mourns only his own passing. Because of the classical gangster film's tragic structure—the film's viewer knows ahead of time that the protagonist will die—viewers are able to distance themselves from the otherwise sad ending of these films. Furthermore, the classical gangster hero is marked by his self-serving desires for monetary and social success (hence his ability to murder and steal without regret), and his lack of penance at the film's conclusion makes it difficult to empathize with his demise. Unlike the hero of the "classical" gangster film, the melodramatic gangster displays the ability, if only at the last minute, to reflect on the needs and desires of others. The gangster heroes in these films ultimately express remorse over their past sins or commit a redeeming act, making their deaths (or the deaths of those they love) seem all the more unfair.

THE MELODRAMATIC-REDEMPTION CYCLE: THE LOVE TRIANGLE

Perhaps the most well known film in the melodramatic-redemption cycle is Josef von Sternberg's *Underworld*. The treatment, written by Ben Hecht, won the first Academy Award for original script, and the film was both a critical and financial success at the time of its release (Rosow, *Born to Lose*, 120). Despite its success, however, *Underworld* is mostly understood as a film that paved the way for the arrival of the classical cycle. For example, Eugene Rosow argues that *Underworld* established several key icons and conventions that would later be lionized by critics as indicative of the genre: the dark, shadowy city seen only at night; a lavish underworld celebration; a detailed depiction of the crowded, run-down city milieu; and the use of newspaper headlines to further key plot points (123). Critics also believe that *Underworld* helped define the classical gangster persona. Bull Weed (George Bancroft), the film's gangster hero, is uneducated and crass but also fearless and street smart; he is aware of and encourages his own media celebrity; and most importantly, he sees himself as being "different" from, or better than, those around him. Like classical gangster heroes Tony Camonte and Rico Bandello, Bull Weed believes he is destined for greater things; early in *Underworld*, he spots a flashing neon advertisement that reads, "The City is Yours," and believes that the sign is addressing him. While almost all these elements had appeared in one form or another in earlier gangster films, "the box office success of *Underworld* simply focused the attention of producers and moviegoers as well as film historians on the genre" (124).

Although *Underworld* is similar in many ways to the films of the classical cycle, the presence of a love triangle among Bull, his sidekick (Rolls Royce, played by Clive Brook), and his moll (Feathers McCoy, played by Evelyn Brent), as well as Bull's sacrifice and redemption at the film's conclusion, places it in the preclassical category and marginalizes it within the gangster film's corpus (McArthur, *Underworld USA*, 34). In *Underworld*, love, passion, and loyalty are more important to Bull than his desire to reach the top. For example, Bull kills his rival, Buck Mulligan (Fred Kohler), not to gain money or power, but because Buck violated Feathers's honor. And once Bull is sentenced to death for Buck's murder, he appears to accept his fate. There is no bargaining (as we see in the conclusion to *Scarface*) or anger (as in *Little Caesar*); Bull accepts his death sentence with a smile, even playing checkers with a prison guard on the eve of his execution. His decision to break out of jail later that night is motivated not by a desire to save his own skin, but rather by his suspicion, spread through newspaper headlines, that Rolls Royce and Feathers are engaged in a secret affair; one incendiary headline reads "Feathers McCoy Proves Fickle: Killer's Girl Takes New Sweetheart." The classical gangster hero's decisions are governed by greed or the desire to get ahead, but Bull Weed's decisions are governed by his romantic and platonic relationships.

Underworld concludes, as many gangster films do, with a climactic shoot out. Bull, Feathers, and Rolls Royce hide from the police, who pepper Bull's hideout with gunfire. As the standoff with the police outside intensifies, Bull realizes two important truths. First, his friends never betrayed him to the police. Instead, they risked their own freedom in an attempt to spring him from jail. Bull also realizes that Feathers and Rolls are happier being in a relationship with each other than they ever were with him. Bull's excessive nature overwhelmed and dominated these relationships, making it impossible for Feathers and Rolls to be truly happy. After coming to this revelation, Bull decides to distract the police so that Feathers and Rolls can make their escape. This selfless decision—the film's emotional climax—is marked with a medium close-up of Bull embracing the wounded Rolls like a lover. Bull then decisively pushes his friends through a secret door in the hideout, explaining, "I've been wrong, Feathers—I know it now—I've been wrong all the way." On the other side of the door, we see Feathers collapse onto the floor, weeping over the fate of her former lover and friend.

When the police finally take Bull back to jail to be hanged, his captors are perplexed by his decision to turn himself in. "And all that got you was another hour!" one policeman remarks. To this, Bull smiles and replies, "There was something I had to find out—and that hour was worth more to me than my whole life." Although Bull had accumulated great wealth, power, and the respect of the criminal underworld, the most important moment of his life was his decision to save the lives of the two people he loved the most. Bull's choice to sacrifice his own life for the sake of others is an act of personal sacrifice. He obtains redemption in the nick of time, even if it comes too late to save his life. Such conclusions, based on emotion rather than action, are melodramatic because "[these protagonists] take on suffering and moral anguish knowingly, as the just price for having glimpsed a better world and having failed to live it" (Elsaesser, "Tales of Sound and Fury," 394). Rather than encouraging the audience to revel in the gangster's death, as in the conclusion of *Scarface* or *Little Caesar*, this ending generates empathy for the gangster hero's demise.

This focus on the love triangle is not limited to its appearance in *Underworld*; it is a convention dating all the way back to one of the earliest surviving entries in the genre, *The Musketeers of Pig Alley*. In this short film, the Little Lady (Lillian Gish) chooses her poor musician husband (Walter Miller) over the much flashier gangster, Snapper Kid (Elmer Booth). The Kid could offer the Little Lady a life of excitement, easy money, and protection from the dangers of the city. Indeed, when they meet at a dance, he intervenes when a rival gangster tries to slip a drug into her drink. Soon after, the Kid becomes embroiled in a back alley gunfight with the same rival and his gang.

The Snapper Kid (Elmer Booth) is puzzled that the Little Lady (Lillian Gish) would choose her milquetoast husband over him in *The Musketeers of Pig Alley* (1912).

Ultimately, the Kid's excessive nature proves less appealing than the stability offered by the Little Lady's penniless but more moderately tempered husband. This choice of mediocrity over excitement is comically illustrated in a three-shot at the film's conclusion. After the Little Lady makes it clear that she will not be running away with the Snapper Kid, the rejected gangster surveys his bland competition, gives the Little Lady a questioning look, as if to say, "Really? Him?" and then shrugs his shoulders and exits the frame.

Manhattan Melodrama (1934, W. S. Van Dyke), as its title implies, offers yet another prominent example of the love triangle. Over the course of the narrative, Eleanor Packer (Myrna Loy) is frustrated with her dashing gangster beau, Blackie Gallagher (Clark Gable), because he is unwilling to relinquish his dangerous gangster lifestyle for marriage and stability. Blackie explains that a "normal" life is antithetical to his character. Eleanor leaves Blackie and begins to date his childhood friend, the district attorney Jim Wade (William Powell). Jim, like *Underworld*'s Rolls Royce, is an educated, law-abiding "gentleman," and more importantly, he is willing to marry Eleanor and give her the stable life she craves. However, Jim's status as an upstanding citizen as well as his bid to become the governor of New York is later threatened by Richard Snow (Thomas Jackson), a former employee of the DA's office, who believes that Jim has covered up Blackie's crimes because of their long-standing friendship. Blackie murders Snow in order to preserve Jim's political aspirations, a selfless act that leads to his arrest and death sentence. As in *Underworld*, *Manhattan Melodrama* features a gangster hero who sacrifices his own livelihood so that his friend and former lover can live happily ever after together.

The conclusion of *Manhattan Melodrama* is mired in sentiment and moral accountability. Jim, now the governor of New York, rushes to Blackie's cell moments before his execution in order to commute his sentence. But Blackie tells Jim that his sentence is just and that death is preferable to a life spent in jail: "If I can't live the way I want, then let me die *when* I want." Blackie accepts his impending death because he is aware that he is an individual out of place in society; he can either be himself or die—there are no other options. Finally, and this is key to the film's emphasis on sacrifice and redemption: Blackie does not want Jim to commute his sentence because it would tarnish the office of the governor as well as Jim's spotless character. "You're going to make a great sacrifice, ruin your career. For what? So's I can rot in this hole?" Blackie's sacrifice also serves an extradiegetic function. A commuted sentence would have implied that the gangster could, in the end, "get away with it," a message prohibited by the Production Code. Thus, Blackie agrees to die so that his friends will be free to live their lives and so that *Manhattan Melodrama* will meet the requirements of the Production Code.

After Blackie marches off to his death, smiling bravely, Jim stands alone in Blackie's empty prison cell. Moments later, the lighting in the frame dims briefly, signifying that Blackie has just been electrocuted (a remarkably speedy execution). In the film's final scene, Jim, ever the rigid pillar of morals, calls a joint session of the legislature to announce that he will resign as governor. The legislators beg Jim to reconsider his decision, but he explains that he won his seat only because a murder was committed on his behalf. Furthermore, he had compromised the office of the governor by his willingness to commute Blackie's sentence. This emotional conclusion is antithetical to the definition of a classical gangster film, which centers on action and the bloody spectacle of the gangster's death; in *Manhattan Melodrama*, the gangster's death is only implied, through a subtle change in lighting. Furthermore, Jim's decision to resign seems an unnecessary act of self-punishment for Blackie's death. As Thomas Elsaesser argues, such "impossible standards," born of the contradictions inherent in the American Dream, are a hallmark of melodrama: "What strikes one as the true pathos is the very mediocrity of the human beings involved, putting such high demands upon themselves, trying to live up to an exalted vision of the human being" ("Tales of Sound and Fury," 394). Thus, at the end of *Manhattan Melodrama*, Blackie's willingness to sacrifice his life to save his friend's reputation allows the viewer to safely mourn the death of a murderer.

Occasionally, love-triangle narratives combine an "in the nick of time" conclusion with a "too late" conclusion. While it may be too late for the gangster, who sacrifices himself, his sacrifice comes in the nick of time for those he loves. We see this formula in *The Roaring Twenties* (1939, Raoul Walsh), which focuses on the love triangle between two former war buddies, Eddie Bartlett (James Cagney) and Lloyd Hart (Jeffrey Lynn), and an aspiring young singer named Jean Sherman (Priscilla Lane). After the war, Eddie goes on to become a successful racketeer, investing in the stock market, nightclubs, and taxicab companies, while Lloyd becomes a district attorney. Both men love Jean, but she has eyes only for Lloyd, whom she eventually marries. After the stock market crash of 1929, Eddie loses everything, while his friends continue to lead an idyllic life in the suburbs with their young son. When Lloyd's life is threatened for pursuing a case against one of the top mobsters in town, George Hally (Humphrey Bogart),

The conclusion of *Manhattan Melodrama* (1934) encourages us to mourn the death of a gangster, Blackie (Clark Gable), for his noble sacrifice.

Panama (Gladys George) mourns the death of the gangster hero Eddie Bartlett (James Cagney) at the conclusion of *The Roaring Twenties* (1939).

Jean begs Eddie to intervene. Eddie's ego is bruised, and his spirits are crushed—he has lost his money, his power, and his girl—but he ultimately agrees to help his old friends.

In the film's final scenes, Eddie confronts George in his well-guarded home and demands that he spare Lloyd's life. Not surprisingly, George does not take kindly to outside input, and a shoot out ensues. When the smoke clears, George is dead, and Eddie, who escapes the melee, is fatally wounded. The camera follows Eddie as he stumbles outside and makes his way to the front steps of a nearby church. The nondiegetic sound track becomes increasingly plangent as the dying gangster, framed in a long shot, climbs the stairs and collapses to the ground. His former moll, Panama (Gladys George), cradles his head in her arms as he dies. A police officer enters the frame and inquires, "What was his business?" Panama strokes Eddie's hair and stares ahead blankly. "He used to be a big shot," she explains. The camera then tracks backward as Panama sobs over Eddie's body. Becoming an almost Christ-like figure in this final scene, the gangster hero is filmed so as to encourage viewers to feel pity for him. While Eddie saved Jean and Lloyd in the nick of time, it is too late for him, and we mourn his death.

This repeated formula of the melodramatic love triangle is significant because it is consistently attached to the same syntax from film to film. In all these gangster films, the protagonist's loss of love or emotional connection is directly tied to his status as the gangster hero. In other words, those qualities that help the gangster succeed in the modern city, to "do it first, do it yourself, and keep on doing it," as Tony Camonte advises in *Scarface*, are the same traits that make the gangster an unsatisfactory lover or friend. The gangster, defined by his individuality or his difference from everyone else (he is more aggressive, more charming, more brutal, and more determined than his peers), cannot successfully function in a relationship requiring the union of two individuals. He cannot maintain healthy long-term relationships with other people because he is simply "too much." In these films, the woman rejects the gangster, even if she initially loved him, for the mate who is willing to be a part of the crowd and accept the status quo. Robert Warshow argues that "the gangster's whole life is an effort to assert himself as an individual, to draw himself out of the crowd, and he always dies *because* he is an individual" ("Gangster as Tragic Hero," 133). Thus, the rejection of the gangster by his lover—which confirms his status as an isolated, excessive individual—is a profound marker of his status *as* a film gangster.

Despite its reiteration in numerous beloved gangster films, including *The Doorway to Hell*, *High Sierra* (1941, Raoul Walsh), *Black Caesar* (1973, Larry Cohen), *Billy Bathgate* (1991, Richard Benton) and *Casino* (1995, Martin Scorsese), the convention of the love triangle is rarely emphasized in studies of the genre. Even the classical cycle, against which such conventions are typically opposed, contains two prominent love triangles. In *Scarface*, Tony might be undone by his desire to "have" the world, but what seals his fate is his unnatural devotion to his sister, Cesca, who, in turn, is in love with his best friend, Guino (George Raft). Likewise, in *Little Caesar*, Rico is cast aside by his best friend, Joe Massara (Douglas Fairbanks, Jr.), who abandons the gang life in order to dance professionally with his love interest, Olga (Glenda Farrell). While Joe's rejection does not lead directly to Rico's downfall, it clouds Rico's judgment, driving him to drink (a vice he had always denounced) and to eventually lose his hold on his power.

The love-triangle narrative is also significant because it highlights the role of women in the gangster genre. Most studies of the genre argue that women play an insignificant role in the world of the gangster film, serving mostly as pious mother figures, as sisters whose chastity must be protected at all costs (Schatz, *Hollywood Genres*, 87), or as emblems of success who may be "traded and acquired at the end of city warfare" (Smith-Shomade, "'Rock-a-Bye, Baby!'" 25). Some critics, such as Jack Shadoian, have acknowledged the importance of female characters in the gangster film. But Shadoian claims that women become integral to the gangster plot only in the 1940s and 1950s, with the appearance of film noir and the femme fatale (*Dreams and Dead Ends*, 106). However, this marginalization of the role of women in gangster films arises from the lionization of the classical cycle, in which the protagonist has no interest in women (*Little Caesar*) or women are merely visible signs of success (*The Public Enemy*). But viewing any of the aforementioned love-triangle films reveals just how integral women were to the plots of these otherwise homosocial, aggressive, masculine films. In fact, in her study of early 1930s gangster films, Esther Sonnet uncovered a host of "love stories and melodramas," such as *Ladies Love Brutes* (1930, Rowland V. Lee) and *A Free Soul* (1931, Clarence Brown), centering on female protagonists and their romantic entanglements with gangsters. In these films, "the dangerous, exciting and coercive gangster provided an imaginative space into which transgressive fantasies of female desire could be projected" ("Ladies Love Brutes," 94). The love-triangle formula was so prevalent at the time that Pare Lorentz, in his 1931 review of *The Public Enemy*, was pleased that the film was not "another one of those gaudy wine-women-and-machine-gun romances" (quoted in Yaquinto, *Pump 'Em*

The body of Blizzard (Lon Chaney) becomes a macabre spectacle in *The Penalty* (1920).

of San Francisco—to destroy the very modernity that fashioned the deformed body he now despises. As he explains to his cohorts: "And for my mangled years the city shall pay me." In a fantasy sequence intended to illustrate Blizzard's grand plan, we see him mobilizing thousands of disgruntled foreign workers to riot and to loot the city's riches. In this sequence, Blizzard imagines leading his followers on two fully functioning legs. While greed is clearly a motivating factor for Blizzard's behavior, his desire to take over the city of San Francisco is also an attempt to retrieve his lost limbs and masculinity.

Later in the film, it is revealed that Blizzard's devious criminal mind was not caused by the unnecessary amputation of his legs during his childhood, but rather by a blood clot that formed at the base of his brain during the same traffic accident that injured his legs. This plot twist enacts the theory that the modern city and its technology—such as the automobile—can literally alter the impressionable mind of a child, skewing his understanding of right and wrong. In the film's conclusion, Blizzard is miraculously cured of his desire to destroy San Francisco when the doctor who performed the botched surgery twenty-seven years earlier removes the evil-inducing blood clot from his brain. Dr. Ferris could have chosen to kill Blizzard, or at least incapacitate him, while he was under anesthetic, but his decision to instead correct the mistake he made decades ago reveals an abiding faith in Blizzard's inherent morality. Dr. Ferris's gamble pays off: opening his eyes after surgery, Blizzard immediately feels regret for his past misdeeds, exclaiming, "I've waked from a terrible dream! I was a devil—I did things that I shudder to think of!" Dr. Ferris later explains to the police that because Blizzard has been under the influence of a blood clot, he was not responsible for his past wrongdoings. The police agree to let Blizzard go free. The message of *The Penalty* is that criminals created by the modern city can be reformed when society takes responsibility for them and recognizes that they are victims, not aggressors.

Another example of the reforming-mentor narrative appears in *Regeneration*. This film depicts, in great detail, the poverty and abuse that characterizes the gangster hero's childhood. Shot on location with a setting emphasizing urban squalor, *Regeneration* reflects the environmental approach to criminality that was emerging in the United States in the 1910s. For example, the film's first image is of the protagonist, Owen (John McCann), as a young boy. He wears dirty, tattered clothing and watches the body of his last remaining parent being loaded into the back of a hearse. Things only get worse for Owen when his equally poor neighbors, the Conways, take him in, subjecting him to the drunken and sometimes violent ministrations of "old man" Conway (James A. Marcus). This emphasis on a socioeconomic explanation for crime is further supported by the film's mise-en-scène, which is filled with dirty, barefoot children who loiter on the front stoop and stairs of Owen's tenement and in the streets. The film highlights these moments through the frequent use of irises, which focus the viewer's eyes on the spectacle of abandoned children. The film creates a direct link between childhood poverty and adult criminality when we see a shot of the young Owen sleeping in the gutter cut to another shot of Owen at seventeen, now fully in the grips of the criminal lifestyle.

As Owen acclimates to life as a criminal, we are introduced to a young socialite, Marie "Mamie Rose" Deering (Anna Q. Nilsson). While on a tour of the Bowery with a group of wealthy friends, Marie takes the admonishments of a socialist soapbox lecturer to heart and decides to become a social worker at a local settlement house. She later meets Owen (Rockliffe Fellowes) and convinces him to abandon his criminal lifestyle in favor of reading, writing, and social work. When Owen is called back to gang life to fulfill one last obligation,

Marie invariably gets caught in the cross fire and is shot by Owen's nemesis, Skinny (William Sheer). However, Marie's death becomes a necessary vehicle for illustrating Owen's regeneration. When Owen has an opportunity to avenge her death by shooting Skinny, he sees an apparition of Marie's face before him. He collapses in tears, deciding to take the moral high ground and turn Skinny over to the police rather than take justice into his own hands. Owen's words, and the film's final line, are both mournful and filled with hope: "It was she, my Mamie Rose, who taught me that within me was a mind and a God-given heart. She made of my life a changed thing and never can it be the same again."

Films like *The Penalty* and *Regeneration* reason that even though their protagonists were essentially reared to be criminals, they can reform and reenter the fold of society with enough determination and the attentions of a good-hearted mentor. Such messages were in keeping with the emerging discourses on criminality in the 1910s, discourses "informed more by psychology and sociology than by biology and beliefs about hereditary influence and that accordingly articulated a different conception of the causes of crime and its possible treatment" (Grieveson, "Gangsters and Governance," 27). Lee Grieveson cites William Healy's 1909 study, *The Individual Delinquent*, as a

Films like *Regeneration* (1915) offer an environmental explanation for criminality.

At the conclusion to *Regeneration* (1915), the ghost of Marie (Anna Q. Nilsson), the reforming mentor of Owen (Rockliffe Fellowes), convinces the gangster not to commit murder.

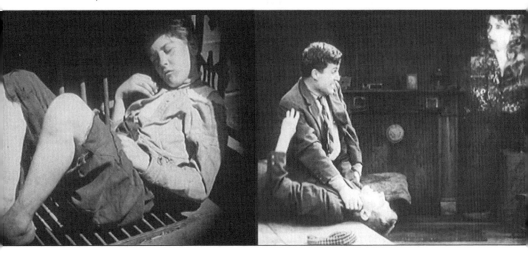

key text in discounting the then-prevalent model of eugenics, which argued that urban crime emanated from "dangerous classes" who had inborn criminal tendencies (Grieveson, "Gangsters and Governance," 27). By 1915, the environmental approach to the criminal began to replace eugenics, and numerous studies were published about the links between criminal behavior and urban living (28). While earlier gangster films like *The Black Hand* (1906, American Mutoscope and Biograph) and *The Silver Wedding* (1906, American Mutoscope and Biograph) painted the gangster or gang as incapable of reform and thus unsympathetic, *Regeneration* and *The Penalty*, with their focus on the decaying mise-en-scène of the modern city, argue that the gangster is a victim of circumstance. Because this victim of circumstance was made, not born, reformation is possible. Therefore, "the insistent theme of reformation eased the contradiction between urban, corporate order and ideals of individual action and character that was particularly pressing for members of the middle class" (26).

Of course, it is important to point out that these reforming-mentor narratives position the gangster both as the fated victim of poverty and as a responsible agent of his own destiny. These gangsters may have had the bad luck to be born into the urban underclass, but they must still make the choice to change. Owen is offered the opportunity to reform numerous times throughout *Regeneration* while under the benevolent tutelage of his upper-class reformer, Marie. But he does not truly reform until he is faced with the devastating consequences of his gangster lifestyle—the death of Marie—which is the direct result of his poor choices. Similarly, *The Penalty*'s message—that criminals are forged in the fires of the modern city and therefore deserve redemption—is effectively tempered in the film's conclusion. We see Blizzard, in a tuxedo and with slicked-back hair, enjoying an evening with his new wife, Rose (Ethel Grey Terry), the undercover agent who infiltrated his crime ring and then fell in love with him. As Blizzard plays the piano, a contented expression on his face, he is shot in the back by one of his previous gang associates. His face seizes up with pain, and he pitches forward onto the piano. "Fate chained me to Evil," he says as Rose clings to his neck, "for that I must pay the penalty." The scene closes with an iris-in on Blizzard's grieving bride; her tears are a signal to the audience that this is a character whose death must be mourned, not celebrated.

Even though Blizzard's criminality is positioned as the work of fate and circumstance, and even though he has reformed, he must, nevertheless, be punished for his past transgressions. Likewise, Owen is punished through Marie's untimely death. These films seem to imply that the gangster can become a productive member of society through the cooperation of high-minded reformers, but the taint of his past transgressions will remain. He must suffer in some way, either through his own death or the death of a loved one, as payment for disrupting the social order. In this way, the reforming-mentor narrative helped contemporary audiences work through their anxieties about the modern city and its many dangers. Audiences could face their worst fears about urban living through their encounter with the screen gangster and then be reassured that they could take part in the gangster's regeneration. Additionally, by having the gangster pay for his sins, law-abiding audience members could feel secure in their decision to obey the law and be productive members of society. The reforming-mentor narrative is even more prevalent than the love-triangle narrative, appearing periodically throughout the gangster film's long history. The cycle was most prevalent in the silent era, but reappeared in the late 1930s with entries like *Angels with Dirty Faces* (1938, Michael Curtiz) and *High Sierra*. The reforming-mentor narrative appeared again in the 1990s, in diverse gangster films like *The Godfather III* (1990, Francis Ford Coppola), *A Bronx Tale* (1993, Robert DeNiro), *Carlito's Way* (1993, Brian De Palma), and *South Central* (1992, Steve Anderson), among others.

CONCLUSION

One of the reasons why well-known gangster films with melodramatic-redemption narratives, such as *Underworld*, *Regeneration*, *The Penalty*, *Manhattan Melodrama*, and *The Roaring Twenties*, have been excluded from a central place in the gangster film's generic corpus is because the concept of redemption is almost wholly rejected in the classical cycle. A true gangster hero, as defined by the classical cycle, is one who is irredeemable and incapable of reform; Rico Bandello and Tony Camonte die, unrepentant, in a hail of bullets. Marilyn Yaquinto consequently criticizes *Underworld*'s conclusion, in which Bull Weed sacrifices himself so that his friends can escape, as "sappy," adding, "*Underworld* had put Bull Weed in the lead but insisted he be redeemed in the end. That sabotaged his integrity as a gangster and turned him into something else" (*Pump 'Em Full of Lead*, 27). A reformed gangster is "soft," a compromised version of the hard-edged heroes that presumably come out of the classical cycle. When these redemption themes reappear in later gangster films like *The Roaring Twenties*, Yaquinto reasons that rehabilitating the gangster at the end of the film is part of his post-Code "defanging" (57). Again, in most critical discourse, the trope of redemption or regeneration represents a compromise of the gangster hero, an anomaly in the genre's blueprint, or the result of the censors' meddling hand. Colin McArthur argues that up until the appearance of post-Code films like *Dead End* (1937, William Wyler), "the explicit attitude of the gangster film to the criminal had been a simple one. Criminals are born, not made; they are incapable of reform and can be stopped only by being destroyed" (39).

Despite these claims, critics like Steve Neale argue that the "topoi of 'redemption, reformation and rehabilitation'" have been prevalent in the genre since its inception. He points out that the perpetuation of these themes in films of the 1930s and 1940s "suggests that they comprised a formula more deep-rooted, more long-lasting and thus more 'classical' than the classical formula itself" (*Genre and Hollywood*, 80). And according to Gerald Peary, themes of sacrifice and redemption were common in 1920s gangster film as well: "In gangster movies of the twenties—*Underworld*, for example—a gang leader who committed terrible deeds, including murder, was allowed to absolve himself gracefully of his sins through heroic sacrifice, often to save the sacred love of a young and innocent couple. By giving up his life for this moral cause, he would instantly bring meaning to his existence, demonstrating knowledge of his sins and a desire for reformation" ("*Little Caesar*," 20).

Although the classical gangster hero is usually understood to be selfish—his ruthless drive to put himself at the top is his defining character trait—the prevalence of films in which the gangster sacrifices his own needs to help the greater good indicates otherwise. I believe that the melodramatic-redemption narratives discussed in this chapter, hinging on either a love triangle or a reforming-mentor figure, constitute one significant, though often overlooked, production cycle within the larger gangster genre. These films deploy a similar set of semantics, including a realistic urban setting, a sympathetic gangster hero, and a pivotal plot moment when the gangster makes a moral choice. They also contain similar themes: criminals are created by their social environment; redemption is possible for even the most hardened criminal; and society must be empathetic if it wishes to solve the problem of crime. By considering this cycle to be significant rather than marginal to the genre, we can expand our understanding of the gangster hero and the genre's overall themes.

As I have demonstrated, viewing the gangster genre through the lens of its classical cycle accounts for only selected elements (the rise-and-fall narrative, the unrepentant hero, the homosocial milieu) in select gangster films (*Little Caesar, Scarface*). The fetishization of these films serves to close down the genre's numerous other potential meanings. For that reason, Tag Gallagher has suggested that "a superficial glance at film history suggests cyclicism rather than evolution" ("Shoot Out," 268). Once we abandon the linear, evolutionary model of generic change in favor of a model more suited to the complexities of genre formation, that is, a cyclical view of generic growth, we can account for why certain groups of films achieve periods of popularity and then lie dormant for decades, appearing again only when the cultural and industrial circumstances permit it (and never in the same exact way). The gangster film genre is composed of numerous smaller, intrageneric cycles, each reflecting a particular sociocultural moment:

- Post-Code G-man films: *G-Men* (1935, William Keighley), *Bullets or Ballots* (1936, William Keighley), *I Am the Law* (1938, Alexander Hall)
- Gangster noirs of the 1940s and 1950s: *T-Men* (1947, Anthony Mann), *The Big Combo* (1955, Joseph H. Lewis), *The Big Heat* (1953, Fritz Lang)
- Self-reflexive French tributes to the American gangster films: *Rififi* (1955, Jules Dassin), *Bob the Gambler* (1955, Jean-Pierre Melville), *Breathless* (1960, Jean-Luc Godard), *Shoot the Piano Player* (1960, François Truffaut)
- 1960s youth-targeted biopics: *Machine Gun Kelly* (1958, Roger Corman), *The Rise and Fall of Legs Diamond* (1960, Bud Boetticher), *Bonnie and Clyde* (1967, Arthur Penn)
- Mafioso films released in reaction to the televised Kefauver hearings: *Murder, Inc.* (1960, Burt Balaban and Stuart Rosenberg), *The Brotherhood* (1968, Paul Fejos), *The Valachi Papers* (1972, Terence Young)
- 1980s nostalgia films: *Once Upon a Time in America* (1984, Sergio Leone), *The Cotton Club* (1984, Francis Ford Coppola), *The Untouchables* (1987, Brian De Palma), *Harlem Nights* (1989, Eddie Murphy)
- 1990s ghetto action films: *New Jack City* (1991, Mario Van Peebles), *Menace II Society* (1993, Allen and Albert Hughes), *Set It Off* (1996, F. Gary Gray)

These intrageneric cycles of the gangster film formed because they capitalized on a contemporary social problem, industrial development, trend, or interest: G-man films resulted from the introduction of industry censorship, while youth-targeted biopics reflected the activation of counterculture politics in the 1960s. A cyclical view of a genre reveals how a genre's themes are taken up again and again throughout the genre's life, but never in the same way or for the same reasons.

The melodramatic-redemption cycle of the gangster film, originating in the 1910s and 1920s, reflected a general trend in silent films toward promoting the ideals of Progressivism, a political movement that arose in response to the vast changes in American cities brought about by industrialism at the turn of the century, including the rise of sweatshop labor and piecework labor (over skilled labor); a swell in the nation's urban population, resulting in crowded tenement living; and decreasing returns and increasing debts among the nation's farmers (Piott, *American Reformers*, 1–5).[13] Progressive leaders sought to improve crowded, unsanitary city living conditions through self-help programs and settlement houses; fought for worker's compensation, child-labor laws, the minimum wage, the forty-hour workweek, and widows' pensions; and attacked government corruption. They also fought to establish building codes for tenements and to regulate sweatshops (5). According to Jonathan Munby, early silent gangster films borrowed their social-realist perspective from the photojournalism of photographers like Jacob Riis, highlighting their "socially reforming point of view" (*Public Enemies*, 21). Much as Riis sought to shed light on the disastrous effects of modernity on the urban poor, the films of the melodramatic-redemption cycle aimed to generate sympathy for their suffering gangster protagonists. Pervasive concerns about burgeoning criminality in turn-of-the-century American cities, the Progressive belief that social reform was necessary to help those who were raised in such an environment, the rise of Prohibition-era racketeering, and the success of early films like *Regeneration* led to the formation of a successful film cycle within the larger gangster genre. However, the labels "preclassical" or "experimental," which are so often attached to these films, allow us to understand these films only according to which elements they contributed to the classical cycle and which elements bar them from being considered "mature" gangster films. These labels do not explain what these films are like, what function they served for their audiences, or what role they played within the genre as a whole. Thus, a cyclical view of a genre offers more detailed information about the cultural climate in which and out of which genre films were produced than traditional genre studies do.

Having abandoned the traditional map of the gangster genre, which places melodramatic films like *Regeneration* and *Underworld* on the borders of the genre, and having replaced that model with a cyclical approach to genre studies, we can now return to the scene of Tom Powers's melodramatic suffering, which opened this chapter. As I mentioned previously, the mode of melodrama is frequently used to produce sympathy for the plight of a particular character. Social injustice generates the suffering of the protagonist. Once viewers have been encouraged to engage with the struggles of the protagonist, they are likely to engage with the social problem depicted in the film. In *The Public Enemy*, this social problem is the poverty and lack of opportunities available to first- and second-generation immigrants in the United States, particularly during the Great Depression. Although Tom could have chosen the path taken by his brother, Mike, who drives a bus by day and goes to school at night, the viewer never sees Mike's hard work bear fruit. In fact, he is bitter and tired throughout the film. Tom's choice to embark on a life of crime and, later, bootlegging appears logical by comparison. Furthermore, the melodramatic conventions used in the conclusion—such as when Tom admits, "I ain't so tough," and apologizes to his family—encourage the audience to sympathize with Tom rather than to feel that he got what he deserved. He is not the social Other, but rather one of us. The social conditions that created Tom Powers were the social conditions experienced by the audiences of the time. If we read a film like *The Public Enemy* only through the lens of the classical cycle, these significant meanings remain dormant, or at least glossed over. When we understand that the classical cycle is but one prominent and influential cycle within the genre—rather than its defining cycle—we can finally shine light on those cycles whose importance and meanings had been previously hidden in the shadows. We can then see that Tom is not the public enemy of the film's title, but rather a victim of the public.

CHAPTER 2

A DYING SERPENT
UNDERSTANDING HOW FILM
CYCLES CHANGE OVER TIME

In 1940, *East Side Kids* (Robert F. Hill), the first entry in the East Side Kids cycle (which was itself a spin-off of the successful Dead End Kids cycle of the late 1930s), was released.[1] In his review of the film, the *New York Times* critic Bosley Crowther expresses his disdain for both *East Side Kids* and the Dead End Kids cycle as a whole: "A less cautious historian . . . might assert flatly that the end [of the Dead End Kids cycle] has been reached, but a cinematic cycle, like the proverbial serpent, dies hard, with its remote tail flicking cynically, long after the last light has expired from its minute, reptilian brain." Crowther's annoyance is somewhat justified: when *East Side Kids* was released, there were already twelve films made under the aegis of the original *Dead End* (1937, William Wyler), the film that inaugurated the Dead End Kids cycle and its spin-offs. Besides criticizing this film, Crowther also appears annoyed by the very concept of the film cycle, likening it to a dying serpent. This serpent simile brings to mind some unflattering images: a dumb animal with a "minute brain," or a predator preying on innocent victims. Indeed, film cycles are often viewed in such polarizing terms: as simplistic, easily accessible films, or as a filmmaking practice aimed at exploiting a successful formula and wringing every last dime out of the moviegoing public. Crowther's reference to the "proverbial serpent" also recalls the image of a serpent eating its own tail; film cycles, at least on the surface, do appear to consume themselves. The process of systemization that generates a successful film cycle is the same process that ultimately destroys it.[2] And just as the proverbial snake does not realize that it is dead or dying, even as it continues to consume itself, the film cycle often continues to generate entries even after it has outstayed its welcome with film critics and audiences.

My purpose is not to dispute these judgments. Rather, this chapter examines an intergeneric cycle, the original Dead End Kids cycle of the 1930s and 1940s, in order to understand how cycles originate, flourish, and then change over time in an attempt to remain financially viable.[3] Although film cycles appear to die or disappear after a few years, in practice their themes and images continue to circulate, even if in a highly diluted or altered form, decades after the original cycle has disappeared.[4] What appears to be a cinematic death is, in fact, the conversion of the original content of a film cycle into a series of affectless cinematic clichés, available for other, seemingly incompatible generic uses, such as comedy, horror, and science fiction. By studying a social-problem-film cycle, we can investigate also how the process of cyclic evolution alters the meaning and function of the social problems being depicted. For example, *Dead End*, an earnest and pessimistic social problem film about the plight of post-Depression urban youth, launched three long-running, primarily comic film cycles. Therefore, while the previous chapter abandoned the concept of generic evolution at the macro level of film genres, this chapter reclaims the concept of evolution at the micro level of the film cycle.

IDENTIFYING THE SEMANTICS OF
THE ORIGINAL DEAD END KIDS CYCLE

A film cycle can come into existence only if its originary film, the first film released in the cycle, is financially or critically successful, addresses a topic of contemporary social interest, and has a set of central semantics, including images, characters, and plot formulas that are recognizable enough to be repeated in several more films. The original Dead End Kids cycle of the late 1930s was created because its first entry, *Dead End*, fits these criteria. *Dead End*, adapted from Sidney Kingsley's successful Broadway play (1935) of the same name, focuses on the necessity of a positive environment, including education, religion, and strong role models, for the creation of good citizens. The film offers two possible outcomes for the children living on a crowded New York City block that dead-ends at the dirty East River: become an upstanding (but poor) member of the community like Dave Connell (Joel McCrea) or turn into a hardened (but wealthy) gangster like Baby Face Martin (Humphrey Bogart). The film asks whether these as-yet harmless juvenile delinquents will grow up to be like Dave or like Baby Face. In the last moments of the film, Tommy (Billy Halop), who has been charged with assault, is on his way to juvenile court to find out whether he will be sent to reform school or will be allowed to leave the Dead End with his sister, Drina (Sylvia Sidney). According to the logic of the social problem film, reform school would guarantee Tommy a future in crime. Thus, Tommy's future—whether he will grow up to be like Dave or like Baby Face—rests in the hands of the juvenile-court judge. Although most classical Hollywood films aim to provide conclusive resolutions, *Dead End* does not reveal Tommy's fate.

The young actors cast to play the Dead End Kids in *Dead End* were not billed as the film's stars, but contemporary reviews consistently mentioned them as being central to the film's appeal. A *New York Times* review claimed: "The show undoubtedly belongs to the six incomparable urchins imported from the stage production" (McManus). However, the Kids were reportedly troublesome on set, and Samuel Goldwyn soon sold their contracts to Warner Bros. (Getz, *Broadway to the Bowery*, 12). Warner Bros. wisely capitalized on the critical success of *Dead End* by releasing a series of films featuring the Kids, including *Crime School* (1938, Lewis Seiler), *Angels with Dirty Faces* (1938, Michael Curtiz), *They Made Me a Criminal* (1939, Busby Berkeley), *Hell's Kitchen* (1939, Lewis Seiler), *Angels Wash Their Faces* (1939, Ray Enright), and *On Dress Parade* (1939, William Clemens). All these films, with the exception of *On Dress Parade*, are social problem films. Social problem films turn contemporary social concerns into popular entertainment and are "generally animated by a humane concern for the victim(s) of or crusader(s) against the social problem and, often, by an implicit assumption that the problem can be treated or even eliminated through well-intentioned liberal social reform" (Mayland, "Social Problem Film," 307). In social problem films, the content must be timely so that the audience will recognize the problem depicted as something that is happening "now." Additionally, the issue being depicted in the social problem film must affect a significant segment of the population and it must be perceived by that segment of society to *be* a problem (306).

The appeal of the original Dead End Kids cycle is directly related to its exploitation of contemporary social problems, particularly the plight of urban youth. In the mid-1930s, increasing attention was paid to the links between urbanization, immigration, and juvenile delinquency. Clifford Shaw's influential 1929 book, *Delinquency Areas*, argued that delinquency could be mapped. Criminality was concentrated in the center of urban areas and was surrounded by zones of receding instances of delinquency (Gilbert, *Cycle of Outrage*, 127). Shaw's findings were bolstered by the fact that jobs for youth were extremely difficult to find during the Great Depression, leading juvenile crime rates to more than double in the 1930s. Furthermore, the large number of children who were orphaned or homeless as a result of the Great Depression was also a growing concern, a problem documented in the social problem film *Wild Boys of the Road* (1933, William A. Wellman). In addition to tapping into fears about crime in the city, the original Dead End Kids cycle also touted the ideals of Progressivism, a broad-based reform movement that arose in the late nineteenth century to address the changes wrought by the industrial revolution. Widespread interest in the plight of the working poor in America's cities reemerged with the onset of the Great Depression and the instituting of the Roosevelt administration's New Deal programs in 1933. At the time, audiences were receptive to movies that critiqued the social order, an extreme case being Mervyn LeRoy's *I Am a Fugitive from a Chain Gang* (1932), with its bleak portrait of Depression-era America. The original Dead End Kids cycle addressed the Progressive movement's emphasis on social justice by examining the socioeconomic causes of criminality and the possibility of reforming those whom society had assumed were incapable of reformation. Given the anxieties surrounding youth, criminality, and the city (and the concomitant desire to rectify those interlinked social problems), it makes sense that the Dead End Kids cycle would strike a chord with contemporary audiences and that studios would continue to make films in this vein.

In addition to its critical success and its ability to exploit contemporary social problems, the original Dead End Kids cycle was also formed because its central semantics were recognizable and easily repeated. First, like all social problem films, the original Dead End Kids cycle emphasized mise-en-scène (and the camera movements that reveal this mise-en-scène) more than any other cinematic element, making the setting "the 'star' of the show" (Ross, *Working-Class Hollywood*, 44). For example, although *Dead End* was shot entirely on a studio back lot, it has a painstakingly detailed set. The film's opening image is a dramatic zoom in to a close-up of a "Dead End" sign, marking where the dirty city block meets the equally dirty East River. The camera movement calls our attention to the film's title while also setting up the fatalistic narrative of the film to follow—the people who live at this location are at a literal and metaphoric dead end. After the credits run, the "Dead End" sign dissolves into an extreme long shot of New York City's skyline, over which runs text detailing a brief history of how the area is being slowly gentrified. The statement "And now the terraces of these great apartment houses look down into the windows of the tenement poor" sets up one of the film's central op-

64

AMERICAN
FILM CYCLES

The set for *Dead End* (1937) highlights the semantics of urban poverty.

positions: between the haves and the have-nots. This explanatory, socially conscious statement, otherwise known as a "square-up," establishes the film's basis in real, contemporary issues and justifies the film's need to address unsavory subjects (Schaefer, *Bold! Daring! Shocking!*, 69). The square-up also signals *Dead End*'s "message with a capital M," and calls attention to its lofty ambition to be something more than mere entertainment; the film aspires to educate its audience. The camera then cranes down from the tops of the skyscrapers into the shadowy depths of the Dead End's tenements, as if to mimic the perspective of the rich tenants who gaze down into the ghetto from the safe vantage point of their opulent apartments. This lengthy opening take (it runs for eighty-two seconds) reveals the semantics of urban poverty: laundry drying on lines strung from window to window, tenants sleeping on fire escapes to cool off during the hot summer night, garbage cans leaning against grimy brick walls, mangy stray dogs wandering the street, and a homeless man sleeping on a bench. The films in the Dead End Kids spin-off cycles likewise emphasize poverty in their mise-en-scène.

Throughout *Dead End* and other entries in the cycle, the camera is our omniscient tour guide through the inner city. The film's use of independent camera movement and unmotivated changes in camera angles—particularly the shift from standard to extreme high and low angles—pulls us out of the classical Hollywood film's seamless narrative spell long enough to make us aware that we are watching a film. These moments of independent camera movement do not appear frequently in the film; rather, their effect comes from appearing at specific, privileged moments. They draw our attention to the fact that the film, as a social problem film, is delivering a message to the viewer (Cormack, *Ideology and Cinematography*, 137). Early in *Dead End*, Kay (Wendy Barrie), a former tenement resident who has upgraded her social standing to that of a kept woman, goes to visit Dave, her sometime beau, in his shabby apartment building. The use of impressionistic, low-key lighting and extreme low- and high-angle shots provides Kay's horrified perspective on the building, a reminder of where she has been and where she could end up again. But then the camera takes on a volition of its own: as Kay walks up the steps, the camera stops, even as she continues to walk, in order to let a garbage man pass by on the rickety, narrow steps. When Kay turns a corner, the camera tilts up sharply to reveal cockroaches crawling over a garbage can. At these moments, the camera becomes detached from its role of forwarding the narrative and instead takes on an active role, "showing" the viewer how bad life can be in the Dead End. In this way, camera movement actively shapes how the viewer feels about characters and their surroundings.

Another important semantic element of the original Dead End Kids cycle and many of its spin-off cycles involves showing how characters master (or fail to master) their city surroundings. In *Little Tough Guy* (1938, Harold Young), the first entry in Universal's Dead End Kids and Little Tough Guys spin-off cycle, Johnny (Billy Halop) is pushed around and threatened by the Dead End Kids gang when he and his family are obliged to move from their upwardly mobile, middle-class neighborhood to a working-class neighborhood with a higher crime rate. Johnny proves himself to the gang (and becomes their leader) only when he is able to defend his turf with a well-aimed punch. This social Darwinism also extends to the boys' ability to manipulate and master their environment in order to find food, shelter, and money. In *Dead End*, the boys cool off in the East River, and when they are hungry, they steal potatoes and roast them over a back-alley garbage can; in *Crime School*, the Dead End Kids steal items off the street, such as tires, bicycles, and even a bathtub, to sell for money.

This ability to navigate the city is also related to each child's reliance on his environment for survival. Characters in social problem films find themselves in restricted economic situations in which they are forced to put objects at hand to use in service of another purpose, such as the conversion of an old metal garbage can into a makeshift stove or the use of a rope as a belt. This conversion of trash into treasure resonates with Claude Lévi-Strauss's concept of *bricolage*. The term *bricolage*, derived from the French verb *bricoler*, means "to tinker" and refers to how "primitive man makes use of the materials at hand which may not bear any relationship to the intended project but appears to be all he has to work with" (Feuer, *Hollywood Musical*, 4). Jane Feuer has argued that the use of bricolage in the integrated musical—when an actor incorporates everyday objects that happen to be lying around, such as a broom or an umbrella, into his or her dance number—creates a feeling of "utter spontaneity" and aids in bridging the gap between audience and performer (3–5). Furthermore, in the context of the integrated musical, bricolage encourages the audience to believe in the "everydayness" and ordinariness of the characters despite their extraordinary singing and dancing abilities. Similarly, bricolage occurs in the social problem film when characters "tinker" with objects in the mise-en-scène that were not intended to be used for their current purposes, but that are all the characters have to work with, given their limited financial situations. As in the musical, bricolage in the social problem film lends a sense of realism to scenes and allows us to believe in the everydayness of the characters.

In all the Dead End Kids cycles, the emphasis on a character's ability (or inability) to navigate the city landscape is especially apparent in how representatives of official society, like police officers and social workers, are depicted. A recurring plot device in the original Dead End Kids cycle and its spin-off cycles is a character who is either wrongly accused of a crime (*'Neath Brooklyn Bridge* [1942, Wallace Fox], *Little Tough Guy, Angels Wash Their Faces, They Made Me a Criminal, Ghosts on the Loose* [1943, William Beaudine]) or whose punishment far exceeds the crime committed (*Dead End, Crime School, Hell's Kitchen*), creating the impression that the police and the judicial system are not to be trusted to uphold social laws. Instead, the Kids must cleverly navigate the city and seek justice for themselves. In *'Neath Brooklyn Bridge*, part of Monogram's East Side Kids series, the boys, despite their lack of formal education and propensity toward goofing off, are able to clear Danny (Bobby Jordan) of false murder charges and to catch the real killers in the act of committing a new crime, all while protecting the stepdaughter of the murdered man. The police are necessary only when the time comes to put on the handcuffs. Not surprisingly, the boys make cracks about the ineptitude of the police throughout the film.

Another important semantic element of these social-problem-film cycles is their emphasis on "down on their luck" characters: working-class white males, ranging in age from adolescence to early twenties, who are raised by abusive or nonexistent families. In *Dead End*, baby-faced Angel (Bobby Jordan) tells the gang about the severe beating he and his mother received from his drunken father the previous evening. Angel's nonchalant account of these events and his friends' blasé responses—at one point they interrupt his story in order to heckle a passerby—indicates that such parental behavior is commonplace and accepted in their world. In the original Dead End Kids cycle and its spin-offs, the best parents are those adults without children. In several films in the original cycle, including *Dead End*, *Crime School*, and *Little Tough Guy*, Billy Halop's character is portrayed as having the most promise of all the boys because he is an orphan being raised by his educated, responsible older sister. The other boys, whose parents are rarely seen or mentioned, find parental figures in Tommy's sister, her upwardly mobile suitors, and neighborhood do-gooders who, unlike everyone else in town, have some faith in the Kids. It is as if the Kids were conceived by the city itself, a parent that feeds, clothes, and, ultimately, corrupts them.

In addition to having similar childhood experiences (extreme poverty, lack of positive adult role models, exposure to violence at an early age), the characters populating these social problem films are marked by their clothing and diction. In the original Dead End Kids cycle, clothing is primarily a reflection of socioeconomic circumstances: the boys wear jeans or khakis, always stained and ripped, with undershirts or sweaters. Often, their clothes are far too big for them, pointing to origins as hand-me-downs or Salvation Army donations. During the course of a Dead End Kids movie, this clothing might be contrasted with that of a wealthy boy of the same age who is dressed in a suit, a private school uniform, or a starched, button-down shirt and dress pants (see *Dead End*, *Little Tough Guy*, *'Neath Brooklyn Bridge*, or *East Side Kids*). Occasionally, when the boys are shown to be making some money (*Little Tough Guy*, *Clancy Street Boys* [1943, William Beaudine]), they acquire gaudy zoot suits and wide-brimmed hats in imitation of the nouveau riche gangsters they see around their neighborhoods.

These characters are also marked by their diction and their use of a specific jargon reflecting their socioeconomic status and education. Most of the gang, particularly Leo Gorcey and Huntz Hall—since they are more caricatured than the other Dead End Kids—speak with a heavy Brooklyn accent.[5] For instance, in *Clancy Street Boys*, part of

The clothing of the financially destitute Dead End Kids is often contrasted with that of a wealthier child.

Monogram's East Side Kids cycle, the gang celebrates Muggs's (Leo Gorcey) eighteenth birthday. After Muggs is presented with a birthday cake decorated with a sign reading "Hapy Boithday," the gang demands a speech. When he struggles to find the right words, Muggs sheepishly admits, "I ignored my vocabulation when I was a kid." A running gag throughout the Dead End Kids cycles involves the boys' malapropisms, usually uttered by Huntz Hall and greeted with a smack by Leo Gorcey. These moments highlight the Otherness of these characters and their difference from the middle and upper classes.

TYING SEMANTICS TO SYNTAX

In the original Dead End Kids cycle, the aforementioned semantic elements, such as the independent camera, a focus on mise-en-scène, and the use of slang, are tied to a consistent syntax, namely, the belief that criminality is rooted in the environment in which an individual is raised. This belief, stemming from the ideology of the Progressive movement, maintains that criminals are not born but made. The most salient semantic element of these cycles, their focus on the mise-en-scène, is used to show the viewer how and why these characters became juvenile delinquents in the first place. As I argued in

Chapter 1, this emphasis on an environment-based explanation for criminal behavior, which dates back to the silent "melodramatic" gangster and social problem films of the 1910s and 1920s, is used to create empathy for characters who commit despicable acts. However, this approach to the depiction of criminality changed in the 1930s with the arrival of the Production Code. The Code, first drafted in 1930, proclaimed that "law, natural or human, shall not be ridiculed, nor shall sympathy be created for its violation" (quoted in Vieira, *Sin in Soft Focus*, 217). The post-Code gangster film, in an effort to gain the PCA's seal of approval (without which films would suffer at the box office), consequently did not attempt to provide a reason, other than greed and a competitive spirit, for the gangster's criminality. To argue that a gangster turned to crime because he had been raised in poverty would create sympathy for his depraved point of view, and, worse, it would imply that the American Dream was somehow flawed. Consequently, many post-Code gangster films veer away from a sympathetic, environmental approach to criminality and criminals.

While the sentimentalized criminal hero, who is depicted as turning to crime as the only way to make ends meet in an antagonistic urban milieu, would not reappear on-screen again until the mid to late 1940s, in film noirs like *Force of Evil* (1948, Abraham Polonsky), the PCA did not seem concerned about depictions of the origins of criminality if the criminal being sentimentalized was a juvenile. The newly emerging concepts of the teenager and the juvenile delinquent did not gain a firm foothold in the American public imagination until after World War II, but a heightened interest in youth and criminality had nevertheless been brewing in the years leading up to the war.[6] Therefore, in many films of the Dead End Kids cycle, we find a doubled perspective on the post-Depression street urchin. On the one hand is the nurture side of the nature-nurture debate, which argues that the juvenile delinquent cannot help his criminality because the city has brutalized him to the point that he must turn to a criminal lifestyle in order to survive. At the same time, these films also promote the nature side: the juvenile delinquent, no matter how brutalized, always has the ability to choose a moral life that will support the needs of the status quo. In these social problem films, the juvenile delinquent is both fated to become a criminal *and* free to choose the straight and narrow path.

The semantics of the original Dead End Kids cycle support this dual syntax. The cycle's fetishistic attention to the garbage on the streets, the small, dingy apartments, the boys' ripped T-shirts, and their thick working-class accents demands that the audience take these factors into account before judging the behavior of the juvenile delinquents on-screen. The use of a "message with a capital M," conveyed through digressive camera movements, in which the camera focuses on a detail unnecessary to forwarding the film's plot or, even more explicitly, through characters' didactic monologues, also provides explanation and context for the delinquents' choices. At one point in *Dead End*, Dave makes an impassioned speech about the Dead End Kids: "They gotta fight for a place to play, fight for the likes of something to eat, fight for everything. . . . 'Enemies of Society,' it says in the papers. Why not? What have they got to be so friendly about?" This idea, whether directly spoken or implied, appears in a slightly varied form in the other films of the original Dead End Kids cycle. In *Crime School*, a juvenile-court judge asks each of the boys why their parents are not present in court, a device alerting the audience to their impoverished childhoods: Frankie (Billy Halop) says he is an orphan being raised by his older sister; Squirt (Bobby Jordan) tells the judge, "My parents couldn't come. They're dead"; and Bugs (Gabriel Dell) explains, "My mother's in jail and my father went to get the check—we're on relief." The boys have committed a serious crime—they accidentally killed an innocent pawnshop owner—but *Crime School* uses this extended sequence to create sympathy for the boys and to remind us that they are not deserving of the cruel treatment awaiting them at the corrupt reform school where the judge eventually sends them.

Although such moments work to convince the audience that the Dead End Kids are essentially good boys who have been raised in the wrong environment, most entries in the original cycle also contain semantic elements supporting an opposing point of view—that no matter how terrible slum life might be, the juvenile delinquent always has the choice to take the moral path. Many of these films contain at least one character who grew up in the slums (like the Dead End Kids) and yet still manages to steer clear of crime in order to become a respectable, even influential, member of society. Prominent examples of these moral characters include Dave Connell in *Dead End*, Father Connelly (Pat O'Brien) in *Angels with Dirty Faces*, Paul (Robert Wilcox) in *Little Tough Guy*, Danny's cop brother Phil (Dave O'Brien) in *'Neath Brooklyn Bridge*, and Officer Pat O'Day (Leon Ames) in *East Side Kids*. Furthermore, the boys are often depicted as being incapable of acting civilized, implying that delinquency is a choice. In *Little Tough Guy*, for example, the gang decides to attend a "Young America" meeting, populated with upwardly mobile boys. The guest speaker regales his eager audience with platitudes like "It isn't where you live and the kind of clothes you wear, it's the way you live" and "Give everything you've got to whatever you're doing." Both statements are reiterations of the myth of the American Dream and its attendant Puritan work ethic. However, earlier in the film, the myth of the American Dream is questioned when Tommy's hard-working father is put on death row for getting caught up in a factory strike that turned deadly; his hard work and patience brings misery, not prosperity, to his family. The speaker's advice is useless to this gang of juvenile delinquents, and so they whack, smack, and curse the crowd of boys at the Young America meeting, eventually whipping the entire crowd into a raucous fight. This scene implies that because the Dead End Kids are cynical about the possibility of living a law-abiding life, they have made the choice to remain delinquents. Because of the combination of PCA strictures as well as a desire to please as large a segment of the audience as possible, the original Dead End Kids cycle provided its viewers with two contradictory views on the contemporary juvenile delinquent.

These mixed feelings toward crime and the juvenile delinquent is best exemplified in the conclusion of *Angels with Dirty Faces*, a film about which Joseph Breen, the director of the PCA from 1933 to 1954, was especially concerned. The film's famous ending, in which Rocky Sullivan (James Cagney), a hero to the Dead End Kids, "turns yellow" during his execution, is purposefully ambiguous. Did Rocky become a coward in order to keep the Kids from admiring him or because he truly was a coward in the final moments of his life? The former reading makes Rocky a diegetic coward but a nondiegetic hero, effectively opposing the PCA's proviso on the depiction of criminals. The latter reading counters the image of Rocky as a fearless gangster hero, thereby appeasing PCA regulations. Regardless of how we interpret Rocky's final act, his behavior convinces the boys that the criminal life is hardly worth emulating. If the film had ended there, with the boys agreeing to change their delinquent ways, we could argue that *Angels with Dirty Faces* is promoting the belief that no matter the environment, an individual always has a choice about embarking on a life of crime. Father Connelly, who committed numerous (albeit petty) crimes as a boy, is living proof of the power of rational moral choice. But then this message is offset by the film's final image, in which Father Connelly, shot at a low angle and bathed in white top lighting (making him appear even holier and wiser than usual), tells the boys, "Let's go say a prayer for a boy who couldn't run as fast as I could." Here, the priest effectively counteracts the concept of free choice by attributing his own decision to go straight as a child to the fact that he did not get caught and sent to reform school as Rocky did. In its final moments, *Angels with Dirty Faces* leads the audience to believe

The final words spoken by Father Connelly (Pat O'Brien) in *Angels with Dirty Faces* (1938) contradict the film's earlier message of free will.

that fate or chance, not choice, has made Father Connelly a respected priest, and Rocky Sullivan a criminal in the electric chair.

The films of the original Dead End Kids cycle suggest that juvenile delinquency, whether caused by nature or nurture, is a serious social problem. However, their conclusions, with the exception of the ambiguous and pessimistic *Dead End*, always provide the audience with visible, though inadequate, individualistic resolutions to the problems depicted. These films argue that poverty can be fixed through "reformed" (that is, uncorrupt) reform schools, kindly juvenile-court justices, community-minded police officers, and good old American pluck. As Marcia Landy argues, a central convention of the Hollywood social problem film is that "the conflicts [are] often resolved through a populist benefactor or through the efforts of an exceptional individual who overcame economic and social constraints in the interests of the community" (*Genres*, 433). In *Crime School*, the problems of the reform school are not attributed to the flawed structure of the criminal justice system as a whole, but to one corrupt individual, Warden Morgan (Cy Kendall). This warden, who violently beats disobedient boys and subjects them to life-threatening labor, is an undisputed villain, and the audience clearly sides with the boys in their quest to escape his clutches. *Crime School*, like other entries in the original Dead End Kids cycle, gains its moral force by playing off agreed-upon beliefs—in this case, that abusing boys and embezzling government funds is wrong—rather than offering a more controversial criticism of the way the criminal justice system handles the rehabilitation of juveniles. With the help of the upright superintendent of state reformatories, Mark Braden (Humphrey Bogart), the Dead End Kids are able to "fix" their reform school merely by ensuring that the corrupt Morgan goes to jail. The film's coda reinforces the feeling that all is well when we see the newly paroled Dead End Kids back in juvenile court. This time around, however, they are wearing suits, sitting with their magically restored families, and discussing the possibility of school and future careers. One boy is even reading a book entitled *How to Break into Society* (perhaps in a cheeky nod to the film's overly rosy conclusion).

These tidy resolutions highlight how social problem films of the 1930s and 1940s generally alert viewers to social problems but then assure them that these problems are easily solved.[7] Social problem films rarely address the true causes of the problems they portray, since the most frequently depicted social problems—inner-city poverty, crime, juvenile delinquency, unemployment, and drug abuse—are far too complex to be sufficiently addressed in two hours or less of entertainment. Social problem films are, at best, "cathartic, purging us for the time being of anxieties and guilt over the state of the world" (Roffman and Purdy, *Social Problem Film*, 305). The original Dead End Kids cycle provides this catharsis, allowing us both to weep over the plight of urban youth and then to feel reassured that there is a feasible solution to their suffering.

A THEORY OF CYCLE EVOLUTION

It is not surprising that concerns about urban youth were translated into a successful cycle of social problem films in the late 1930s—the topic was timely and understood by a large portion of the audience to be a problem. Film reviews, one of the first ways in which a film's structures of meaning are communicated to a mass audience, also helped exploit audience interest in these problems by consistently describing these films as capable of addressing timely social issues. In a 1937 issue of the *National Board of Review Magazine*, for instance, New York City's tenement house commissioner described *Dead End* as a film that exposed "the horrible influences surrounding the children of the slums" (quoted in Stead, *Film and the Working Class*, 94). A *New*

York Times review claimed that *Dead End* "deserves a place among the important motion pictures of 1937 for its all-out and well-presented reiteration of the social protest that was the theme of the original Sidney Kingsley stage play," and that it made a *"prima facie* case for a revision of the social system" (McManus). A review in *Time* magazine (6 September 1937) concludes: "The not unhappy ending of the screen version of Dead End is no less valid than that of the stage original, and should strike even the most critical cinemagoers as art rather than artifice." Finally, the *New York Post* proclaimed: "The best thing that could have been done at the last session of Congress would have been to show the film *Dead End* to the committee which crippled the Wagner Housing Act" (quoted in Getz, *Broadway to the Bowery*, 11). *Dead End* also earned numerous Academy Award nominations, further solidifying its status as an important picture (Roffman and Purdy, *Social Problem Film*, 141; Getz, *Broadway to the Bowery*, 11). The uniformity of these discourses about *Dead End*—commenting on its realism, social importance, and timeliness—indicates how certain patterns of interpretation, motivated by the filmic text, historical context, actor interviews, and advertisements, coalesce into a single narrative and help preemptively define the content of a film or group of films. In this case, the narrative insisted that *Dead End* was socially important.

While it is nearly impossible to understand exactly how economically, racially, and ethnically diverse viewing audiences in the 1930s and 1940s read and understood the Dead End Kids cycles at the time of their release, it is possible to examine the public discourses circulating around these texts by analyzing reviews, editorials, and studio advertising campaigns. By analyzing this range of texts, the film historian can reconstruct the interpretive strategies available to the films' original viewers. I am borrowing this methodology—the idea that a viewer's understanding of a text is always dependent on an interaction with other viewers as well as with public discourses—from Janet Staiger's concept of historical reception studies. Her approach "attempts to illuminate the cultural meanings of texts in specific times and social circumstances to specific viewers, and it attempts to contribute to discussions about the spectatorial effects of films by moving beyond text-centered analyses" ("Taboos and Totems," 162). Staiger argues that in this type of study, the film is less an object of analysis than it is an "event" or "a set of interpretations or affective experiences produced by individuals from an encounter with a text or set of texts within a social situation" (163). Though all viewers make independent readings of texts, we are nevertheless profoundly shaped by the information circulating around us at the moment we happen to watch a film. As Staiger tells us, "free readers" do not exist (143). What I hope to uncover in the remainder of this chapter is a tentative theory of cycle evolution by analyzing the affective experiences originally produced by these film cycles and how these experiences changed over time.

As previously mentioned, the films released in the wake of *Dead End*'s success offered "solutions" to the problems of juvenile delinquency by reinforcing the status quo and reconciling the boys with society. Even though the films in this original cycle were derivative—offering the same plots and character types over and over—film reviewers continued to describe the early entries in this cycle, such as *Crime School* and *Angels with Dirty Faces*, as capable of effectively addressing contemporary social ills. For instance, a *Photoplay* capsule review of *Crime School*, the second film in the original Dead End Kids cycle, explains: "Those 'Dead End' boys are here again, and you'd better go to see them, as they lift a somewhat grim social problem picture to fascinating entertainment" (6). This review defines the core of the social problem film's appeal—disturbing social problems serve as objects of fascination and entertainment. A review in the *New York Times* is slightly more critical of *Crime School*, noting that it "bears a family resemblance to 'Dead End' and to 'San Quentin,' not to mention the old Cagney film, 'The Mayor of Hell'" (Nugent). While Frank Nugent is annoyed with what he sees as a distinct pattern forming in these films—the boys are delinquents who eventually reform—he also writes that the "close range study of the screen's six best bad boys" is, nevertheless, "fascinating."

By the third entry in the cycle, *Angels with Dirty Faces*, the cycle's formula was clear, with the Kids revisiting the delinquent personas first established in *Dead End* and *Crime School*. Given the success of United Artists and, later, Warner Bros. with exploiting the topic of juvenile delinquency, it is not surprising that several other studios began releasing films with similar characters and themes around this time.[8] Monogram released *Boys of the Streets* (1938, William Nigh) and *Streets of New York* (1939, William Nigh); Columbia made *Boys' Reformatory* (1939, Howard Bretherton); MGM made *Boys Town* (1938, Norman Taurog); and RKO released *Boy Slaves* (1939, P. J. Wolfson).[9] *Boy Slaves* even uses an actor who resembles Dead End Kids star Huntz Hall, perhaps with the hope that audiences might get confused and think that the film was part of the original Dead End Kids cycle. In addition, female variations on the Dead End Kids formula were released concurrently with the original cycle, including *Girls on Proba-*

Films like *Boys Town* (1938) replicated the semantics and syntax of *Dead End.*

tion (1938, William C. McGann) and *Beloved Brat* (1938, Arthur Lubin). These two films starred Dead End Kids regulars Ronald Reagan and Leo Gorcey, respectively, and were released by First National, a production company under the umbrella of Warner Bros. And Million Dollar Productions, a production company specializing in "race pictures," created a black-cast version of the formula in 1939, titled *Reform School* (Leo C. Popkin). The cast of this film was dubbed the Harlem Tuff Kids, presumably in an attempt to kick-start another film cycle about juvenile delinquents.[10] Thus, from approximately 1937 to 1939, the film market was saturated with images of juvenile delinquents—African American and white, male and female—suffering from various social injustices.

Concurrent with this surge in films about juvenile delinquency in the late 1930s was a change in the public discourses surrounding these films. While *Dead End* was considered a piece of "social protest" upon its release, a *Photoplay* review of Monogram's *Streets of New York*, a B film starring popular street urchin Jackie Cooper and released just two years later, describes the film's depiction of "an underprivileged kid's regeneration" as "routine" (8). The appearance of juvenile-delinquent-themed films, released by different studios, also affected the reception of the original Dead End Kids cycle. A *Photoplay* review of

Hell's Kitchen claims that by the end of the film, the boys have "made a 'Boys Town' out of *Hell's Kitchen*" (86), implying that the film is simply an imitation of MGM's *Boys Town*. Bosley Crowther was likewise wearied by the repetitiveness of *Hell's Kitchen*: "The Dead End Kids, Inc., have been so stubbornly anti-social for so long that it might surprise you to discover them in their latest film, 'Hell's Kitchen,' at the Globe, as a stalwart band of misused youngsters, tucked away in a shelter home for boys, just awearying for a quick regeneration from which (this time) they are brazenly deprived." Crowther's mocking tone and use of the term "Dead End Kids, Inc." indicates that these characters were becoming less and less convincing as victims as they received more and more exposure on the big screen. The glut of juvenile delinquent films as well as the predictability of the Dead End Kids formula, this time in its fifth iteration, had clearly weakened the cycle's capacity for social critique. They were parts of a franchise now ("The Dead End Kids, Inc."), not realistic depictions. Crowther's apparent boredom with the cycle's repetitive plots is representative of the critical reaction to these films as the cycle aged.

In fact, as early as 1939, most critics found the Dead End Kids–initiated juvenile delinquent cycle to be "routine" and clichéd (Roffman and Purdy, *Social Problem Film*, 144). The main source of this cycle's appeal—its exploitation of contemporary social problems—was no longer believable. To list just a few examples: *Photoplay*'s review of *Little Tough Guy*, the first entry in Universal's spin-off cycle, the Dead End Kids and the Little Tough Guys, comments on its approach to plot: "If you examine the rather fabricated story too closely, you will find both this idea and that of '*Crime School*' had the same origin" (70). And the *New York Times* review of *Pride of the Bowery* (1941, Joseph H. Lewis), which was part of the East Side Kids cycle, laments: "There was a time when . . . we, too, believed that the Dead End Kids or their current facsimiles could be converted to the better and finer things of life. No more. For after an innumerable series of soul-launderings and glib regenerations they are bobbing up again. . . . That spark of decency invariably fanned into a bright pure flame in the last reel is again given the bellows by the authors, but we don't trust it" (T. S., 15). It is significant that the reviewer attributes his annoyance with *Pride of the Bowery* not so much to the film itself, but to the sheer number of similar films being made at the time. It is difficult for the reviewer to continue to buy into the "truth" of these characters. They have become mere facsimiles, empty replicas, of the earnest and comparatively "realistic" characters found in *Dead End*.

Similarly, Bosley Crowther notes in his review of *Angels Wash Their*

Faces that "the Dead Enders (though the traffic in them seems more worthy of an arterial highway) are pitting themselves against the injustices of an adult world with unsurprising success, considering the way they've grown." And by 1941, Crowther had become positively fed up. In a column entitled "Gnashing of Teeth: Here Are a Few of the Things to Which This Column Took Exception This Year," Crowther concluded his long list of grievances with this plea: "But the truly wonderful thing would be a liquidation of the 'Dead End' Kids and all their assorted gangs of hoodlums which have been offshoots thereof. The picture we are waiting to see is the one in which those kids are rounded up, faced against a wall and mowed down with machine gun fire, followed by a notarized caption, 'This is absolutely the last appearance of the Dead End Kids.'" Crowther's annoyance with the Dead End Kids, revealed in his 1940 review of *East Side Kids*, grew exponentially in the space of one year. He went from hoping for the end of the cycle to fantasizing about the violent murders of its characters. Crowther's strong reaction to these film cycles is a testament to the film cycle's ability to quickly endear itself to audiences and then, just as quickly, to annoy them.

The Dead End Kids films were popular enough among audiences to justify a slew of imitators, but the repetitiveness of the films' plots made it difficult for viewers to accept the reality they were presenting. Even coverage of the cycle's cast began to change in tone over time. When the *New York Times* did a piece on the young actors just before the release of *Dead End* in 1937, the reporter, Thomas Pryor, described them as kids from the streets of New York who were bowled over when director William Wyler showed up on set riding a motorcycle. The kids also told Pryor that it was difficult for them to relate to costar Sylvia Sidney, since "guys like us just don't get along with dames" ("Local Boys Make Good"). The actors are characterized as sincere ingénues, appropriately dazzled by the excitement of Hollywood and nervous around starlets and women in general, like any regular teenage boys might be. However, a little more than two years later, in January 1940, the *New York Times* portrayed the same group of actors as consumed with the Hollywood life of "dames, cars and pictures" (Franchey, "Victims of Café Society"). Even the title of the piece mocks the boys' new socioeconomic status and its incongruity with the type of characters they portray on the big screen. John Franchey describes the actors as "professional street urchins," and his article lingers on details, such as the fact that Leo Gorcey was particular about the way his cocktails were prepared. The boys, once depicted as real and earnest, are now egotistical and demanding Hollywood poseurs, a transformation mirroring how the semantics of the Dead End Kids cycle were perceived by critics over time. If part of a social problem film's claims to authenticity are predicated on the use of unknown or character actors—whose screen presence cannot easily be associated with that of a real-life actor or the glamour of Hollywood—then the increasing fame of the Dead End Kids would have also affected the ability of these films to convey a sense of realism to audiences familiar with their offscreen personas.[11]

Even though the themes and images of the Dead End Kids were expanded into an industry-wide, intergeneric cycle (that is, a cycle whose films are released by multiple studios at the same time) within one year of their cinematic debut in 1937, this juvenile delinquent cycle never developed into a stable and coherent genre of its own. This example runs counter to Rick Altman's theories about cycle growth. Altman has argued that during the reign of the studio system, as long as a film cycle was associated with the contract actors and proprietary characters of a single studio, other studios would not attempt to release similar films. Altman reasons that a small studio like Monogram would have had little to gain by emulating Warner Bros.' established film properties because Monogram would only have been adding to the buzz surrounding Warner Bros.' "proprietary" cycle. He explains that only "when conditions are favorable can single-studio cycles be built into industry-wide genres" (*Film/Genre*, 61). By "favorable conditions," Altman refers to the moment when a cycle can be defined by elements that are both widely perceived by audiences and "easily" shared by studios (that is, recognizable plots and settings as opposed to recognizable actors). But as I have just demonstrated, *Dead End* knockoffs were released by several different studios less than one year after *Dead End*, and concurrently with the remainder of the original Dead End Kids cycle, and yet this industry-wide juvenile delinquent cycle never developed into its own stable juvenile delinquent genre. Consequently, while I agree that the industry-wide adoption of a cycle can sometimes lead to the formation of a stable and coherent genre, it may also lead to an opposing effect—the decline and eventual collapse of that cycle.

A MOVE TO COMEDY

The critics' reactions to the Dead End Kids, Dead End Kids and Little Tough Guys, and East Side Kids cycles indicate that these cycles were no longer effectively communicating their social messages to audiences by the late 1930s and early 1940s. But why? It appears that the process of cycle formation and proliferation had a profound impact on the ability of these film cycles to effectively communicate with film critics (and by extension, the moviegoing audience). Critics expressed an increasing exhaustion with the narratives, characters, and thematics of these films as more and more of them were released. As mentioned in the Introduction, for a cycle to form, it needs to repeat the same images and plots over and over within a brief window of time. This derivative type of repetition occurs because film producers frequently act as "film critics," analyzing and isolating the most bankable elements of a financially successful film and then repeating only those elements in their next release in order to maximize their profit potential (Altman, *Film/Genre*, 43). In the case of the Dead End Kids cycle, its semantics were its most bankable elements, and so they were isolated and repeated in film after film. However, these films were also social problem films, and the very process of cycle formation worked to vitiate the social problem film's primary appeal: its ability to depict social problems in a realistic fashion.

In other words, by attempting to replicate the success of previous films, later films in the Dead End Kids cycles reproduced the signifiers of *Dead End*—plucky street urchins, urban settings, and run-ins with the police—but not their signifieds—the message that the current social and economic structure was creating a generation of criminals. After so much repetition, these signifiers became referents not of real people suffering in a real world, but of the images found in previously successful films. Jean Baudrillard argued that without the dialectic between signifier and signified, which allows for the accumulation of information and meanings, it is not possible to determine significance, gain knowledge, or place any value on anything: "Released from any 'archaic' obligation it may have had to designate something, the sign is at last free for a structural or combinatory play that succeeds the previous role of determinate equivalence" (*Selected Writings*, 129).

Without a dialectic between signifier and signified, the images of the Dead End Kids cycles could no longer be linked in any meaningful way with the real-world concerns they once represented; the cycles' characters, to quote the aforementioned *New York Times* review, had become "facsimiles" of their former selves. A similar breakdown occurs between the semantic and syntactic elements of the social-problem-film cycle over time. The semantics of the original Dead End Kids cycle—such as the image of a smudge-faced street urchin—were once capable of generating awareness and concern about a timely social issue (its syntax). But as these semantic elements were duplicated too often in too short of a time period, they increasingly lost their ability to convey the same thematic meanings. Without sympathy—an emotion integral to the effectiveness of the social problem film—the entries in this cycle could no longer function as social problem films.

Once the semantics of the Dead End Kids cycles lost their grounding in their original social-problem-film syntax, they had to be attached to a new generic syntax in order to continue to pull in an audience. From the patterns established by the Dead End Kids cycle and its spin-off cycles, the first response appears to have been a move into comedy. This transition made sense, since film comedy has a weak, inconsistent set of semantic elements and therefore is able to easily "combine with or to parody virtually every other genre or form" (Neale, *Genre and Hollywood*, 66). For this reason, Thomas Schatz labels genres like the musical and the comedy as "genres of indeterminate space," since they rely "less upon a heavily coded place than on a highly conventionalized value system" (*Hollywood Genres*, 29). In *Dead End*, the image of a boy stealing potatoes in order to get his daily sustenance is tied to the social problem film's syntax: when we read this image, we understand that this boy is poor and destitute and in need of society's intervention. But in a comic East Side Kids film like *'Neath Brooklyn Bridge*, this same image of a boy stealing food is attached to the syntax of the comedy, and consequently bears very different meanings. Rather than indicating that the little boy needs our help, these images invite the viewer to both marvel and chuckle at the delinquent's mastery of his urban landscape and his ability to outsmart the law and its restrictions. *'Neath Brooklyn Bridge*, because it is a comedy, does not ask us to ponder why this boy should have to steal or whether he can be reformed or what his home life might be like. These are the concerns of a social problem film like *Dead End*, not a comedy like *'Neath Brooklyn Bridge*.

How are films able to make this switch? What cues the viewer to laugh rather than cry at a particular image? In his essay "Horror and Humor," Noel Carroll explores a similar question, namely, to understand how two "broadly implausible affects [horror and humor] can attach to the same stimulus" (145). Of particular interest to my purposes here is Carroll's discussion of how the same semantic cue, the Frankenstein monster, elicits fear in one film, *House of Frankenstein* (1944, Erle C. Kenton), but laughter in another, *Abbott and Costello Meet Frankenstein* (1948, Charles Barton). One reason for this shift in affect is the frame or climate created by each film. If the characters being threatened by the Frankenstein monster are "clowns," that

The once-frightening Frankenstein monster becomes humorous in the context of a comedy like *Abbott and Costello Meet Frankenstein* (1948).

is, indestructible, then the fictional environment is marked as "safe": "Within the comic frame, though injury, pain and death are often elements in a joke, we are not supposed to dwell on them, especially in terms of their moral or human weight or consequences" (152). Comedy, which Carroll labels an "amoral" genre, does not invite viewers to feel empathy for characters—this is why we laugh rather than scream when Wyle E. Coyote is smashed flat with an anvil in a Road Runner cartoon. Similarly, we are not asked to feel sympathy for the adolescents in *'Neath Brooklyn Bridge*, and so we are able to laugh at them instead. Semantic elements, like a young boy forced to steal, are freed of all the serious or weighty obligations of the social problem film once they are placed within the comic frame. For example, getting arrested and thrown into jail or reform school is an event with grave consequences in a social problem film like *Dead End*, but it is merely another bump along the road to a happy resolution in an East Side Kids comedy like *Smart Alecks* (1942, Wallace Fox).

Gerald Mast argues that the comic frame is created through "a series of signs that lets us know the action is taking place in a comic world, that it will be 'fun' (even if at some moments it will not be), that we are to enjoy and not worry" (*Comic Mind*, 9). He further explains that this climate can be established through a silly title, iconic comic actors, the presence of one-dimensional comic types, improbable plots, the reduction of a serious subject to a trivial one, absurdist dialogue, self-consciousness or artificiality, and film style (9–11). In addition to the establishment of this comic frame, it is the inherently repetitive nature of film cycles that allows for their easy transition into new generic climates. For instance, the two films cited by Carroll, which employ the image of the Frankenstein monster for two very different effects, were each part of long-running film cycles: *House of Frankenstein* was part of Universal's monster cycle, and *Abbott and Costello Meet Frankenstein* was, of course, part of the Abbott and Costello franchise. The humor of the latter hinges on the immediate recognizability of the Frankenstein monster, Bud Abbott, and Lou Costello, and the incongruity of their meeting. But these semantic elements could be redeployed for other syntactic purposes only after they had been repeated enough to be recognizable even in a radically different context. *Abbott and Costello Meet Frankenstein* would not have worked in the same way had it marked the first cinematic appearance of the Frankenstein monster or the first appearance of the Abbott and Costello comedy duo.

The more a particular image or character is repeated in a series of films, the easier it is to recognize and define that image or character, even if very little information is provided in the new text. Colin McArthur describes this process of meaning accumulation as the "curious alchemy of the cinema": "Each successive appearance in the genre further solidifies the actor's screen persona until he no longer plays a role but assimilates it to the collective entity made up of his own body and personality and his past screen roles" (*Underworld USA*, 24). Thus, while *Dead End* needed to spend screen time establishing the personalities and backgrounds of each of the Dead End Kids, *Boys of the City* (1940, Joseph H. Lewis), an East Side Kids film released just three years later, jumps right into the plot, confident that viewers will already be familiar with the characters and their basic traits. The oft-repeated semantics used by *Boys of the City* are capable of signifying a host of meanings instantly, merely by appearing in the film. Furthermore, the inherently repetitive process of cycle formation frees certain images to be used for any purpose whatsoever. These images or signs "exchange among themselves, without interacting with the real" (Baudrillard, *Selected Writings*, 128) or without an origin in the "real." Consequently, the image or sign (the smudge-faced juvenile delinquent in *Boys in the City*) detached from its signified (a poor little child who requires social intervention) is all surface and no meaning.

And this state of meaninglessness is conducive to the all-important comic shtick, allowing us to laugh rather than cry at the image's presence in a new context.

It is not surprising then that the majority of the films in Monogram Studio's successful East Side Kids cycle—initiated in 1940, just after the completion of the first Dead End Kids cycle—retain the basic semantics of the original cycle, but are comedies.[12] Placing the semantics of a film like *Dead End* into a comic frame facilitated the East Side Kids cycle's transition from the syntax of the social problem film to that of the comedy. This comic frame was established primarily by altering the destitute socioeconomic backgrounds of the boys. As I mentioned, in the original Dead End Kids cycle, the boys' biological parents were usually only mentioned as people who inflicted beatings, got drunk, and yelled at their sons. The East Side Kids cycle, however, takes a decidedly less hostile view toward parents and other authority figures. In *Kid Dynamite* (1943, Wallace Fox), there is significant characterization of the protagonists' mothers, while in *Clancy Street Boys*, the entire plot revolves around the subject of Muggs's family. In all cases, parents and guardians are depicted as supportive and loving. Moreover, while the East Side Kids are always strapped for cash, they are not the impoverished street urchins of the original Dead End Kids cycle. For instance, when it is necessary to don suits in order to participate in a jitterbug contest in *Kid Dynamite*, none of the boys have any problem locating one. In this cycle, the gang's day-to-day outfits, which remain consistent from film to film, have been upgraded from torn, oversized hand-me-downs to the clean but casual attire of a lower-middle-class teenager.[13] Finally, rather than hanging out on the docks or on someone's front porch, the gang has a clubhouse, for which they presumably pay rent (since the East Side gang charges monthly dues).

These changes ease the transition from social problem film to the comedy, since the boys are released from their previous positions as social victims; the boys never wonder where their next meal will come from or whether they will sustain a beating from an angry parent. They are thus free to become picaresque heroes, and each film provides them with new opportunities to showcase their comedic talents. As in most "clown comedy," or comedies centering on a comic figure or troupe, the East Side Kids' story lines are a "convenience on which the film clown can 'hang' his comic shtick" (Gehring, "Comedy Genres," 189). By contrast, the outcome of the social problem film's narrative is always significant: will the juvenile be sent to reform school or be given a second chance? Within the comic frame, the an-

Muggs (Leo Gorcey) and Danny (Bobby Jordan) are able to find suits for a dance in *Kid Dynamite* (1943).

swer to this question is of little to no importance. In the switch from social problem film to comedy, the significance of the plot is subjugated to the significance of the image or sight gag. The image is valued over its context and content, effectively severing the relationship between semantics and syntax.

Another way to understand the change in affect from the original Dead End Kids cycle to its spin-off cycles is through the difference between two viewing positions: the "gaze" and the "glance." According to Janet Staiger, the gaze is a mode of reception generally aligned with classical Hollywood cinema, since it emphasizes reading and interpretation: "The gaze cinema creates a fixed subjectivity and unified identity through its narrative continuities, closures, central characters, and flexible realism" (*Perverse Spectators*, 15). By contrast, the glance, a mode of reception generally aligned with preclassical and postmodern cinema, encourages "sporadic attention to the screen" (15). Staiger, however, argues that these two modes of reception are not necessarily time bound and have existed side by side throughout the history of cinema. She sees certain film genres as being more or less aligned with particular modes of reception: melodramas, gangster films, and thrillers invite the gaze, while action-adventure films, slapstick or gag comedies, fantasies, and westerns all invite the glance

(22). I would add the category of the social problem film to Staiger's list of gaze genres. Social problem films require emotional investment or sympathy on the part of viewers if they are to think of the characters as existing in a real world and suffering from real problems. Social problem films require audiences to become absorbed in the narrative and invested in their characters. Glance genres do not require the same degree of emotional investment in order to fulfill their generic purposes. Viewers can be distracted, skimming over the surface of the text without becoming too attached to characters and their problems. The differences between these two viewing positions further explain why the same images can create different emotional reactions in audiences, depending on the context into which they are placed. For example, in the original Dead End Kids cycle—a group of films characterized by the gaze—Huntz Hall's propensity for malapropisms was developed as a way to show how the boys had not been properly educated, serving as a veiled social commentary about America's class inequities. However, in spin-off cycles like the East Side Kids—a group of films characterized by the glance—Hall's verbal confusion is transformed into one of his recurring jokes and an excuse to endure physical violence at the hands of Leo Gorcey. The social commentary generated by the engaged viewing position of the gaze becomes the comedic shtick generated by the distracted viewing position of the glance.

Laughter is also possible in the comedic East Side Kids cycle because its character have become clichés, images repeated so often that they are capable of instantly signifying a series of traits. A viewer familiar with the original Dead End Kids cycle knows that Huntz Hall's character, even if he appears under different names or in wildly different settings, will always be unintelligent, lazy, and clumsy. Throughout the course of a film, we can expect to hear him mispronounce a word, get smacked by Leo Gorcey, or fall down. The East Side Kids cycle also imported clichés from outside the original Dead End Kids cycle and used them as shorthand for various social and political issues. The most interesting and ideologically fraught example of this cycle's deployment of clichéd images is Scruno ("Sunshine" Sammy Morrison), the only recurring African American character in any of the Dead End Kids cycles.

The original Dead End Kids cycle was consistently identified in public discourses as realistically addressing the problems of underprivileged urban youth, yet it conspicuously avoided any discussion of the problems of nonwhite youth living in American cities.[14] The oppression experienced by the cycle's characters was based on social and class differences rather than on racial, ethnic, or religious differences. The cycle's omission of African American characters is significant: since the early 1900s, northern industrialized cities such as New York, Chicago, and Detroit had been becoming increasingly populated with African Americans migrating from the South. This Great Migration, taking place between 1910 and 1930, increased "the black populations in the northern urban centers by 300 percent" (Massood, *Black City Cinema*, 12). Monogram's apparent corrective to the absence of racial difference and urban blackness in the original Dead End Kids cycle is the addition of Scruno to the East Side Kids cycle. In these films, Scruno is treated like "one of the gang," and he is an equal to his friends (though Muggs is the undisputed leader of the group). Despite these apparent equalities, Scruno frequently makes out-of-place, racially charged comments during the course of any given East Side Kids film. In *Boys of the City*, to name one prominent example, Scruno is the only character to be served a giant hunk of watermelon during a formal dinner, leading him to exclaim, "I don't like that woman and I don't like that graveyard, but watermelon is watermelon *anytime*!" He then plunges his entire face into the fruit. Later in the same film, when exploring a haunted mansion, Scruno makes a casual reference to slavery, "Man, I sure do miss that old plantation!" The "joke" is that the haunted mansion is far more terrifying than the violent and corrosive legacy of slavery in the United States.

What is most interesting about these moments—and there are many of them in the East Side Kids cycle—is that they are out of place in the narrative: other characters rarely react to Scruno's one-liners, and often his jokes are delivered directly before the transition to a new scene, denying other characters the opportunity to productively engage with these comments. The incoherence of these moments and the narrative's inability to seamlessly incorporate Scruno and his outbursts of racial difference within the diegesis highlights this cycle's inability to properly address issues of race at a time when Hollywood cinema was beginning to grapple with America's racial problems.[15] By 1942, frustrations with the Hollywood film industry led the National Association for the Advancement of Colored People (NAACP) to demand that it amend its exclusionary hiring practices as well as improve its depiction of African American characters.[16] Walter White, then the head of the NAACP, demanded "a truer picture of the Negro as a normal member of society" (quoted in Nickel, "African American Men," 25). As a result, a series of social problem films were released—such as *Home of the Brave* (1949, Mark Robson)—that portrayed African Americans as "normal" and like "everyone else" in an attempt to close the racial divide in America. Consequently, in Hollywood films released after World War II, African American characters served a very particular function. If they appeared as a main character, then their race was the subject of the film or, rather, the "problem" of the film. The presence of an African American protagonist in a film of this era could mean only that the film was a social problem film and that that problem was race.

However, Scruno is not a social problem in the East Side Kids cycle, and neither are any of his white costars. Rather, because the East Side Kids cycle merely recycles the images of previous films and is no longer capable of engaging with real social problems, the character of Scruno is instead representative of earlier depictions of African Americans in Hollywood films. He is a mere cipher. For example, *Smart Alecks* opens with a scene in which Scruno is dancing in order to raise money for the gang's baseball uniforms. The first image is a high-angle medium shot of a pair of legs tap-dancing on a city sidewalk. Offscreen, we can hear the sounds of a harmonica playing and a crowd of onlookers enthusiastically cheering on the dance. As the camera tilts up, we see that these feet belong to Scruno, and that, as usual, he is the only African American character within the frame. While Scruno dances, the other members of the East Side gang goad the crowd of spectators by commenting on Scruno's dancing skill ("That boy gets more and more hep every day" and "Cut that rug, boy!") and panhandling. Throughout the scene, Scruno dances continually, smiling for the crowd but not speaking. This scene replicates the images of black performance found in earlier films like *The Little Colonel* (1935, David Butler), in which Walker (Bill Robinson) serves as racial spectacle, performing within an all-white milieu. In this and other Shirley Temple vehicles (for example, *The Littlest Rebel* [1935, David Butler] and *Rebecca of Sunnybrook Farm* [1938, Allan Dwan]), Robinson's characters are depicted as being happy to perform for the diegetic (and the nondiegetic) white spectator.

In his discussion of these Temple-Robinson pairings, James Snead writes: "We never see black families or significant relationships between black men and women. Blacks are not here for themselves, clearly, but mainly for others, and more precisely, *for whites*" (*White Screens*, 58). Scruno is similarly isolated from the black community; the only time other African American characters appear in the East Side Kids cycle is when they are explicitly identified as being Scruno's relatives (and this occurs very rarely). Scruno thus exists, as Snead argues, *for* whites, making racially charged jokes, eating watermelon with gusto, or performing a "hep" dance. These moments hark back

Scruno (Sammy Morrison) performs before a crowd of white onlookers in *Smart Alecks* (1942).

to images of blackness familiar to the audience from previous Hollywood films.

If, as Sander Gilman has noted, "stereotyping is a universal means of coping with anxieties engendered by our inability to control the world" (*Difference and Pathology*, 12), then the deployment of this fixed, stereotyped image of blackness, which denies the possibility of alternate readings or an engagement in contemporary social issues, is a way to alleviate this anxiety. By using Scruno as nothing more than a cliché of cinematic blackness retrieved from the past, *Smart Alecks* removes the burden of social commentary, found in so many other films of this era, from Scruno's slight shoulders. To treat Scruno's racial difference in any other way would be to engage in a different syntax— that of the social problem film. If *Smart Alecks* were a social problem film, as opposed to a comedy–crime caper, then Scruno might have complained about how his friends called him "boy" or about having to perform alone before a crowd of white spectators, leading to a discussion of contemporary race relations. Scruno's racial difference would then become the film's "issue," and the film would no longer be a light comedy. But in the East Side Kids cycle, Scruno's blackness inspires only passivity and an unchanging acceptance of the contemporary racial climate. The presence of this character forcefully highlights how the East Side Kids cycle trafficked in one-dimensional images borrowed from previous texts.

GENERIC HYBRIDS AND TIMELY TOPICS IN B FILMS

Once a film cycle's semantics are incapable of conveying their initial syntax, they must be revised or attached to a new syntax in order to continue to generate box-office dollars. While comedy is the most common mode taken up by a dying film cycle, any stable genre or cycle will do the trick. Here I am using the word "stable" to refer to long-established genres whose popularity has remained consistent throughout film history (even if this popularity waxes and wanes), such as the comedy, the western, the gangster film, the musical, and the horror film. I am also using the term "stable" to refer to the periodic bankability of certain film cycles—such as the self-reflexive teen slasher cycle of the mid to late 1990s—or even the periodic upwelling of a sentiment—such as the predictable resurgence of patriotism during times of war. Combining the proven moneymaking elements of a particular film cycle with the proven moneymaking elements of one or more different genres or cycles also ensures that studios can appeal to the widest segment of the audience with just one product. As Rick Altman puts it: "Studios are like candidates for political office, above all concerned to avoid alienating any particular group of voters" (*Film/Genre*, 128).

Attaching the semantics of a faltering cycle to a more stable genre or cycle, or to a timely topic or sentiment, is a way to extend a cycle's cultural relevance and thus squeeze more revenue out of it. This process explains why most film cycles never completely disappear or die. Traces of a cycle's images and themes continue to circulate throughout films, and when they stop appearing on the big screen, they can still be located in other forms of visual media, like television shows, music videos, video games, comics, and even YouTube videos. In particular, the clichéd material of a dying film cycle often finds a welcoming home in B films. The terms variously attributed to B films, like "quickies," "cheapies," or simply "low budget," "imply pictures that were regarded as secondary even in their own time, and the 'B' label has often been used to imply minor pictures or simply poor filmmaking, anything tacky or produced on a low budget" (Taves, "The B Film," 313). Despite their lowly cultural status, not only do B films keep studios in business, but their ability to consistently generate profits also indicates that audiences pay money to watch these films (315).

Film cycles thrive in a low-budget, B-film environment because much of the work (and, by extension, much of the cost) has been completed before production even begins: actors know their motivations from previous films, scriptwriters recycle dialogue and plot formulas, and set designers reuse or reconstruct soundstages. The overused semantic elements of a faltering film cycle, each carrying its own detailed backstory, are welcomed in low-budget films that rely heavily on an economy of action. Therefore, it should not be surprising that entries in the spin-off cycles of the original Dead End Kids cycle, including the East Side Kids, the Dead End Kids and Little Tough Guys, and, later, the Bowery Boys, were all B films.

After Warner Bros. had exhausted the narrative and thematic possibilities of the original Dead End Kids cycle after seven films, Universal and Monogram Studios took the characters (and the actors who played them), images, and settings and attached them to a different syntax. This pattern occurs in Monogram's aforementioned East Side Kids cycle. While these B films address, if only implicitly, the lower-class origins of the boys and the problems created by growing up poor, their main story lines usually classify them as something other than social problem films. This move into new (and often multiple) generic climates allows filmmakers to continue to exploit a familiar, moneymaking concept—the personas developed in the original Dead End Kids cycle—while simultaneously providing audiences with the novelty of new story lines: *Boys of the City* is a comic murder mystery; *Ghosts on the Loose* is a comic horror film; *Kid Dynamite*, *Bowery Blitzkrieg* (1941, Wallace Fox), and *Come Out Fighting* (1945, William Beaudine) are sports or boxing movies; and *Flying Wild* (1941, William West) and *Spooks Run Wild* (1941, Phil Rosen) are spy stories.

Attaching some of the most recognizable semantics of the original Dead End Kids cycle—the kids, the Brooklyn setting, their delinquent antics and moneymaking schemes—with another genre's semantics and syntax also streamlines the filmmaking process. Monogram understood that the presence of the original Dead End Kids in a film would sell tickets, so all the studio needed to do was to plug those characters into new contexts and slightly varied plots in order to keep the audience paying. In *Spooks Run Wild*, Monogram inserted the Dead End Kids into the established framework of the horror film. In a repetition of the basic plot structure of *They Made Me a Criminal* and *Boys of the City*, the Kids are sent to a mountain camp as an alternative to reform school. Predictably, the camp is being terrorized by the much-feared "Monster Killer." Here we have two primary semantic elements of the original Dead End Kids cycle: the Kids and the convention of the reformatory, albeit in an altered form. The film also contains some of the primary semantics of the horror film: a creepy mansion, several red-herring suspects, and a horror film icon, Bela Lugosi (who, at this point in his career, was appearing in B films in order to support a morphine habit). This film spawned a sequel of sorts, *Ghosts on the Loose* (also featuring Lugosi), which has the Kids roaming around what they believe to be a haunted house. This East Side Kids entry also manages to tie in a wedding and a Nazi spy plot, bringing its generic count to four (social problem, comedy, horror, and war film). This process of genre hybridization ensured that there were an endless number of plotlines for the Dead End Kids beyond the world of the Bowery, stretching the cycle's appeal to the widest swath of audience.

As spin-off cycles like the East Side Kids and the Dead End Kids and Little Tough Guys moved further and further from their origins in the social problem film, they needed to find other ways to connect with audiences. Since both cycles coincided with U.S. involvement in World War II (1941–1945), many of their plots revolve around patriotic, prowar story lines. Furthermore, the brevity of their production schedules—most B films were shot within five to seven days—meant that their topics could be extremely timely. This quick turnaround time was one of the few advantages that Poverty Row studios like Monogram and Republic had over the Big Five studios (20th Century Fox, MGM, RKO, Paramount, and Warner Bros.). They could take an event and turn it into a timely film plot while the news was still at the forefront of the public's mind. *Pride of the Bowery*, an East Side Kids film, is a particularly fascinating example of this cycle's ability to capitalize on current events. Released in January 1941, *Pride of the Bowery* takes place at one of America's Civilian Conservation Corps (CCC) camps, which were in service from 1933 to 1942. The film is essentially an advertisement or plea for the continuation of the CCC program, which had been deprioritized because of the war-generated increase in employment for young men (Encyclopedia.com, "Civilian Conservation Corps"). For example, during their first meal at the camp, the boys eagerly gorge themselves while one of them exclaims, "Can you believe we get all this and they pay you for it?" Likewise, Muggs, a character who is normally defined by a preternatural resistance to authority, evolves from a cocky tough to an obedient cadet over the course of the sixty-two-minute film.

Although Monogram Studios, like all studios at the time, was "encouraged" by the Office of War Information to use their films as "a means of propaganda to achieve [the government's] military and diplomatic objectives" (Murphy, "Motion Pictures during World War II," 59), a more likely explanation for *Pride of the Bowery*'s pro-CCC message is the timeliness of the story. It was in Monogram's best interests to appear pro-American at a time when patriotism defined the nation. Indeed, many Poverty Row studios, whose chief market was the Midwest, the South, and the Southwest, created films infused with so-called traditional values like "patriotism, conservatism, self-reliance and justice" (Dick, *Star-Spangled Screen*, 46). What is especially interesting about *Pride of the Bowery* is that images, like one of the boys digging ditches in the hot sun, had they appeared in the original Dead End Kids cycle, would have been attached to an entirely different syntax. Backbreaking work in a social problem film like *Crime School* is an indicator of exploitation and social injustice. In the original Dead End Kids cycle, hard labor is something to fight against, not embrace. Yet in *Pride of the Bowery*, this kind of work is considered patriotic, "American," and capable of turning useless juvenile delinquents into model citizens (which was, in fact, the original goal of the CCC camps). Furthermore, it appears that the East Side Kids cycle's turn to patriotism had a positive effect on its reviews. As discussed earlier, the *New York Times* had taken to bashing the cycle for its formulaic plots and one-dimensional characters. However, it had this to say about *Pride of the Bowery*: "Some of the curse of triteness is removed from the tale by the unpretentious and straight-forward manner in which it has been projected" (T. S., 15). While the film employs just as many clichés as its predecessors, the decision to base the film on a timely, patriotic topic made it more palatable to critics.

In films released before and during World War II, those characters once considered enemies on the home front, the Others to the middle-class white majority—including gangsters, white juvenile delinquents, and African Americans of all ages—were now needed to help fight the "real" enemies overseas. For instance, gangster heroes, whose presence had been heavily censored in the mid to late 1930s for their unassimilable Otherness, were enlisted in service of the Allied cause in 1940s films like *Lucky Jordan* (1942, Frank Tuttle) and *All Through the Night* (1942, Vincent Sherman). Similarly, the East Side Kids and the Dead End Kids and Little Tough Guys films released at this time function to recuperate the deviants of the original Dead End Kids cycle back into the warm embrace of the nation and its hegemony. Whereas *Dead End* addresses the social problem of juvenile poverty but finds no solution to the boys' destitution and delinquency, *Pride of the Bowery* addresses a similar problem but is able to offer up a believable "solution": nationalist zeal and hard work. Thus,

Though they played juvenile delinquents in other film cycles, Bolts (Huntz Hall), Billy (Billy Halop), and Creaseball (Bernard Punsly) are saboteur-catching American heroes in the *Junior G-Men of the Air* (1942) serials.

Monogram's East Side Kids cycle as well as Universal's Dead End Kids and Little Tough Guys cycle effectively tap into the national project of consolidating the population behind the war effort and of glossing over individual differences in an effort to present a united American front. The Dead End Kids and Little Tough Guys cycle used the popularity of the Dead End Kids cycle to sell cheaply made films and serials with action-packed, interchangeable plots. The first *Junior G-Men of the Air* serial (1942, Ford Beebe and John Rawlins), for example, has the boys joining forces with the FBI in order to hunt down a terrorist organization. This organization, known as the Order of the Flaming Torch, was clearly reacting to the growing public apprehension over Adolph Hitler's actions in Europe. Likewise, *Keep 'Em Slugging* (1943, Christy Cabanne) centers its plot on the boys' decision to get jobs so that draft-age men will be free to fight in the war, inspiring one of the boys to say, "We're not old enough to fly a bomber, drive a tank, or man a machine gun. We all know there's a war going on. Get legitimate jobs! Keep things moving over here!"

Likewise, in the East Side Kids film, *Let's Get Tough!* (1942, Wallace Fox), the boys finally discover a useful outlet for their normally menacing delinquency—terrorizing the Japanese residents living in their community. After a military parade stirs the boys' national pride, they head to the recruiter's office, only to discover that they are too young to enlist in the military. Still determined to do their part for the Allied cause, the boys decide to "teach a lesson" to a grumpy antiques dealer, Mr. Keno, whom they assume is Japanese (we find out later he is Chinese, an ally as opposed to an enemy). At one point in the film, the boys threaten Mr. Keno en masse and bombard him with racially inflected insults. Muggs threatens to turn the innocent antiques dealer into "chop suey," but then reconsiders, reasoning that Keno is probably "too yellow" to make good chop suey. Even Scruno's racial difference is eradicated when he joins the boys in terrorizing the country's new Other, the Japanese saboteur. Scruno sees nothing wrong with making assumptions about Keno's character based on his ethnicity and, as result, blends in with his group of white friends. In fact, *Let's Get Tough!* is one of the few East Side Kids films that does not single Scruno out because of his racial difference; the gang has bigger fish to fry. After their heated altercation with Keno, Danny (Bobby Jordan), often typecast as the wishy-washy or sensitive member of the gang, questions whether they should be terrorizing the man. Muggs explains, "Its open season on Japs!" which convinces Danny.

The entire plot of *Let's Get Tough!* is based on the then-popular notion that every Japanese American must have been a saboteur working for the Japanese government.[17] For that reason, it is not surprising that the Japanese community objected to this film, and television stations in Los Angeles, San Francisco, and Las Vegas refused to play it (Hayes and Walker, *Bowery Boys*, 67). The film also exploits public awareness of Executive Order 9066, signed by President Roosevelt on February 19, 1942 (three months before the release of this film), which resulted in the compulsory internment of 120,000 Japanese residents, two-thirds of whom were American citizens with no record of subversive behavior (Burton, *Confinement and Ethnicity*, ix). The quick turnover rate of the East Side Kids films enabled Monogram to capitalize on timely issues of interest to the American public; the relocation of Japanese residents had begun just one month before *Let's Get Tough!* hit theaters. Again, this support of government policies was probably less a reflection of the studio's patriotic spirit than an attempt to create films reflecting, reinforcing, and capitalizing on contemporary public opinion. Monogram was also on target with the rest of Hollywood, which, by the spring of 1942, had begun loading its films with anti-Japanese sentiments (Dick, *Star-Spangled Screen*, 230).

Many East Side Kids films also use plots derived from the boys' desire or lack of desire (which is always rectified) to join the fight against the Axis powers. This "awakening of the neutral" plotline was a common theme in World War II–era cinema (Dick, *Star-Spangled Screen*, 165). *Kid Dynamite*, which is illustrative of this plotline, depicts Muggs, a jobless loafer, as being clueless about current events and what it "means to be an American." Halfway through the film, while Muggs is playing pool, a distraught Czech boy runs into the local pool hall to show a newspaper headline to the hall's owner, Nick (Charles Judels). The headline, which reads "Peaceful Czech Town Wiped Out by Nazis: Male Population Face Firing Squad; Women and Children Held in Concentration Camps," is likely a reference to a wholesale massacre in the small Czech village of Lidice, which took place in June 1942, approximately seven months before the film's release. The introduction of this piece of news elicits a lengthy lecture from Nick about the Bill of Rights and what it means to be an American. Nick is currently studying to become an American citizen, and his speech serves as a lesson in patriotism to Muggs as well as the audience. As in the social problem film, this focus on the "message with a capital M" brings the film to a standstill. Even the normally loquacious Muggs becomes silent, nodding and lowering his eyes as Nick explains why "our boys are joining the army."

While the boys' problems in the original Dead End Kids cycle are eradicated through the intervention of an "exceptional" individual capable of righting society's wrongs one at a time, conflicts in the films from the 1940s were resolved by World War II; it provided studios with a solution satisfying the needs of the narrative, which requires the boys' recuperation, and one satisfying the needs of the nation, which required patriotism and unity. Though a character like Muggs was a true social outsider in the original Dead End Kids cycle, an Other who could not be reformed or recuperated, in *Kid Dynamite*, he is recognized as an American, as "one of us." At one point during his patriotic speech, Nick assures Muggs that he does not need to memorize the Bill of Rights, even though Nick, as a foreigner, must do this in order to obtain his American citizenship. The film implies that Muggs has internalized the concepts of freedom and protection simply by being born an American: "Americans are born with [the Bill of Rights] in their hearts," Nick tells Muggs. The film concludes with Muggs, Danny, and Glimpy (Huntz Hall) decked out in navy, army, and marine uniforms (respectively), meeting up with the other four East Side Kids, who are collecting scrap metal for the war effort (they are a year too young to join the armed forces).[18] In this conclusion, all seven East Side Kids have found their purpose—as American heroes. This happy conclusion is a far cry from their earlier days of spitting at doormen, robbing their social betters, and taunting the elderly.

CONCLUSION

Film cycles form around the financial or critical success of one or two films that address a timely subject and have iconography or plot formulas that readily lend themselves to duplication. Once a film's semantics begins to lose their ability to connect with audiences, studios select the most successful elements of the original cycle and attach them to one or more stable genres or cycles. Studios usually select generic modes that maintain a steady popularity with audiences, such as comedies, horror films, or science fiction films. Studios may also capitalize on a timely sentiment or current event—such as a war— in order to further extend the financial viability of the original cycle. As long as the familiar icons, formulas, conventions, and themes of these cycles are deployed in a new way or in a new generic setting, they are capable of resonating again with audiences. Therefore, while the previous chapter rejected the concept of generic evolution at the macro level of genres, this chapter recuperates the concept of evolution at the micro level of the film cycle. However, this model of cycle evolution excludes the concept of a cycle's "death" by insisting that highly visible film cycles rarely disappear completely; the images of the Dead End Kids cycles continue to circulate in texts throughout film history, such as juvenile-delinquent-themed teenpics of the 1950s and the ghetto action cycle of the 1990s.[19] Furthermore, an examination of these films and their alterations over time reveals how film cycles can form around the exploitation of the public's interest in a particular social problem—in this case, the plight of urban youth. The fact that these cinematic social problems crop up periodically over the course of film history testifies to the fact that our nation is cyclically concerned about the state of "today's youth" and our cities, and that social problems have historically made for fascinating and profitable films.

Studying the manifestations of the original Dead End Kids cycle also reveals how the suffering urban youth of the social problem film can be put to other, more lucrative purposes once they have ceased performing their original function of educating the audience and possibly even motivating some kind of prosocial action on the part of the viewer. The East Side Kids and the Dead End Kids and Little Tough Guys cycles offered up the same images of urban youth getting

Huntz Hall (*top row, third from the right*) on the cover of the Beatles' *Sgt. Pepper's Lonely Hearts Club Band* (1967) album.

into trouble found in the original Dead End Kids cycle, but discovered a more timely and, therefore, more plausible solution to the problem: transforming them into patriots. Hence, these spin-off cycles effectively tapped into the national project of rallying the population behind the war effort by transforming the unrecuperable social problem of the late 1930s—the urban juvenile delinquent—into a useful social product for the 1940s—the patriot or the soldier. The problems of class and, to a lesser extent, racial difference represented by the original Dead End Kids, which could no longer be remedied in the generic context of the social problem film, is effectively glossed over in later cycles in an effort to present a united American front at a time when consensus was a necessity.

Since film cycles are woven into the social fabric as active parts of their audiences' lives, it is not surprising that two of the Dead End Kids cycle's biggest stars, Huntz Hall and Leo Gorcey, were represented in the famous photo collage on the original cover of the Beatles' *Sgt. Pepper's Lonely Hearts Club Band* album (1967). Although Gorcey demanded $400 for the use of his likeness, and subsequently had his image removed from the album, it is telling that these two B-film actors, whose repetitive films drove Bosley Crowther to distraction, could be placed alongside such prominent cultural figures as Albert Einstein, Bob Dylan, Marlon Brando, Marilyn Monroe, and Gandhi. While it is difficult to imagine that the Beatles believed that Leo Gorcey and Huntz Hall offered the same cultural capital as Karl Marx or Oscar Wilde (who also appear on the cover of the album), their presence on that very significant piece of music literalizes how film cycles occupy a significant space in the cultural imagination.

CHAPTER 3

I WAS A TEENAGE FILM CYCLE
THE RELATIONSHIP BETWEEN YOUTH
SUBCULTURES AND FILM CYCLES

American International Pictures' *I Was a Teenage Werewolf* (1957, Gene Fowler, Jr.) offers a useful starting point for a discussion of how teenagers and their subcultural behaviors were both depicted and exploited by the cinema in the 1950s. In this particular entry in the juvenile-delinquent-themed teenpic cycle, we meet a moody, lower-middle-class white teenager, Tony Rivers (Michael Landon). Tony's short fuse, as the film's opening scene demonstrates, frequently gets him embroiled in schoolyard brawls. Later in the film, Tony attends a Halloween party at which practical jokes are the evening's entertainment. However, when it is Tony's turn to become the butt of the joke—someone blows a party horn in his ear—he reacts by repeatedly punching the trickster in the face. Tony's friends are appalled by his violent reaction: a panning shot reveals their shocked expressions. This incident finally convinces Tony to seek counseling for his anger. He agrees to see Dr. Alfred Brandon (Whit Bissell), a psychiatrist recommended by a concerned mentor figure, Detective Donovan (Barney Phillips).

During their first meeting, Dr. Brandon explains that "the only hope for the human race is to hurl it back to its primitive dawn." He promises Tony that his own special brand of "regression therapy" will restore the troubled teenager to his "true self." Like any teenager, Tony just wants to fit in and be like his peers, so he consents to being Dr. Brandon's guinea pig. After just one session, the experimental procedure proves to be a success—Tony is restored to his true self. Unfortunately, Tony's true self is a violent, sex-crazed werewolf who murders one of his teenage classmates later that evening. Neither Tony nor the rest of his community realizes that he is the source of the gruesome murder, and so Tony continues his therapy with Dr. Brandon, oblivious of the consequences.

During Tony's second visit to the psychiatrist, the audience is privy to the effects of Dr. Brandon's unconventional treatment. As the doctor "regresses" Tony, we see close-ups of the doctor's mouth as he counts backward and of Tony's mouth as he sweats profusely, grimaces, and bites his lip. These shots culminate in a series of close-ups of each man's eyes. The doctor's eyes are anxious, watching Tony's every move with delighted anticipation, while Tony's eyes are clenched shut. These alternating close-ups allow the audience to take up Dr. Brandon's sadistic, curious viewing position as well as Tony's passive, suffering one. The close-ups of Tony's agonized expression allow the audience to sympathize with him as a victim of society, while the close-ups of Dr. Brandon's face encourage us to see the deviant teenager as a scientific curiosity to be studied, experimented upon, and tortured. Dr. Brandon even tells to his assistant that it does not matter whether Tony dies during the experiment, since he is "headed for the electric chair" anyway. Thus, as Cyndy Hendershot argues, "the film associates the horrors of science that shaped the Fifties—the A-bomb, then the H-bomb, both leading to the threat of an impending nuclear war—with the problem of psychotic teens" ("Monster at the Soda Shop"). The film concludes with Tony killing Dr. Brandon, the man who has been exploiting his teenage angst, with his bare hands. Tony is later shot and killed by Detective Donovan, his friend and mentor, further proving that there is no solution to the problem of juvenile delinquency.

It is no wonder that *I Was a Teenage Werewolf* was such a hit with

Tony (Michael Landon) as the teenage victim in *I Was a Teenage Werewolf* (1957).

Dr. Brandon (Whit Bissell) examines the teenage monster in *I Was a Teenage Werewolf* (1957).

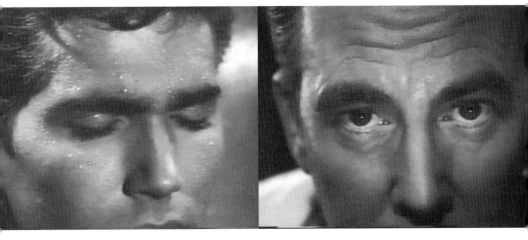

its target teenage audience.[1] The film is an apt metaphor for how, in the 1950s, film studios milked the teen ethos for profit while simultaneously making teenagers appear to be out-of-control monsters worthy of the dark fates visited upon their screen surrogates. Studios discovered this lucrative teenage demographic as a result of a series of economic, industrial, and social factors. First, movie attendance had dropped precipitously for several reasons: the Supreme's Court's decision in *U.S. v. Paramount* (1948), which forced Hollywood studios to divest themselves of their theater holdings; the rising popularity of television; and the mass migration of white middle-class families to the suburbs and away from city-based movie theaters (Lewis, *American Film*, 233–234). Despite the drop in movie attendance, three films that were initially marketed to a general adult audience—*The Wild One* (1953, Laslo Benedek), *Blackboard Jungle* (1955, Richard Brooks), and *Rebel without a Cause* (1955, Nicholas Ray)—all became huge hits with youth audiences. In other words, teenagers were still paying to see movies. Studios took notice of this surge in young moviegoers and began making films, later known as teenpics, specifically for this new market demographic. While films like *Blackboard Jungle* and *Rebel without a Cause* view youthful delinquency from the standpoint of adult culture—as strange and threatening but ultimately "fixable"— the teenpics that followed attempt to depict teenage behaviors from the point of view of teenagers.

This juvenile-delinquent-themed teenpic cycle exploited sensational topics of the 1950s, including the newly emerging concepts of the teenager, juvenile delinquency, and rock 'n' roll music, which quickly snowballed into "moral panics." In *Folk Devils and Moral Panics*, Stanley Cohen loosely defines "moral panic" as "the mobilization of public opinion . . . by the media and public figures" over a perceived threat to social values (xxiv). Moral panics are triggered by actual events but are amplified when those events are associated with larger abstract problems in society. The moral panics forming the core of the juvenile-delinquent-themed teenpic conveniently allowed studios to exploit contemporary concerns while also making claims for the educational value of their films; in fact, many of the films in the 1950s juvenile-delinquent-themed teenpic cycle open with a square-up, or a prefatory statement, about the social or moral ill the film is depicting (Schaefer, *Bold! Daring! Shocking!*, 69). The typical teenpic square-up usually explains that the story the audience is about to see is happening "right now," and that while addressing such topics might be unpleasant, it is necessary to do so if society is ever going to eliminate this significant social problem. The square-up safeguarded studios from the censorious hands of the Production Code Administration (PCA) by allowing them to preemptively criticize the salacious material they were selling and to cloak a film's sensational content in the guise of civic duty.

The presence of a square-up in so many of these films points to the fine line that teenpics walked between titillation and education (Schaefer, *Bold! Daring! Shocking!*, 70). Indeed, film studios appealed to teenagers precisely by making a spectacle of their so-called deviant behaviors: listening to and dancing to rock 'n' roll music, racing hot rods or stealing cars, engaging in "confrontation dressing," and taking or distributing illegal drugs.[2] After allowing the viewer to vicariously indulge in these images of rebellion, juvenile-delinquent-themed teenpics almost always conclude with a containment of the offending subcultural behavior or style; the majority of films in this cycle end with images of teenagers reforming, going to jail, getting killed, or being exiled from society. On occasion, these films conclude that the offending behavior depicted throughout the story has been "misread" by the mainstream—that it is prosocial rather than antisocial—leading to a joyous celebration of teen subcultures in the final reel.

This chapter will analyze how the culture industry of the 1950s, including record labels, magazine editors, clothing manufacturers, and film studios, exploited the deviant imagery of 1950s youth subcultures in order to create an intergeneric film cycle: the juvenile-delinquent-themed teenpic, or JD teenpic. Despite the fact that the film studios behind the 1950s JD teenpic cycle ultimately defused much of the potentially political, racial, and class-based protests of the youth subcultures they depicted, I argue that they also widened the "cultural space," thereby permitting the "selective re-working and re-appropriation of the [teenage] style by geographically-dispersed groups" (John Clarke, "Style," 186). While elements of youth subcultures were selectively reproduced and potentially bastardized by their successful exploitation in the JD teenpic film cycle, this cycle was also integral to the proliferation, diffusion, and active shaping of how subcultures and their teenage participants understood themselves. Cultural theorists like Bill Osgerby have argued that "rather than being a consistent and unvarying stage in human physical and psychological development . . . the distinguishing features of 'youth' are the product of wider social, economic and political structures" (*Youth Media*, 8). In other words, if the teenager is a biological reality as well as a construct of criminologists, politicians, newspaper reporters, studio heads, and record-label executives, then film cycles play an integral role in the process of differentiating teenagers as a specific grouping of people. The two went hand in hand: teenpics came into existence based on the economic and social presence of teenagers, while the category of the teenager, specifically the threatening and yet strangely lucrative "juvenile delinquent," was further rarefied through its depiction in the 1950s JD teenpic cycle.

The cinema is a useful medium for the transmission of youth subcultures because of its ability to create a spectacular display, providing an opportunity for the studio's costume department to outfit actors in up-to-the-minute fashions. These moments of spectacle form a major part of the JD teenpic cycle's appeal. Furthermore, since subcultural styles exist in order to provoke a reaction from those who see them, they are ready-made for the cinema. Dick Hebdige argues that subcultural styles are "maps of meaning": "As such, they are gestures, movements towards a speech which offends the 'silent majority,' which challenges the principles of unity and cohesion, which contradicts the myth of consensus" (*Subculture*, 18). It is simple to depict teenage rebellion on film when rebellion can be signified visually by the juvenile delinquent's blue jeans and black leather jacket, or aurally, through a contemporary rock 'n' roll sound track. Youth subcultures, in their desire to be seen—to be the object of the parent culture's wary gaze—are the perfect subject for a medium that thrives on provocative imagery. Hebdige describes this relationship as circular, explaining that "fractions of youth now aspire to the flatness and stillness of a photograph," adding, "They are completed only through the admiring glances of a stranger" ("Posing," 295). Teenage rebellion is "completed" by its reproduction in the JD teenpic cycle, and the JD teenpic cycle needs the teenager as its visual model: each feeds the other in a continual loop.

Film studios should therefore not be read as faceless corporate monsters that made teenagers appear to be the root of all of society's problems and then took their money to boot. Rather, the relationship between studios and subcultures is one of mutual benefit. Teenagers displayed a to-be-looked-at-ness, and film studios complied by projecting those looks back into the movie theater. While many contemporary subcultural studies discuss the integral role that mainstream media play in the formation and dissemination of subcultural style, few have addressed the multivalent, symbiotic relationship between film cycles and subcultures in any detail.[3] As Sarah Thornton explains, the media is "crucial to the definition and distribution of cultural knowledge. . . . The difference between being *in* or *out* of fashion, high or low in subcultural capital, correlates in complex ways with degrees of media coverage, creation and exposure" ("Subcultural Capital," 187). Analyzing those film cycles created out of a desire to exploit the existence of controversial youth subcultures will uncover the complex process by which film studios convert subcultural signifiers into film language and how that film language, in turn, helps to further promote and shape subcultures. I see this process not as a linear, back-and-forth exchange, but as a fluid process, which makes it difficult to determine the line between subcultural "creation" and mainstream "exploitation." Youth subcultures of the 1950s needed film cycles to reflect their trends for them—to "complete" their images. And film studios needed teenagers to provide the raw materials for their film cycles. This dialectical relationship illuminates the film cycle's intimate relationship with its audience members as well as its ability to interact with them and respond to their needs.

DEFINING SUBCULTURES

In the introduction to their 1975 study of subcultural behavior, *Resistance through Rituals: Youth Subcultures in Post-war Britain*, Stuart Hall and Tony Jefferson describe subcultures as "smaller, more localized and differentiated structures, within one or other of the larger cultural networks" (13). Subcultures are defined by a set of social rituals that "underpin their collective identity and define them as a group rather than as a collection of individuals" (45). Furthermore, unlike groups taking a separatist stance toward mainstream culture, such as the Amish, subcultures are not autonomous; they always exist in relation to, and are dependent on, the dominant culture (Doherty, *Teenagers and Teenpics*, 47). In his seminal 1979 study of British working-class youth, *Subculture: The Meaning of Style*, Dick Hebdige argues that subcultures are commonly created as a resistance to the dominant hegemony and represent a "'solution' to a specific set of circumstances, to particular problems and contradictions" within the current hegemony (81). These solutions manifest themselves in an identity marked by clothing styles, music preferences, behavioral patterns, and choices in language and peer groups. In this way, each subculture represents "a different handling of the 'raw material of social existence'" (80).

For example, the 1950s teenage subculture was broadly associated with interlinked activities such as listening to or creating rock 'n' roll music, building and racing hot rods, being part of a gang (or affecting the posture of a gang member), and using a specialized slang ("dig," "crazy," "the most," "cats," etc.). Such activities can be read as a way for teenagers to assert their newfound postwar independence as well as a desire for the danger denied them in the safe confines of their affluent, postwar suburbs (Doherty, *Teenagers and Teenpics*, 108). These subcultural activities contested an ideology demanding, among other things, that teenagers be asexual, docile, and racially segregated.[4]

While subcultures represent countercurrents within the larger hegemonic structures of society, they are nevertheless "magical solutions" to lived contradictions. Lawrence Grossberg argues that "style/identity can only respond at the level of culture/ideology/identity, and thus, the contradictions remain firmly in place" ("Youth and Youth Culture," 29). In other words, although subcultures initially pose "symbolic challenges to a symbolic order," these subcultures are inevitably, almost instantaneously, recuperated into the very system they are challenging (Hebdige, *Subculture*, 92). According to Hebdige, this process of recuperation, in which "the fractured order is repaired and the subculture incorporated as a diverting spectacle within the dominant mythology" takes two forms: the conversion of "subcultural signs" into mass-produced objects, and the "labeling" or redefinition of this style by dominant groups (94). These twin processes are important to keep in mind, since our understanding of subcultures is, more often than not, shaped almost entirely through their representation in print media, films, television, popular music, clothing trends, and, most recently, the Internet. Only a small portion of the population witnesses subcultures in their initial, raw form (which is why they are *sub*cultures); instead, what the rest of society sees of a particular subculture is what has been translated into a commercially viable product by another mediating force. This process of "spectacular consumption," or "the process by which the material and symbolic relations among the culture industry, the life worlds of persons, and the ontological status of cultural forms are transformed in terms generated by public consumption," is a defining feature of subcultural imagery (Watts and Orbe, "Spectacular Consumption," 228).

It is important to keep in mind that the subcultural imagery depicted in teenpics cannot be so marginal that it appeals only to a small slice of the teenage demographic; dominant culture, represented in this case by film studios, must defuse or deradicalize certain aspects of a subculture in order to ensure that its product is marketable to a more general audience. Nevertheless, these images must retain some element of their (perceived) threat to the status quo in order to continue to appeal to their target market. Audiences enjoy consuming images of delinquent teenagers not for their sameness, but for their difference and for their ability to generate anxiety in others (Watts and Orbe, "Spectacular Consumption," 230). These images must be simultaneously novel and familiar, antisocial and welcoming, threatening but not too threatening. Furthermore, members of a subculture seldom have a choice about which elements of their style will be promoted to the rest of society; rather, "the news media select those aspects of the style which are to be made public, according to the dominant culture's perception of its significance" (John Clarke, "Style," 186). In this way, the media plays an integral role in shaping the future of subcultures by singling out certain elements of the subculture and redefining them for mass consumption.

The early models of subcultural theory articulated by the influential Centre for Contemporary Cultural Studies in Birmingham, England, in the 1970s posited what Oliver Marchant has identified as the "incorporation myth" ("Micro-Macro Gap," 85). The incorporation myth assumes that subcultures are intrinsically subversive or resistant to mainstream culture and that there is a definitive line between a subculture and the parent culture (that is, the mainstream). However, more recent subcultural theorists argue that in today's media-saturated landscape, there is no privileged moment when a subculture can be free of co-optation, when we might experience it "in the raw" (Weinzierl and Muggleton, "'Post-Structural Studies,'" 8). Although the "dichotomy between subcultures and an undifferentiated 'general public' lies at the heart of subcultural theory," there is no clear dividing line between parent culture and subculture (Gary Clarke, "Defending Ski Jumpers," 172). Rather, the concepts of "mainstream" and "subculture" are born at the same moment, since these forces simultaneously construct each other, relying on each other for their existence (Stahl, "Renovating Subcultural Theory," 29). The mainstream exists as a social pastiche in which fragments from the margins are incorporated, and fragments of the mainstream are likewise "excorporated" back into the margins (31). As a result, the mainstream cannot be seen as "monolithically Other" (31), since a subculture is always dependent upon the mainstream for its existence (and vice versa). It is my contention that film cycles capitalizing on teenage subcultural interests are integral to this exchange between parent culture and subculture.

TEENAGERS, JUVENILE DELINQUENTS,
AND THE ROCK 'N' ROLL MENACE

If movies are a reflection and refraction of contemporary belief systems, then throughout the 1930s, when social problem films were an especially popular genre, juvenile delinquency was perceived to be a problem rooted in definable causes (poverty, lack of good parenting, etc.). Thus, the troubled youths appearing in the Dead End Kids cycle are the sympathetic victims of their destitute environments, and with the right intervention, they can be reformed.[5] Likewise, classic exploitation films such as *Are These Our Children?* (1931, Wesley Ruggles), *Reefer Madness* (1938, Louis Gasnier), *Where are Your Children?* (1943, William Nigh), and *I Accuse My Parents* (1944, Sam Newfield) portray troubled or delinquency-prone teenagers primarily as the innocent victims of manipulative adult forces (Betrock, *Teenage Juvenile Delinquent*, 9). This fairly sympathetic view of adolescents changed in the 1940s with the postwar baby boom, when youth became a symbol of the American public's fear and expectations about the impacts of World War II on the nation's future. Several events—like the 1942 creation of the Commission on Children in Wartime, the 1943 *March of Time* newsreel series *Youth in Crisis*, and the 1946 national conference devoted to the prevention and control of juvenile delinquency— contributed to a generalized moral panic over "the state of American youth" (Gilbert, *Cycle of Outrage*, 24–40).[6] In 1956, Ralph W. Whelan, a New York City Youth Board official, issued a statement in which he argued that too much publicity was being given to teenage crime: "Because of 'three isolated incidents of crime among youth,' Mr. Whelan said, 'the press picked it up and the first thing we knew we had an almost hysterical situation on our hands" (*New York Times*, "Youth Crime Rise"). Thus, most Americans in the 1950s were made aware of juvenile delinquency through mediated sources, including politicians, moral pundits, the media, and film cycles, rather than through direct personal experience (Gilbert, *Cycle of Outrage*, 27). Stanley Cohen adds that moral panics are usually exacerbated by the media's emphasis on the novelty of a "social problem," making it appear more threatening "than something which has been coped with in the past" (*Folk Devils*, 68); in the 1950s, teenage delinquency was often (erroneously) described as new and unprecedented in American society.

It was not just World War II and the mass media that changed America's perception of the juvenile—adolescents' perceptions of themselves were also changing at this time. In the 1940s, while government and social agencies were wringing their hands over juvenile crime, adolescents, particularly white middle-class adolescents, were gaining increased autonomy by taking part-time jobs. The postwar shift in consumer industries, along with changes in traditional labor markets, created an increase in job availability, particularly for youth workers (Osgerby, *Youth Media*, 9). This new source of income gave teenagers a (limited) financial and social freedom from adult society. The money they made, which was not necessary for the maintenance of their middle-class households, went toward the purchase of cars (which were sorely needed in the isolated suburbs where many of these households were now located) as well as for less expensive leisure products like clothing, magazines, records, and movie tickets.[7] Youth as a social group existed in the popular cultural imagination before the 1950s, but the category of the teenager was not solidified as an exploitable market reality until this time (Palladino, *Teenagers*, 96–115).[8] Savvy marketers soon began to develop and target products at this new independent consumer and social group.

This new awareness of the teenager was also marked and generated by the release of several book-length studies of teenagers or youth experiences. One of the first contributions to this canon was Robert and Helen Lynd's 1929 study, *Middletown: A Study in Modern American Culture*. *Middletown* began as a sociological analysis of the "typical American city" (in this case, Muncie, Indiana). But during the course of their study, the authors discovered what they saw as a new phenomenon: the high-school-aged residents of Middletown had formed their own "social cosmos," separate from the adult world and complete with its own hierarchies and rituals (211). This sense of society can be partially attributed to the fact that as America moved from an agrarian to an industrial economy, more and more adolescents had the luxury of completing their high school educations. "Today," the Lynds discovered, "the school is becoming not a place to which children go from their homes for a few hours daily but a place from which they go home to eat and sleep" (211). This transition allowed adolescents to see themselves as a distinct social group, independent of their traditional familial sphere. The Lynds' influential book was later followed by a slew of studies, including A. B. Hollingshead's *Elmstown's Youth* (1949), Dorothy W. Baruch's *How to Live with Your Teenager* (1953), William C. Meninger's *How to Be a Successful Teenager* (1954), Paul Landis's *Understanding Teenagers* (1955), Benjamin Fine's *1,000,000 Delinquents* (1955), and S. N. Eisenstadt's *Generation to Generation* (1956) (Doherty, *Teenagers and Teenpics*, 67; Tropiano, *Rebels and Chicks*, 30).

TEEN MAGAZINES

During and after World War II, popular magazines also began featuring articles on this nascent social group, a development that further shaped the contours of the teenager's self-image. In December 1948, *Life* magazine devoted its cover story to the creature known as

Popular magazines like *Life* supported the vision of teenagers as members of an independent, like-minded community with its own set of rituals ("Teen-Agers: They Are Still Changing Their Customs to Suit Themselves," *Life*, Dec. 1948, 67–75).

the "teenager" and its strange leisure activities. The articles in this issue, covering topics like music, clothing, haircuts, kissing, sock hops, and general teenage dos and don'ts, describe American adolescents as if they were a newly discovered tribe whose exotic behaviors are incomprehensible to adult society (*Life*, "Teen-Agers," 67–75). One section explains teen rituals in this way: "A . . . greeting is a simple thing that adults deal with every day. But to teen-agers simplicity is a challenge; they have to find a way to make it complicated and turn it into a game. On meeting instead of just shaking hands, they go through the violent contortions of a 'beer drinker's' or a 'politician's' handshake" (68). Another section in the issue offers a series of photographs depicting various teenage behaviors, broken down step-by-step, such as the "sniff game" (68). Thus, a decisive element in the formation of the modern teenager was not just financial independence and baby-boom numbers, but also "an acute sense of themselves as a special, like-minded community bound together by age and rank," an awareness that was "carefully nurtured and vigorously reinforced by the adult institutions around them" (Doherty, *Teenagers and Teenpics*, 46).

Throughout the early to mid 1950s, entire magazines catering exclusively to this newly discovered teenage market started to appear, including titles like *Dig!*, *'Teen*, *Teen World*, *'Teen Life*, *Flip*, *Youth*, and *Miss* (Gilbert, *Cycle of Outrage*, 23). Though youth-oriented magazines existed before the 1950s, these newly created publications were different in that they recognized the teenager as part of a special subculture and spoke to him or her as a "friend" (Doherty, *Teenagers and Teenpics*, 59). An editor's letter from June 1957 claims that the new *'Teen* magazine is "the first" magazine to delve into all aspects of teen life: "*'Teen* magazine, born into a generation that has finally come to recognize persons between the ages of 13 and 19 as a distinct cultural group, now opens its pages to the future" (*'Teen*, "Editor's Letter" [June 1957], 1). One year later, the same magazine told its readers: "Teenagers today have double the responsibility, and double the self-reliance of yesterday's teener. The 1958 'teen is a first-class citizen of the world who has tackled and conquered problems that he would never have faced if he had been this age only a few years ago" (*'Teen*, "Editor's Letter" [May 1958], 7).

In the 1950s, teenagers were informed, on a mass scale, that they were separate, special, and different from mainstream adult society—and were told so by that very same adult society. To that end, each teen magazine claimed to be the publication that truly understood and recognized the significance of "today's teen." Magazine editors claimed to understand the teenagers' world and promised to continue to provide content specifically for them—as long as teenagers continued to spend their disposable income on magazines.[9] This mode of address appears to have been successful with contemporary teenagers. One teenager wrote in to *'Teen* magazine in 1958 to thank it for creating a publication that "we can understand and moreover, that understands us! . . . Your magazine has picked up on our line of thought and put it down on paper. Music, movies, clothes, and sports—just the way we like it" (Harrison, letter to the editor, 7).

Given this heightened awareness of teenagers as a social group and the burgeoning fears about teenage independence after World War II, it is not surprising that by the mid-1950s, the concepts of teenagers and juvenile delinquents would become almost interchangeable in public discourses. Moral policing groups, such as Estes Kefauver's Senate Judiciary Subcommittee, which investigated juvenile delinquency in the 1950s, made social problems out of contemporary youth merely by stating that they *were* social problems. Daniel Dotter explains: "[Ruling] social groups create deviance by making the rules whose infraction constitutes deviance, and by applying those rules to particular people and labeling them as outsiders" ("Here to Stray," 89). The criminal patina of teenage subcultural behaviors was further heightened by intense media scrutiny, resulting in what Stanley Cohen has labeled "deviation amplification," or the process by which increased attempts by the public, politicians, and, most especially, the media to understand a deviant act results in an increased awareness of said deviance (though not an actual increase in deviance) and in the subsequent creation of a moral panic (*Folk Devils*, 18–20). As one annoyed teenager wrote in a 1960 letter to *Ingénue* magazine: "Teenagers used to be known as 'the younger generation' and conversation usually began with 'What is this younger generation coming to?' Now it's teenagers and its synonym, juvenile delinquency. (According to our elders in the spotlight, anyway.) Just new words for the same old problem" (Bromley, "It's Your Turn," 9). Not only were teenagers defined as a separate social group, but they were also becoming a social problem for older generations. This generation gap is reflected by the teenpic convention of having characters who represent mainstream society—usually the white middle-class Protestant segment of adult society—act frightened, outraged, or concerned by a particular subcultural style or behavior. Of course, the very fact that these behaviors are shunned by squares or the mainstream adult community is precisely what marks them as contemporary and enticing to the target teenage market.

THE WILD ONE

The Wild One, released in 1953, was one of the first films to acknowledge this fundamental split in politics, consumption, and lifestyle choices between the youth subculture and the mainstream, adult society of the 1950s. The film also helped establish the image of the cinematic juvenile delinquent or "JD," including the leather jacket, specialized language, and the souped-up motorcycle or hot rod. Like so many social problem or exploitation films, *The Wild One* opens with a square-up that justifies the film's content by indicating that it is based on the true story of a marauding motorcycle gang that terrorized a small town.[10] Although 1930s and 1940s social problem films like *Dead End* almost always open with lengthy shots of the mise-en-scène in order to establish the poverty-stricken milieu against which juvenile delinquents must struggle, *The Wild One* offers no such context for its juvenile delinquents. Instead, the film opens with a low-angle shot of a generic paved road, dappled with shadows. This opening sequence implies that the delinquents in *The Wild One* have no explainable origin; rather, they emerge, fully formed, out of thin air. Even Johnny (Marlon Brando), the gang's leader, does not seem to understand the gang's purpose; his voice-over informs the audience: "It begins here, for me, on this road. How the whole mess happened, I don't know." In the background of the shot, we see figures on motor-

In *The Wild One* (1953),
Johnny (Marlon Brando)
inspired rebellious
teenagers to don leather
jackets and blue jeans.

cycles approaching quickly, paired with the sounds of revving motorcycle engines. These motorcyclists, the Black Rebels, zoom through
the frame and over the camera, as if they were going to ride right out
of the movie screen and into the audience. This image then cuts to
a medium close-up of the Black Rebels, who ride their bikes against
a rear-projected landscape. The use of rear projection here bolsters
the feeling of placelessness and the idea that these delinquents have
emerged from nowhere and everywhere.

With their taste for bebop music and slang, their identical leather
jackets and blue jeans, and their unifying distrust of authority, we
can assume that the Black Rebels are, at least in style and mentality,
part of the contemporary youth subculture (even though their ages
are never specified). In fact, the image of Johnny straddling his motorcycle with a defiant stare has become an icon of angst-filled, direction-
less 1950s teen rebellion and anomie; after the film's release, the sale
of black leather jackets and motorcycles rose dramatically as teens
tried to imitate Marlon Brando's defiant swagger (Dirks, review of *The
Wild One*). Jon Lewis explains this character's appeal specifically as
a reflection of generational conflict: "Brando's Johnny epitomized a
kind of fifties' male ego ideal, empowering the rigid, working-class,
teenage male with the very masculinity a generation of fathers so ob-
viously lacked" (*Road to Romance*, 29). Nevertheless, since the majority of the Black Rebels appear to be in their twenties (or even older),

the film is not so much about teenagers as it is about the clashing of values and tastes in America. The people of Wrightsville and the Black Rebels clash because they cannot understand one another: the Rebels see the townspeople as "squares" who will never accept them, while the townspeople see the Rebels as an exotic, frightening mob.

THE ROCK 'N' ROLL CRAZE

Much of the fear over youth subcultures and their strange new behaviors was rooted in the teenage hysteria for rock 'n' roll music. The basis for rock 'n' roll—rhythm and blues—had been on the "black charts" since at least 1947.[11] However, most music historians agree that the genre first gained recognition in 1955, coinciding "with the demographic and sociocultural development of a white middle-class youth subculture" (Dotter, "Here to Stray," 91). The music of rhythm-and-blues performers like the Chords, Fats Domino, Little Richard, Chuck Berry, and others, with its emphasis on the backbeat (the second and fourth beats of a four-beat measure) and the frequent use of licentious lyrics, was "perceived [by the white, adult population] as being overtly sexual in both lyrics and performance—and this bordered on immorality" (Friedlander, *Rock and Roll*, 18–23). By contrast, the music targeted at white middle-class teenagers in the late 1940s and early 1950s was characterized by sugary, beatless romantic ballads sung by "song stylists" or crooners like Perry Como, Frank Sinatra, Patty Page, Nat "King" Cole, and Rosemary Clooney, and was meant to appeal to both teens and their parents (26). It is therefore not surprising that teenagers wishing to break away from their parents and the conservative environment of the 1950s gravitated toward rhythm and blues, which was later dubbed "rock 'n' roll," a slang term meaning "rowdy sex." Indeed, in the 1950s, much of the adult community—particularly parents—viewed rock 'n' roll music as the beginning of a vast social decline into immorality, sexual promiscuity, juvenile crime, and drug abuse.

Rock 'n' roll was especially objectionable to the white middle-class parents of rock-'n'-roll-crazed teenagers because of the genre's roots in the African American community.[12] In 1956, Asa Carter, the executive secretary of the North Alabama White Citizens Council, asked jukebox operators in Birmingham and the surrounding areas to throw out their rock 'n' roll records, believing that the music was a plot hatched by the NAACP to "infiltrate" southern white teenagers (*New York Times*, "Segregationist Wants Ban"). These sentiments circulated, both explicitly and implicitly, in the many articles devoted to outbreaks of violence associated with rock 'n' roll music in the 1950s. Indeed, coverage of rock-'n'-roll-related violence in the mainstream press frequently mentioned the race of performers or the race of the concertgoers involved in the violence. In a 1957 article about a teenage knife fight, to offer one example, the *New York Times* reported that teenagers involved in the melee had recently attended a "rock 'n' roll show featuring a majority of Negro performers" just before the fight ensued, and that, according to the police on the scene, "the Negro youths were responsible for [the stabbings]" ("Rock 'n' Roll Fight"). And three months later, the *New York Times* reported that knife fights and gunfire "erupted from a mass of 6,000 *interracial* rock 'n' roll fans" ("Six Dallas Youths Hurt"; emphasis added). In both cases, the reporters felt a need to mention that violence stemmed from shows containing either African American performers or that facilitated the mingling of African American and white fans.

Another tactic used to demonize rock 'n' roll was to compare the music with "primitive" tribal rituals that put impressionable listeners into a trancelike state and inspired deviant behaviors. One psychiatrist, Dr. Joost A. M. Meerlo, of Columbia University, compared the teenage desire to dance to rock 'n' roll to the "contagious epidemic of dance fury" that "swept Germany and spread to all of Europe" in the fourteenth century. Later, in the same *New York Times* article, Dr. Meerlo compared the effects of rock 'n' roll on teenagers with "Tarantism," an uncontrollable to desire to dance supposedly caused by a toxic tarantula bite (Bracker, "Experts Propose Study," 12). Outrageous as these beliefs might seem, they were not limited to Dr. Meerlo. A November 1956 issue of the teen magazine *Dig!* reprinted one particularly egregious newspaper article with the headline "Has 'Rhythm of Death' Invaded America? 'Voodoo Beat' Blamed for Teen Age Riots Coast to Coast as Music-Maddened Maniacs Maul Many!" The article attributes the success of rock 'n' roll to the "deadly rhythm of the jungles which sets off a hidden charge within the brain of its hearers, and incites them to acts of violence, murder, rape." Rock 'n' roll, the article reasons, "can make a murderer out of the nice kid next door" (*Dig!*, "'Rhythm of Death,'" 39). Again, the use of words like "tribal" and "primitive" is an implicit reference to the music's origins in African American culture.

These fears about teenagers and rock 'n' roll music were further bolstered by actual incidents of violence at rock concerts and dances. Throughout the late 1950s, there were several high-profile incidents linking rock 'n' roll music, teenagers, and acts of violence or destruction. In 1956 alone, all the following occurred: several people were injured when police used tear gas to break up a "rock 'n' roll riot" at a Fats Domino show in Fayetteville, North Carolina (*New York Times*, "Gas Ends Rock 'n' Roll Riot"); the antics of "rioting rock 'n' rollers" at a show in San Jose, California resulted in 11 injuries and $3,000 worth of damage (*Time*, "Rock 'n' Roll"); a rock-'n'-roll-related riot in Asbury Park, New Jersey, sent twenty-five teenagers to the hospital, causing Mayor Roland J. Hins to ban rock 'n' roll from all city dance halls (*Time*, "Rock 'n' Roll"); and Roman Catholic leaders demanded that all rock music be boycotted in Boston (*Time*, "Yeh-Heh-Heh-Hes, Baby"). And in 1957, 15,220 teenagers stood in line to attend an all-day rock 'n' roll show hosted by Alan Freed, the white American disc jockey credited with both naming and promoting rock 'n' roll music on his radio program. This event, held at the Paramount Theater in New York City, resulted in several injuries when attendees tried to push past wooden barriers set up by the 175 policemen on the scene (Asbury, "Rock 'n' Roll Teen-Agers").

As a result of these outbreaks of teenage resistance, authority figures including police superintendents, admirals, and mayors made headlines by banning rock 'n' roll music from civic buildings, teenage dance parties, and naval stations. In San Antonio, Texas, rock 'n' roll was even banned from swimming pool jukeboxes because the city council felt that "its primitive beat attracted 'undesirable elements' given to practicing their spastic gyrations in abbreviated bathing suits" (*Time*, "Rock 'n' Roll").

While many segments of the adult population fretted that, at best, rock 'n' roll music was decreasing the intelligence of the nation's youth and, at worst, turning them into destructive, sex-obsessed maniacs, the film industry was busy capitalizing on the teenage craze for rock music. Film studios used the popularity of rock 'n' roll to help sell teenpics, which often included musical performances having little or no relation to the central narrative of the film (see Jerry Lee Lewis's unmotivated musical performance at the opening of *High School Confidential!* [1958, Jack Arnold]). The inclusion of rock music in teenpics served a double function: to sell the featured music to the target audience and to make a spectacle of the film's contemporaneity and its privileged knowledge and production of teenage desires. For example, *Blackboard Jungle* was initially released as a mainstream melodrama about the problem of juvenile delinquency in urban schools. However, the studio's decision to play Bill Haley and His Comets' 1954 single "Rock Around the Clock" during the film's opening credits—the first time that rock 'n' roll music appeared in a major motion picture—created some unexpected reactions among America's youth population (Doherty, *Teenagers and Teenpics*, 76). In Minneapolis, Minnesota, a group of teenagers danced through the downtown and smashed windows after seeing the film, causing a theater manager to withdraw the film from his theater (*Time*, "Yeh-Heh-Heh-Hes, Baby"). Once again, the idea that rock 'n' roll put teenagers into a deviance-inducing trance was promoted and reinforced.

PUTTING THE TEENAGER ON FILM

It was not just the inclusion of the "Rock Around the Clock" that made *Blackboard Jungle* so appealing to teenagers. As Thomas Doherty points out, the film revealed "that the terms of the social contract between young and old have changed" by depicting teenagers who fully reject the social, cultural, and political tastes of their parent's generation (*Teenagers and Teenpics*, 76). In one of the film's most famous scenes, a meek math teacher, Mr. Edwards (Richard Kiley), brings in his prized collection of jazz 78s to illustrate how jazz is based on mathematics. Mr. Edwards believes that he can connect with his students by bringing in his music collection, not realizing that none of his young students would be fans of jazz (let alone *obscure* jazz). While he has intended this lesson for his more advanced students, his remedial class of juvenile delinquents begs him to play "just one record" before they take their exam. Mr. Edwards finally relents and plays a rare jazz recording for the JDs. Predictably, the boys become bored with the music and complain, "How 'bout some bop?" The restless teens soon get out of control, and the escalating mayhem is marked by the film's shift from long shots to low-angle close-ups. The increasingly aggressive diegetic sounds of the trumpet and saxophone serve as a menacing counterpoint to on-screen action: the boys smash Mr. Edwards's precious disks on the floor, push him around, and dance wildly with one another. Although the boys are rejecting the "square" music of their parent's generation in this scene, they manage, via their destructive actions and the film's unconventional cinematography (close-ups, extreme high- and low-angle shots, etc.), to make this safe and familiar music sound foreign and threatening. The final shot of the scene is an aerial view of the silent and empty classroom. Mr. Edwards stands alone, holding a shard of one of his jazz records—the sad aftermath of one miscalculating adult's attempt to bridge the widening generation gap.

The success of *Blackboard Jungle* and Haley's song with teen audiences indicated that teenagers, like their screen counterparts, wanted to differentiate themselves from their parents' generation.[13] However, the film's narrative—which depicted teenagers beating up their teachers in back alleys, stalking and threatening a pregnant woman, and attempting to rape a female teacher, generated protests from people who felt the film did not reflect the reality of either the nation's youth in general or urban vocational schools in particular. Moral crusader Senator Estes Kefauver denounced the film for its emphasis on sex and violence. The film was withdrawn from the Venice Film Festival after U.S. ambassador Clare Boothe Luce announced that she would not attend a screening of the film (*Time*, "Manicured Fistful"). Luce claimed that she did not want to lend "official sanction" to a film portraying such a "distorted view" of American life (*New York Times*, "Mrs. Luce Upheld").

Despite, or rather because of, this controversy, movie executives attempted to capitalize on *Blackboard Jungle*'s success by making a series of rock-'n'-roll-themed teenpics, including popular titles like *Rock Around the Clock* (1956, Fred F. Sears) and *Shake, Rattle and Rock!* (1956, Edward L. Cahn). These teenpics were integral to the distribution of rock 'n' roll imagery and sounds to eager teenage moviegoers. While many rock 'n' roll teenpics were nothing more than glorified musical revues, offering a loose narrative structure that allowed for the showcasing of contemporary musicals acts (see *Rock, Rock, Rock* [1956, Will Price]), others contained more substantial narrativization of the rock 'n' roll phenomenon and its relationship to teenagers and deviance.[14] In *Go, Johnny, Go!* (1959, Paul Landres), Johnny's (Jimmy Clanton) deviance is tied to his preference for rock 'n' roll music over devotional church music. A flashback sequence in which the audience learns about the protagonist's early days as a juvenile delinquent opens with Johnny practicing with his church choir. With no adults in the room, Johnny and the other kids begin singing rock 'n' roll music, accompanying themselves on the church organ. A priest sternly reprimands the group for engaging in such delinquent behavior and then kicks Johnny out of the choir permanently. The priest's explanation for singling Johnny out for dismissal is simple: he is an orphan and therefore beyond adult control. Later in the film, Johnny plots to steal a gold pin for his girlfriend. However, this robbery is aborted when Alan Freed, who plays himself in the film, finds Johnny contemplating the pin in a jewelry store window and offers him a recording contract instead. Johnny's decision to choose a life spent making rock 'n' roll music over a life spent in reform school cements his fame in the frame story. Thus, in *Go, Johnny, Go!*, rock 'n' roll both sets Johnny on a path of deviance and also rescues him from a life of crime. Rock 'n' roll is the primary signifier of teenage deviance as well as the juvenile delinquent's saving grace. Perhaps the film's ultimate message is that rock 'n' roll is safe for teenagers only when it is controlled by adults like Alan Freed, who decides which teens are worth making into stars and which are simply hopeless delinquents.

In addition to rock 'n' roll, the teenpic also portrays teenage behaviors like hot-rod racing (*Hot Rod Girl* [1956, Leslie Martinson]), drinking and drug abuse (*High School Confidential!*), and premarital sex (*Date Bait* [1960, O. Dale Ireland]) as dangerous and alluring. Scenes of teenage deviance are usually staged with bravado: the music is alternately tense or epic; the cinematography becomes more stylized; and the dialogue is more earnest and fraught with youthful angst than usual. One deviant subcultural behavior tailor-made for the cinema because of its visual dynamism was hot-rod racing, a hobby that swept the entire nation in the late 1950s.[15] As one teen explained in a 1956 letter to *Dig!* magazine: "Do you know what the two most important things in the world are to a teen-age boy? First is a car to drive, and second is a license to drive it. Why? Because teen-age life centers around anything with four wheels and a motor, and if you don't have access to such a device, lots of people you'd like to impress simply don't know you exist" (Tubbs, letter to the editor, 23).

Numerous magazines devoted to cars and hot rods began to appear on newsstands around this time (*Hot Rod, Rod & Custom, Car Speed and Style*, etc.). And as early as 1956, teen magazines like *Dig!* and *Modern Teen* had their own "custom car editor" and featured regular articles on hot rods, driver safety, and tips for customizing your car, marking these activities as belonging to youth culture.[16]

This fetishization of hot rods as well as the potentially fatal activities associated with them, such as drag races and "chickie runs" (in which two cars head for a cliff or each other until one driver "turns chicken" and drives off course to avoid certain death), was first translated into the language of cinema in *Rebel without a Cause*, a film that Timothy Shary describes as "the most influential demonstration of pure teen angst in American cinema" (*Generation Multiplex*, 4). The film's chickie-run scene is, I would argue, the seminal moment in the JD teenpic, a crystallization of the cycle's ability to translate the aura of teen rebellion into an alluring cinematic image. This iconic scene opens with Buzz (Corey Allen) and Jim (James Dean) preparing for their race, which will take place on a seaside cliff. To emphasize the danger of this activity, we see the steep drop to the ocean from Jim's perspective in a dizzying high-angle shot as he and Buzz contemplate what they are about to do. "That's the edge. That's the *end*," Buzz points out with a laugh. "Why do we do *this*?" Jim asks. "You gotta do

119

I WAS A
TEENAGE
FILM CYCLE

something, don't you?" Buzz replies. This exchange, beyond signifying the ennui so characteristic of the 1950s teenpic, also highlights
the sense of dire self-importance that appeals to a teenager's sensi-
bilities. This is not the conversation of two boys who have the ability to choose whether they will participate in such a dangerous game.
Rather, the boys sense that they must participate in this race; lacking
any other responsibility or commitment, the chickie run is something
they can commit to with the gravitas of a soldier heading off to war.

Indeed, when Buzz and Jim approach their vehicles at the start of
the race, excitement ripples through the crowd of teenage onlookers, who are instructed to drive their cars into a line along the im-
provised racetrack. When everyone is in place, Judy (Natalie Wood),
the love interest of both boys, moves to the center of the track, raises
her arms in the air, and shouts, "Hit your lights!" The camera immediately cuts to an extreme long shot, making Judy a small figure on the
darkened road. When the headlights come on, Judy is transformed
from an ordinary teenager on a dirt road into a performer on a stage.
To emphasize the gravity of the moment, the nondiegetic music, composed of brass and drums, becomes louder, while a rising string glis-
sando further elevates the tension. Judy then gives the signal for the
race to begin, and the camera immediately cuts to a close-up of car
tires squealing. This frantic cutting between long shots and close-ups
adds to the uncertainty and anxiety pervading the scene. The score
continues to intensify throughout the sequence, becoming louder and
more frantic. As the cars race past Judy, her expression is one of almost orgasmic pleasure and excitement; she turns to chase after the
boys as they race out of the shot and toward the edge of the cliff. Here
the viewer is meant to take up Judy's passive viewing position as she
thrills over the vision of two tough, strong young men being willing
to place themselves in real danger, merely to prove who is tougher
and stronger. However, the point of view then shifts to the speed-
ing cars, with alternating medium close-ups of Buzz and Jim as each
driver concentrates on the race.

These shots are exhilarating until we see a close-up of Buzz's sleeve
getting caught on his car door. He cannot exit his vehicle. When his
car goes over the seaside cliff, the viewer is "trapped" in the car with
Buzz. We see the plummet into the ocean from Buzz's point of view—
a shot that is simultaneously terrifying and thrilling. This accident,
culminating in Buzz's death, makes him the "winner" of the chickie
race. Despite, or rather because, Buzz never intended to make this
sacrifice, his death highlights the real stakes involved in such a race,
making the spectacle all the more alluring to the teen spectator—

both within and outside the film. Teenagers who participated in drag racing may not have had a literal death wish, but the fact that death was a possibility elevated their antics to the level of something more epic than pointless teenage horseplay. Such self-destructive teenage behavior is, according to Donna Gaines, a direct result of the boredom, isolation, alienation, and anomie of bourgeois, suburban teen life ("Suburban Scenes," 48). In other words, middle-class youth engage in delinquent behavior not so much out of economic need, but primarily in defiance of adult rules and restrictions (51). The success of *Rebel without a Cause* and its acknowledgment of both teen angst and car culture inspired and encouraged a cycle of JD teenpics centered on hot rods and drag racing, including such imaginatively titled entries as *Hot Rod Rumble* (1957, Leslie Martinson), *Hot Rod Gang* (1958, Lew Landers), *Joy Ride* (1958, Edward Bernds), and *Teenage Thunder* (1957, Georg Tressler).

As *Rebel without a Cause* demonstrates, to squeeze the most drama out of the teenpic's scenes of deviant spectacle, the high stakes of the activity, such as the loss of credibility among one's peers, loss of the respect of an adult mentor, jail time, or even death, must be stressed early in the film. In *Dino* (1957, Thomas Carr), we know that if the newly paroled Dino (Sal Mineo) goes through with his plan to rob a local service station, he will not only go back to jail, but also forfeit the hard-won emotional progress he has made with his psychiatrist, Dr. Sheridan (Brian Keith). Similarly, in *Go, Johnny, Go!* we know that if Johnny goes through with his plan to steal a gold pin for his best girl, he will lose his dream of becoming a famous rock 'n' roll star, a scenario highlighted by the fact that Johnny's song is playing on the radio—and generating buzz among teenagers across the country—at the exact moment that he stands contemplating the coveted pin in a jeweler's window. By portraying these high stakes, the teenpic heightens the excitement and danger of teenage deviance.

Another important convention of the JD teenpic is that it must present "authentic" depictions of teenage subcultural activities in order to attract the capricious teen audience. Teenagers are not likely to support a film that purports to be about teenage life but portrays slang, music, or clothing trends that are completely out of date. As Sarah Thornton argues: "Nothing depletes [subcultural] capital more than the sight of someone trying too hard" ("Subcultural Capital," 186).[17] *High School Confidential!* aptly illustrates Thornton's argument. In the film, a young teacher, Mrs. Williams (Jan Sterling), gives her students an English lesson on contemporary slang, offering definitions for terms like "square," "chicken," "doll," and "scram." However her attempts to "speak the language" of the students only highlights Mrs. Williams's exclusion and distance from the subculture—the students even tell her that her slang is "old-style jive." When the teacher leaves the classroom to take a disruptive student to the principal, another student, J. I. (John Drew Barrymore), posited as the "hippest" member of the student body by virtue of his position as leader of the Wheelers and Dealers gang, provides the class with a corrective to Mrs. Williams's dated lesson. J. I. reclines lengthwise on the teacher's desk as he delivers his "history lesson." The vertical compositions used during Mrs. Williams's lecture on slang are thus replaced with horizontal lines that complement the favored position of the contemporary teenager: in repose. J. I. delivers a slang-heavy narrative, telling his classmates: "One swingin' day when Chris [Columbus] was sittin' at the beach, *goofin'*, he dug that the world was round!" Throughout his lecture, the camera cuts to medium close-ups of J. I.'s teenage audience, representing a range of teen types, who whoop and laugh at each joke. These teenagers, who are stand-ins for the film audience, inform us that this is the language and humor that appeals to today's teenagers.

The students' uproarious laughter—which stands in stark contrast to the derisive giggles Mrs. Williams's lesson generated—indicates that J. I. is speaking the proper slang of contemporary teens. J. I. rewrites the story of Christopher Columbus's discovery that the world is round as a teenager's easy epiphany, arrived at while relaxing on the beach. History is made not through the hard work and self-abnegation characterized by the Protestant work ethic and validated by adult culture, but rather by teenage "goofin'." Teenagers and their specialized language overtake the adult universe, in which history is made, written, and passed on by adults. However, the moment Mrs. Williams re-enters the classroom, J. I. quickly ends his story and, in his haste to get off of her desk, tumbles to the floor. This moment of clumsiness, so unlike the cool demeanor J. I. has just displayed, foregrounds the disruptive effect that adults have on the teenage sphere.

Rock Around the Clock, the first post–*Blackboard Jungle* teenpic to capitalize on the rock 'n' roll craze, works in a similar fashion, telling the story of two (adult) big-band promoters who are frustrated by the decreasing number of patrons in their dance halls. It appears that nobody wants to go out dancing anymore. One night while traveling through a small town on their way to New York City, the promoters happen upon a dance hall packed with grooving teenagers. The men, who are baffled by the teenagers' ecstasy over the featured band, Bill Haley and His Comets, are initially depicted as clueless squares, especially when the teens' "jive" talk proves incomprehensible. One of the adults, Steve (Johnny Johnston), repeatedly attempts to find out the name of the band on stage as the teenagers dance, only to be thwarted by their cryptic replies. When he politely asks a young man, "Say, pardon me, friend, but could you tell me what the name of that band is?" the teenager replies, without missing a dance step, "Later, man, later. I'm gone now. I don't dig *nothin'*." As the teen dances out of the shot, Steve and Mike (John Archer) give each other quizzical looks. Later in the scene, Steve wants to know why the kids are clearing the floor for a pair of dancers. He is informed, "Dig man. When the most is on the floor, we give 'em room!" Even though the adult promoters eventually catch on and later profit from the rock 'n' roll subculture they "discover," their initial disorientation, along with the film's use of supposedly up-to-date lingo, music, and dance steps, provides hip teens with a mirror of their contemporary activities and square teens with a model to emulate (or scorn, if the teen really *is* a square). As Doherty points out, the narrative of the teenpic "provides at least a recognition, at most a validation, of the subcultural ways of the target audience" (*Teenagers and Teenpics*, 85).

Both *Rock Around the Clock* and *High School Confidential!* illustrate the dual function of JD teenpics: to exploit teen interest in subcultural behaviors and to further disseminate these subcultural behaviors to a broader audience. In *Rock Around the Clock*, the entrance of the adult squares into the dance hall provides an opportunity for the film to display teenage subcultural behaviors, much as if they were the ceremonial dances of a foreign culture. In fact, these teenpics depict teenage tastes in much the same way that *Life* magazine did in 1948. For example, at first the men are unable to label the genre of music being played by Bill Haley and His Comets. "It isn't boogie, it isn't jive, and it isn't swing. It's kind of all of them," says the befuddled Steve. In desperation, Mike asks a teenager, who is slung sideways across her partner's back, "Hey, sister, whattya call that exercise you're gettin'?" "It's rock 'n' roll, brother," she explains, amid her dance-generated ecstasies, "and we're r-r-r-rockin' tonight!" This line is followed by a series of aerial shots of the dance floor showing teenage couples performing contemporary dance steps. These shots are alternately cut with views of Bill Haley and His Comets performing and floor-level shots of the dancers from the waist down. This extended dance sequence, since it is not explicitly filmed from the perspective of our adult tour guides, Steve and Mike, serves instead as pure spectacle. These lengthy dialogue-free sequences, which appear throughout the film and do nothing to further the film's plot or develop its characters, are the primary draw of this film.

In fact, when *Rock Around the Clock* was marketed, its distributor,

The spectacle of teenage subcultural activities, divorced from any particular character's point of view, are highlighted in *Rock Around the Clock* (1956).

Columbia Pictures, did not emphasize its story, director, or its actors; rather, its theatrical posters highlight the musical acts that perform in the film, like Bill Haley and His Comets and the Platters. And the film's taglines, including "It's the Whole Story of Rock 'n' Roll!" and "The Screen's First Great Rock 'n' Roll Feature!" clearly address the film's appeal to teenage subcultural tastes. In both *Rock Around the Clock* and *High School Confidential!*, extended scenes of teenage subcultural styles are the films' raisons d'être. They are also the primary ways that these styles and behaviors were disseminated to a larger audience. After watching *High School Confidential!*, teenagers who were not in the know could catch up on the argot of their generation, while audiences for *Rock Around the Clock* could learn the latest dance steps. Film studios and individual directors and writers selected the songs, dance steps, slang, and clothing styles that thousands of teenagers would see and, if the film was successful in its address to teenagers, emulate. Here we can see how the proliferation of a film cycle helps further define and shape the contours of an emerging subculture.

Since Mrs. Williams, Steve, and Mike are initially depicted as dopes—adults who desperately want to connect with today's teenagers, but who are barred from a true communion with them because of age—it is sometimes easy to forget that these teenpics were produced, written, and directed by adults looking to exploit the teenage zeitgeist. Despite having the patina of being "hip," films like *High School Confidential!* and *Rock Around the Clock* were always already "square." Consequently, to enjoy these films, teenagers had to have undergone a willing suspension of disbelief, much as viewers of classical Hollywood films have to ignore the fact that they are watching a constructed piece of studio product in order to fully immerse themselves in the film's fantasy world. For teenage consumers of teenpics, these films offered a fantasy of a teen-centric world in which adults exist as active tormentors or flimsy annoyances, but not as figures of any importance. But to enjoy this fantasy, teenagers had to disavow their knowledge of the teenpic's origins in adult-controlled businesses.

Another important feature of the JD teenpic is its implicit and explicit fixation on class differences among teenagers. American International Pictures' *Teenage Doll* (1957, Roger Corman) depicts the antagonism between the Black Widows, a female gang composed primarily of working-class teenagers, and Barbara Bonney (June Kenney), a middle-class "square." The film begins just after Nan, a member of the Widows gang, attacks Barbara for dating Eddie (John Brinkley), the rebellious leader of the Vandals gang. During the fight, which takes place on a rickety stairway, Nan falls off the landing and dies. The rest of the Widows target Barbara for her role in Nan's death; however, it is clear that the Widows also despise Barbara because she is a privileged "good girl." Indeed, in *Teenage Doll*, the distinction between good kids and bad kids, between squares and gang members, boils down to a distinction between the middle and working classes. All the Black Widows, with the exception of Betty (Barbara Wilson), a policeman's daughter, come from poor, immigrant, working-class, or broken homes. This class bias is illustrated in the film's opening shot: we see a man tossing a bucket of dirty water into a back alley. He does not notice that he has doused the lifeless body of Nan, who is laid out like the trash that surrounds her. As the film's square-up explains: "What happens to the girl is unimportant . . . what happens to the others is more than important; it is the most vital issue of our time." In other words, we are not to mourn the death of this low-class hoodlum—an identity signified by the victim's members-only jacket, low-cut top, and bleached hair—who has literally become nothing more than street trash; we must instead concentrate on those girls who are worth saving, namely, those in the middle classes. Furthermore, *Teenage Doll* demarcates class visually through a teenager's ability to conform to or reject prescribed gender roles. Before we ever see Barbara's home life, the audience is cued that she is a square—a good middle-class girl—by her long, full-skirted dress, demure cardigan, and curled hair. By contrast, the Widows wear less-feminine attire: sneakers, jeans, matching Members Only jackets, and ponytails.

Early in *Teenage Doll*, each Widow returns home to scrounge for money, a plot device that offers the viewer a peek into the girls' family lives (or lack thereof). The nastiest, most ruthless Widow, Lori (Sandra Smith), is depicted as having the most aberrant home life: she lives in a dilapidated shack with her younger sister, who sits alone in the dark all day, chewing on cardboard. The scene in which we meet Lori's sister is over the top and grotesque: the sister has dirty, matted hair, crawls around on the floor, and begs Lori for "breakfast," though the scene takes place in the evening. The child looks to be about six years old, but she can barely formulate sentences. Instead, she makes sounds resembling the grunts and growls of a wild animal. Clearly, Lori and her sister have no parents or adults to care for them. The scene concludes when Lori tosses the little girl a box of stale crackers and turns off the light, leaving the child alone in darkness as she goes to seek her revenge on the privileged Barbara.

These scenes are meant to indicate that the Widows are, as Janet (Barboura Morris), the older sister of one of the Black Widows, puts it, "too rotten to save." But what is interesting and potentially subversive about *Teenage Doll* is that middle-class life—as embodied by the Bonney family—does not appear to be any more nurturing or stable than Lori's disturbing existence. We first see the Bonney living room in a wide shot; it is neat, quiet, and tastefully furnished. Mr. Bonney (Damian O'Flynn) appears in the foreground, working at a desk.

Barbara Bonney (June Kenney) is marked as a middle-class square by her conservative feminine clothing in *Teenage Doll* (1957).

In *Teenage Doll* (1957), Helen (Fay Spain) and Squirrel (Ziva Rodann), both members of the Widows gang, wear tougher, more masculine clothing, signifying their delinquent, and working-class, status.

Barbara attempts to sneak into the house quietly in the background of the frame. Without looking up from his work, Mr. Bonney reprimands his daughter for returning home past curfew. So far, the Bonney household, while strict, appears normal and peaceful. The "normal" tone of this scene changes quickly, however, when Barbara's mother, Estelle Bonney (Dorothy Neumann) appears. Although she is middle-aged, Estelle is dressed like a young girl. She wears a childish flower-print dress with short puff sleeves and a scooped neck that is too large for her slight frame. Her thinning grey hair is styled in pigtails, and a large satin bow is tied around her head. At one point, she scolds Barbara for getting into trouble, telling her, "A sixteen-year-old girl shouldn't be out where a truck can hit her." Barbara has to correct her, "I'm eighteen, Mother." Mrs. Bonney appears to be surprised by this news, confirming that she is suffering from delusions or memory loss. Later in the scene, it is revealed that Mrs. Bonney, like her daughter, was once in love with a "cheap, worthless, and treacherous" man, a "bad boy" like Eddie. We get the impression that had Mrs. Bonney stayed with her bad boy, her true love, she would be a very different (and possibly saner) person in the present. Her clothing choices, a caricature of a little girl's Sunday best, reflect her own arrested development, caused by her imprisonment in a sanitized, unfulfilling, overly structured middle-class relationship.

Barbara, feeling stifled by her middle-class existence, searches for excitement in the dangerous world of teen gangs, just as her mother did a generation ago. One of the Vandals hits the nail on the head when he later mocks Barbara for her attempts to rebel against her parents. "My mommy and daddy don't understand me, so I gotta go out and be a juvenile delinquent!" he teases. Here we can see how delinquency, previously explained as a matter of economics, was eventually depicted as a problem affecting all classes (Doherty, *Teenagers and Teenpics*, 124). It was, as *Teenage Doll*'s square-up warns, "a sickness, a spreading epidemic that threatens to destroy our very way of life."[18]

Although teenagers enjoyed the teenpics flooding the market in the 1950s, they were not always pleased with how they were being portrayed in these films. In a November 1956 issue of *Dig!*, a teenage reader complained about how *Teenage Crime Wave* (1955, Fred F. Sears), advertised itself as "The story of today's wild youth." The teen writes: "This type of phony advertising misleads the adults into thinking that *all* teenagers are bad, instead of realizing that it's only 2% of the teenagers that get into trouble" (Pelath, letter to the editor, 5). And in a 1960 issue of *Dig!*, a teenager wrote in to complain about the portrayal of teenagers in contemporary movies: "Adults say [the problems in contemporary society are] our fault because we have 'corrupt, vulgar minds.' Did they ever stop to realize that our minds wouldn't be so 'corrupt and vulgar' if *they* didn't give us the atmosphere in which to build these thoughts?" The teen explains that it is impossible to avoid "filthy" movies, adding, "And who creates this filth? Adults. . . . The same adults who blame us, the victims of their horrid money-making schemes, for the trouble in the world today" (Travers, letter to the editor, 24). This letter raises a valid point: teenagers were being blamed for their seemingly endless appetite for crime, sex, and horror, yet teenagers were able to consume these films only because adult-run film studios created them for and marketed them to the teenage audience.

Teenagers were also increasingly frustrated with how their clothing choices demonized them and marked them as juvenile delinquents. For example, in a March 1961 issue of *Teens Today*, a girl wrote in to complain about how her parents did not like her new boyfriend, because he dresses like a "juvenile delinquent." "I've been dating a wonderful boy named Jerry," she writes, "but if you saw him on the street, I guess you'd think he was a hood. He wears sideburns, a black leather jacket and he rarely says more than two words to most people" ("He Looks Like a Hood," 5). And in the November 1956 "Letters to the Janitor" (that is, the "Letters to the Editor") section of *Dig!*, numerous teenagers wrote in to comment on another teenager's letter. The offending letter critiqued the new "delinquent" style being sported by contemporary teens. According to the *Dig!* editors, they received 4 letters in praise of the "square's" letter and 233 against it. Those opposed viewed the conservative teenager, who was advocating the new "Ivy League" style, as a "hopeless square." One teen responded: "Would you kindly tell that 3D square that just because teenagers like to use hep talk and wear ducktails . . . it does not make us juvenile delinquents! So what if a lot of teenage boys act like Marlon Brando" (*Dig!*, "Letters to the Janitor," 4). Teenagers were aware that certain styles and speech patterns marked them as juvenile delinquents—and this knowledge alternately pleased and annoyed them.

CONTAINING THE TEENAGER

In addition to providing viewers with a visual and aural display of teenage subcultural styles and behaviors, the films in the JD teenpic cycle had to eventually recuperate these images of rebellion and social difference in order to fulfill the contract brokered with the viewer (and society at large) in the film's square-up. The square-up promises the viewer that the filmmakers would never create such amoral images for the sake of mere titillation. Therefore, the teenpic must conclude with some solution to the problem at hand in order to make good on the square-up's promise of moral clarity. The teenpic's recuperative solution usually plays out in one of three ways: the delinquent commits an act of redemption or reformation (Jim Stark in *Rebel without a Cause*, Dino in *Dino*, Johnny Melody in *Go, Johnny, Go!*); his or her delinquent behavior is shown to be innocent and harmless after all (the rock 'n' roll lovers in *Rock Around the Clock* and *Rock, Pretty Baby* [1956, Richard Bartlett]); or the delinquent proves to be unrecuperable and is therefore eliminated though his or her death, incarceration, or rejection by the teenage community (Artie West [Vic Morrow] in *Blackboard Jungle*, Tony Rivers in *I Was a Teenage Werewolf*, Matt Stevens [John Ashley] in *High School Caesar* [1960, O. Dale Ireland]). This recuperative strategy proved useful for studios because they were able to capitalize on images of teenage deviance without provoking the ire of the PCA, moral watchdog groups, or irate parents.

The containment, correction, reincorporation, or punishment of deviant teen behavior is almost always demonstrated via a visual tableau at the teenpic's conclusion. The last shot of *High School Confidential!*, for example, shows the film's protagonist, Tony (Russ Tamblyn), his girl, Joan (Diane Jergens), and their square teacher, Mrs. Williams, all sitting together in the front seat of Tony's car. This image is comforting because Joan, the formerly marijuana-addicted juvenile delinquent, has finally been integrated back into the fold of adult conformity. Likewise, throughout *Teen-Age Strangler* (1964, Ben Parker), Curly, the leader of the local hot-rod gang, the Fastbacks, is resolutely antiauthoritarian. He refuses to cooperate with Lieutenant Anderson (Bill Bloom), who is trying to solve the case of the "teenage strangler," and gets himself permanently banned from Marty's diner, the local teen hangout. However, after some finger-pointing, a fiery hot-rod crash, and the arrest of the killer (it was the janitor), the rebellious juvenile delinquent, newly repentant and bandaged from his accident, is completely reconciled with the adult community. In the final scene, Curly, who is now allowed to return to Marty's diner, is given a soda "on the house" while Lt. Anderson puts his arm around the recuperated teenager's shoulders. In the JD teenpic, it literally pays to conform.

And *Dino* concludes with the title character deciding not to rob the local gas station and returning to the office of his therapist, Dr. Sheridan, to ask whether he might bring his troubled younger brother in for some counseling as well. As Dr. Sheridan closes the door to his office so that Dino can begin his therapy session, the camera pans to the left, catching Dino's love interest, Shirley (Susan Kohner), walking around the corner. The camera follows her into the main room of the James Street Settlement House, where teenagers from all over the neighborhood are busy decorating for the evening's big dance. The camera continues to track Shirley in one long take as she emerges from the settlement house and out into the streets of her busy urban neighborhood. The shot fades to black, with triumphant music playing on the sound track, signifying that these once-dangerous streets are safe now that the neighborhood's juvenile delinquents are engaged in wholesome, prosocial activities created and supervised by the adult community.

Teenpics of the 1950s also frequently conclude with formerly rebellious teenagers accepting the rule of their middle-class parents and, by extension, mainstream social norms. In *Rebel without a Cause*, to name one well-known example, Jim Stark spends most of the film raging against the hypocrisy and disingenuousness of the adult world and the impotence of his father (Jim Backus). He rejects his parents' middle-class conformity for the excitement of an alternative community created with like-minded alienated youth like Plato (Sal Mineo) and Judy. Yet despite the fact that the film continually emphasizes Jim's inability to communicate with his parents and the adult world in general, *Rebel without a Cause* concludes with a narrative and visual reconciliation between father and son. In the final scene, Jim mourns over the body of his new friend, Plato, who was accidentally shot by the police after an evening of delinquent antics. Here, Jim looks much like he did in the opening shots of the film, when he was drunk and lying on the street, playing with a child's wind-up toy. But this time, rather than rejecting adult authority, Jim is embracing it. In a medium close-up, we see Jim hugging his father's legs, much as a child would. His father then kneels down to lift his son up into a standing position. He tells Jim, "Stand up, and I'll stand up with you." Jim had earlier criticized his father for allowing himself to be emasculated by his overbearing mother, but this scene restores patriarchal power to the father of the middle-class family. As the men embrace, the camera cuts to a close-up of Jim's mother (Ann Doran), who appears to be both alienated and annoyed by this scene of male bonding and power. Jim then solidifies his transition into responsible adulthood and away from his juvenile, countercultural antics by tenderly zipping up the red jacket Plato is wearing. Plato had borrowed the now iconic jacket from Jim moments before he was shot, and it makes sense that it should remain with him, since his untimely death has

The teenagers Joan (Diane Jergens) and Tony (Russ Tamblyn) enjoy the company of their teacher (Jan Sterling) in the final scene of *High School Confidential!* (1958).

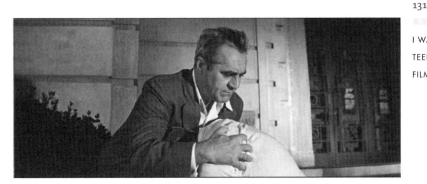

The reformed juvenile delinquent Jim (James Dean) accepts the embrace of adult rule at the conclusion of *Rebel without a Cause* (1955).

made him a rebellious teenager forever. By contrast, Jim swaps the loud red jacket for the more subdued, adult sports coat of his father, signifying his abandonment of youthful rebellion for adult responsibility. In one of the film's final shots, Jim stands with his arm around Judy, accepting his role as the male half of a responsible heterosexual couple.

Teenage Doll concludes similarly. At the film's climax, Barbara, the middle-class square, finds herself trapped in a warehouse with three options: give herself up to the police and possibly end up on death row for the (accidental) murder of Nan, flee to Arizona and start a new life alone, or face the wrath of the vengeful Widows, who wish to kill her. When Barbara complains that none of these choices are acceptable, her ex-boyfriend Eddie, a career juvenile delinquent, tells her, "Look, kid, you're lucky. You still *got* a choice." Barbara ultimately decides to turn herself in to the police. In the film's final shots, we see her slowly approach the detective and then collapse in his arms, as if relieved to be returning to a world of adult rules after an evening immersed in a terrifying, teen-run judicial system. When Betty, the Widow who also happens to be the daughter of a police officer, sees this emotional exchange from afar, she too realizes that she must abandon the gang and go straight. Earlier in the film, Betty stole her father's gun, a symbol of his power over the nuclear family and society, in order to sell it for cash. But now Betty agrees to repent and restore that (phallic) power to its "rightful" owner. She explains to her friends: "I've gotta take this gun back to my father." Likewise, Squirrel (Ziva Rodann), whose family, although poor, is depicted as being stable and loving, also decides to turn herself in.[19] As in the conclusions of *Teen-Age*

Strangler and *Rebel without a Cause*, this compromise with adult society is marked visually, with adults and juvenile delinquents grouped together in a final reconciliation. While *Teenage Doll* recuperates the deviance of girls like Barbara, Betty, and Squirrel, who were reared in relatively stable, two-parent homes, the other juvenile delinquents in the film, who lack such domestic support, are positioned as being "beyond help." The implication of this conclusion is that the only teens who merit saving are those from the middle classes or the upwardly mobile working classes. The rest are street trash, worthy of what will assuredly be a violent, untimely death (like Nan's). As a reflection of the times, *Teenage Doll* implies that juvenile delinquency was a major social problem primarily because deviance had spread from the confines of the city to the suburbs.

Occasionally, though, the juvenile delinquent cannot be recuperated. He or she rejects the ministrations of big-hearted social workers, concerned parents, or idealistic English teachers, opting instead to live by his or her own nihilistic code or, worse, to inflict it on others. When patience, therapy, and adult sympathy prove to be ineffective, brute force is the only option for dealing with such intractable delinquents. In *Blackboard Jungle*, well-meaning English teacher Mr. Dadier (Glenn Ford) is unable to get through to his classroom's most degenerate delinquent, Artie West. Their antipathy comes to a head when Artie refuses to turn in a paper and Mr. Dadier orders him to go to the principal's office. Rather than comply with this adult-issued order, Artie stands his ground and provokes Dadier into engaging in a physical battle. "You're gonna have to take me to the principal's office," he snarls. The room is silent except for the diegetic sound of a ticking clock. As the confrontation escalates, we see a series of shot–reverse shot exchanges between Dadier and Artie. Like the boys in the classroom, who intently watch to see how this conflict will unfold, the audience is being asked to determine who is tougher and who deserves our support: Dadier, representing adult rules and conformity, or Artie, representing danger and juvenile rebellion.

When Artie pulls out his switchblade, Dadier is left with no choice but to disarm the boy. After a long standoff, in which the majority of the classroom jumps into the fight to aid to their teacher, Artie is disarmed. However, once Dadier is able to get his hands on Artie, he loses his sense of control and slams the boy against the chalkboard over and over while muttering gibberish. This action is filmed from over Dadier's shoulder, providing the viewer with a full view of Artie's pained expression as his furious teacher throttles him. Given that *Blackboard Jungle* was initially aimed at adult viewers, this moment is cathartic, fulfilling the viewer's own desire to stifle teenage independence. However, the film does not end on this pessimistic moment of generational conflict and the breakdown of law and order. After Artie and one of his supporters are duly deposited in the principal's office, the film offers up a more congenial image of the relationship between teenage delinquents and adult rule makers: the formerly rebellious Greg Miller (Sidney Poitier) and his teacher, Mr. Dadier, both agree not to quit high school (attending it and teaching it, respectively). The final shot of the film shows both men framed against the front of North Manual High School, an image restoring authority to adult-run institutions.

The possibility or impossibility of recuperation in the teenpic is not always tied to class. Occasionally, affluence is depicted as a corrupting factor (a theme only hinted at in *Teenage Doll*). *The Violent Years* (1956, William Morgan) tells the story of Paula Parkins (Jean Moorhead), the leader of an upper-middle-class gang of remorseless teenage toughs. Paula, who lives in a lavish home with seemingly normal parents, explains the reason behind her juvenile delinquency: "I'm not interested in the money. There's plenty of that at home. . . . It's the thrill that gets me." The film concludes with all the girls in the gang dead, except for Paula, who is soon brought to trial and convicted of first-degree murder. While in jail, Paula, who was impregnated by an older man before her incarceration, dies in childbirth. The film's final shot is of the shadows of jail bars paired with the offscreen cries of a newborn baby, implying that the sins of the mother will be revisited upon the child. Indeed, though the film establishes Paula's behavior as monstrous, her parents are also blamed for her behavior. The film implies that their busy modern lives keep them from fulfilling their parental responsibilities; Mr. Parkins (Arthur Millan) is a newspaper editor who works constantly, and Mrs. Parkins (Barbara

Weeks) spends most of her time doing charity work. The court judge declares them to be unfit to raise their newly orphaned grandchild, explaining, "Juvenile delinquency is rooted in adult delinquency."

The Violent Years abandons the possibility of recuperating or containing the deviant teenager. Death or incarceration is the only possible solution to juvenile delinquency. By the mid to late 1960s most teenpics, had adopted a similar stance. Delinquent teenagers, some of whom had at least the possibility of being recuperated into the dominant hegemony in earlier teenpics, are now completely outside the bounds of society. In *Teenage Gang Debs* (1966, Sande N. Johnson), gang members and their "debs" (that is, girlfriends) engage in torture, murder, and gang rapes. As the film's poster promises: "They all talk, fight, and love, just one way . . . DIRTY!" Although earlier teenpics like *High School Confidential!* created a teen-centric universe, *Teenage Gang Debs* differs in that adult rules are completely absent. The kids' parents have no say over what they do or where they go, and justice is administered by the juvenile delinquents rather than by representatives of adult society. When one deb, Annie (Sandra Kane), gets out of line, alpha female Terry (Diane Conti) orders the boys in the gang to rape her. "She's dirt! Show her!" Terry commands. At the film's conclusion, Terry is sentenced to disfigurement by switchblade. This attack is filmed from Terry's point of view as several snarling debs creep toward the camera, wielding small switchblades. These scenes of physical and sexual violence are made all the more disturbing by the film's gritty black-and-white cinematography.

And in *The Sadist* (1963, James Landis), two gun-crazy teenagers, Charlie (Arch Hall, Jr.) and Judy (Marilyn Manning), hold a group of people hostage at a gas station. The film's trailer describes Charlie, who dons the characteristic JD uniform of jeans and a matching jean jacket, as "a human volcano of unpredictable terror: rejected by society, twisted by mental anguish, tortured by complexes. Man or monster, sane or insane, but driven to shock and kill." As an unrecuperable juvenile delinquent (he tortures and kills all but one of his victims), Charlie must suffer a suitably macabre fate: death by rattlesnakes.

Concurrent with these bleak depictions of teenage behavior in the 1960s was a new teenpic cycle that viewed teenagers not as unrecuperable rebels but as "clean-cut kids who just wanted to have fun" (Betrock, *Teenage Juvenile Delinquent*, 100). In 1963, American International Pictures released William Asher's *Beach Party*, starring "clean teenpic" staples Annette Funicello and Frankie Avalon. Despite the initial reservations of the executive producer, Samuel Arkoff, the film was a huge success with teenagers (102). *Beach Party*, and the cycle of clean teenpics it spawned, depicts a teenage world free of angst, rebellion, drugs, and, most importantly, parents. The film opens with a shot of a sunny beach paired with upbeat rock 'n' roll music, which then cuts to a close-up of Frankie (Frankie Avalon) and Dee Dee (Annette Funicello) smiling as their convertible speeds along the highway. They sing, without a care in the world, "Vacation is here! Beach party tonight!" The biggest concerns these teens face is whether the evening's bonfire will be a success and whether they will find true love that summer—a far cry from the drug addictions, pregnancies, and murder charges endured by their JD teenpic forbearers. Alan Betrock believes that these films were successful in the mid-1960s because as the world was threatened with assassinations, the escalation of the Vietnam War, and violent racial uprisings, the beach-party films offered "a fantasy vision of life without serious problems" (102). While many teenagers were embracing the counterculture of the 1960s, with its protests, long hair, and progressive rock 'n' roll, a segment of the youth population "fought steadily to hold onto what was safe, fun and familiar" (105). By the late 1960s, then, the JD teenpic cycle, at least in its original 1950s incarnation, had effectively run its course.

CONCLUSION

Dick Hebdige has argued that the concept of the subculture, that is, a culture that is somehow separate from and in defiance of the dominant culture, is a paradox: "It is . . . difficult . . . to maintain any absolute distinction between commercial exploitation on the one hand and creativity/originality on the other, even though these categories are emphatically opposed in the value systems of most subcultures" (*Subculture*, 95). For a subculture to spread beyond a few individuals and *become* a subculture, it must be publicized or packaged in some way, whether through a mass-produced CD or clothing style, a nationally published article, a televised news report or, more recently, through websites, weblogs, and social-networking sites. Thus, while subcultures initially pose a "symbolic challenge to a symbolic order," these subcultures are inevitably, sometimes instantaneously, recuperated back into the very system they are supposed to be challenging. The paradox of these subcultural behaviors is that despite their ability to provide marginal voices with a forum for critiquing the dominant hegemony, the moment of their exposure beyond a small group of individuals marks the moment when these behaviors became products to be marketed and sold by the mainstream. It would appear then that as soon as the media reproduces a subculture, that subculture's authenticity starts to degrade.

Michael Jarrett argues that most histories of the popularization of modern music (and, I would add, any subcultural phenomenon in general) employ a similar, physical science model. Specifically, histories of popular music follow the law of entropy, or the belief that "energy tends toward a state of equilibrium" ("Rock & Roll," 168). For subcultures, this law translates to the idea that whatever is hip or innovative will inevitably become conventional. Likewise, this narrative of conventionalization almost always uses what Jarrett calls the "rhetoric of degeneration": as a new musical genre or subculture ages, its quality, originality, and purity degrade. The rhetoric of degeneration would argue, for example, that when artists like Fats Domino and Little Richard began playing what came to be known as rock 'n' roll music in the late 1940s, the genre was "authentic" and pure. But as white musicians like Buddy Holly and Elvis Presley began to play rock 'n' roll music, thereby increasing its popularity among white teenagers, the purity of the genre became degraded. By the time a film like *Sing, Boy, Sing!* (1958, Henry Ephron), which was made to capitalize on the "clean teen" rock 'n' roll sensation Tommy Sands, was released, rock 'n' roll music had been stripped of its original creativity, its authenticity, and, of course, its sexual bite. This model of conventionalization is appealing, Jarrett argues, not only because it accounts for how certain marginal cultural tastes become mainstream, but also because it is politically correct, explaining how (white) commercial interests have historically plundered and degraded black, "authentic" cultures (169).

However, Jarrett offers a more positive counterreading of this physical science model, suggesting that conventionalization is a necessary component of all forms of creative expression because it helps "digest" the decaying matter of culture, refertilizing it so that new material can grow. Jarrett argues that before artistic innovations can occur, the material of popular culture must first be properly digested—that is, it must be consumed by a mainstream audience. The process of conventionalization, rather than destroying art, "fosters artistic renewal by generating conditions which allow for aberrant readings" ("Rock & Roll," 174). Once a form of cultural expression has become an entrenched part of the mainstream, it is possible for innovators to "misread" this expression, creating an innovation or a new interpretation of the initial expression: "In every case the rock musician perceived as innovative is the one who has creatively misread the popularized or conventionalized version of the compost pile produced by a previously recognized innovation" (176). Conventionalization is a "compost pile" that allows for the growth of new art forms both predictable and novel, conventional and avant-garde.

Jarrett's arguments can be usefully applied to the relationship between subcultures and film cycles. Film producers take the aspects of a subculture that they perceive to be to new, exciting, or scandalous—such as teenage interest in hot-rod racing—and translate these fragments into saleable filmic images. These fragments of youth subcultures are eventually conventionalized by their appearance in film cycles, spreading out through mainstream culture and exposing a broader public to styles and images that were once contained within a small, isolated subculture. At that point, these conventionalized images become available for numerous "aberrant" readings, including the following cycles and films:

- Clean teenpics: *Beach Party, Beach Blanket Bingo* (1965, William Asher), *How to Stuff a Wild Bikini* (1965, William Asher)
- Youth-on-drugs films: *The Trip* (1967, Roger Corman), *Psych Out* (1968, Richard Rush), *Easy Rider* (1969, Dennis Hopper)
- 1980s "Brat Pack" films: *The Outsiders* (1983, Francis Ford Coppola), *Sixteen Candles* (1984, John Hughes), *The Breakfast Club* (1985, John Hughes)
- Ghetto action films: *Boyz N the Hood* (1991, John Singleton), *Juice* (1992, Ernest R. Dickerson), *Menace II Society* (1993, Allen and Albert Hughes)
- Teen sex comedies of the 2000s: *Road Trip* (2000, Todd Phillips), *Van Wilder* (2002, Walt Becker), *Superbad* (2007, Greg Mottola), *Nick and Nora's Infinite Playlist* (2008, Peter Sollett), *Fired Up!* (2009, Will Gluck), *Adventureland* (2009, Greg Mottola), *Easy A* (2010, Will Gluck)

While the exploitation of 1950s youth subcultures seemed to rob them of their originality and creativity, it also spread rock 'n' roll music and other subcultural styles and interests to a broader population, offered teenagers a sense of community, and, ultimately, created a rich array of film cycles that are still being produced today. Here we can see how the existence of many film cycles are predicated on subcultures, and how subcultures are dependent on the culture industry, including film cycles, for their existence and sustainability. Film cycles are not the parasitic organs of mainstream culture, sucking the money (and originality) out of subcultural innovations; rather, they are better understood, as Jarrett might put it, as popular culture's "recyclers." They break down the organic material of popular culture to such an extent that, over time, this material can become the basis for future innovations. While many critics deride film cycles as structures that kill previously fresh, innovative concepts or characters, I argue that film cycles are a necessary part of the distribution, distillation, and transformation of commercial imagery.

CHAPTER 4

NOT ONLY SCREEN BUT
THE PROJECTOR AS WELL
THE RELATIONSHIP BETWEEN
RACE AND FILM CYCLES

In 1991, a series of independent films dealing with black themes and directed by African Americans were all slated for release at once, including titles like *Daughters of the Dust* (Julie Dash), *Livin' Large* (Michael Schultz), and *Boyz N the Hood* (John Singleton). This phenomenon generated an abundance of press coverage on the subject of African American filmmaking. The general tone of this coverage balanced excitement for the future of black cinema with a tentativeness about what African American filmmakers should do with their newfound Hollywood clout. A *Los Angeles Times* article from 1991 is characteristic of the early coverage of what came to be known as the "black film boom": "In an era still dominated by special effects extravaganzas and feel-good romance and comedy, these black-themed films provide some of the most compelling social and political material in Hollywood today" (Easton, "New Black Films"). This boom was even more significant coming in the wake of the whitewashed 1980s, when very few films about the African American experience were released (Guerrero, *Framing Blackness*, 125). Of course, Hollywood's new open-door policy toward African American filmmakers was rooted, like all decisions made in the industry, in a strong economic incentive—in this case, the periodic marketability of black cultural productions. *New York Times* reporter Karen Grigsby Bates presciently noted in July of 1991: "The frenzy for black product that allowed [John] Singleton, who has no previous professional credits, to direct his own film has become so great that black film properties may be to the '90s what the car phone was to the '80s: every studio executive has to have one" ("'They've Gotta Have Us'").

Bates's forecast was correct: in the early 1990s, African Americans had more directing, writing, and acting opportunities than ever before. And what was even more exciting, unlike the blaxploitation cycle of the 1970s, the black film boom of the early 1990s encompassed a diversity of stories, filmmaking styles, and perspectives: from Reginald Hudlin's lighthearted, mainstream-targeted teenpic, *House Party* (1990), to Charles Lane's black-and-white homage to Charlie Chaplin, *Sidewalk Stories* (1990), to Robert Townsend's glossy period piece about a singing quintet, *The Five Heartbeats* (1991). African American female directors, who still found themselves marginalized, struggled to obtain studio funding, but nevertheless, the black film boom inspired a general sense of hopefulness about the possibilities of contemporary black cinema.[1] This change in the film industry was thought to be a harbinger of bigger and better things for African American producers, directors, writers, actors, and moviegoers. As the African American director Charles Lane optimistically predicted: "The Berlin Wall, having been pulled down, will not be re-erected" (quoted in Bates, "'They've Gotta Have Us'"). This time, critics, pundits and filmmakers argued, the black film renaissance would not be a repeat of the public relations disaster that was the 1970s blaxploitation cycle, which incited the ire of several activist groups, including the Coalition Against Blaxploitation, Blacks Against Narcotics and Genocide, and Jesse Jackson's People United to Save Humanity. These groups claimed that the blaxploitation cycle, with its emphasis on pimps, pushers, and prostitutes, was racist, promoting negative stereotypes about the urban African American community (Guerrero, *Framing Blackness*, 101). The black film boom of the 1990s, with its diversity of representations and perspectives, appeared, at least initially, to be very different from the blaxploitation cycle.

From within the diversity of styles produced by the black film boom of the 1990s, a distinct cycle of films, using similar characters, settings, themes, and even filmmaking styles, began to emerge. I refer to this film cycle collectively as the "ghetto action cycle," a term I borrow from S. Craig Watkins's article "Ghetto Reelness: Hollywood Film Production, Black Popular Culture, and the Ghetto Action Film Cycle." The ghetto action cycle, which includes releases like *New Jack City* (1991, Mario Van Peebles), *Boyz N the Hood*, *Straight Out of Brooklyn* (1991, Matty Rich), *Juice* (1992, Ernest R. Dickerson), *South Central* (1992, Steve Anderson), *Menace II Society* (1993, Allen and Albert Hughes), *Fresh* (1994, Boaz Yakin), *Clockers* (1995, Spike Lee), *New Jersey Drive* (1995, Nick Gomez), and *Set It Off* (1996, F. Gary Gray), emphasizes just one aspect of the contemporary African American experience: the tragic and difficult lives of young African American men (and, occasionally, women) who are either directly or indirectly involved in a criminal lifestyle.

These films generated awareness about a pressing social problem:

the state of the American inner city in the early 1990s. Critics, academics, audiences, and filmmakers, both within and outside the African American community, felt that the ghetto action cycle (much like the Dead End Kids cycle of the 1930s and 1940s) could be effective in generating awareness about urban problems like poverty, joblessness, drug abuse, violence, and gang activity. In addition, boosters felt the cycle could speak to those who might be tempted to turn to violence as a solution to their dire living conditions. For example, in the press kit for *New Jack City*, the first entry in the ghetto action cycle, the director, Mario Van Peebles, is quoted as saying, "[Drugs are] an amazing, terrible thing to witness, but it's also a lesson that can be learned and acted upon. We hope we can generate both responses [with this film]."[2] And in a *Jet* piece about the theater violence that erupted at screenings of his and other ghetto action films, Van Peebles told the interviewer, "When I did *New Jack City*, I saw an opportunity to make a movie that kids would go see; to make edutainment" (*Jet*, "Who Should Be Blamed?" 57). Despite the violence occurring at some of the showings of his film, Van Peebles saw *New Jack City* as an opportunity to educate the public about the dangers of drugs, violence, and gang life.

Ultimately, these lofty hopes were not realized. The ghetto action cycle proved extremely controversial and problematic, not only for the black film boom and its filmmakers, but also for the urban African American population as a whole. In the days following the March 1991 premiere of *New Jack City*, newspapers and television news programs across the country reported on isolated incidents of violence—shootings, stabbings, and rioting—linked with the screening of the film. In Brooklyn, two teenage boys from "warring" housing projects allegedly fired more than one hundred bullets in and around a theater where the film was playing, culminating in the death of a nineteen-year-old man. In Los Angeles, several hundred moviegoers who were denied admission to the Mann Theater's screening of *New Jack City* "rioted" through the streets of Westwood, California (Brode, *Money, Women, and Guns*, 188). Four months later, when John Singleton's *Boyz N the Hood* premiered, media reports linked the film with violence, including two fatalities and more than thirty injuries (Leland, "New Jack Cinema").

Violence is not unprecedented at movie screenings; films like *The Godfather III* (1990, Francis Ford Coppola) and *The Warriors* (1979, Walter Hill) were also associated with incidents of theater violence at the time of their release. However, the primary difference between *The Godfather III* and *The Warriors* and the films of the ghetto action cycle is that the first two were targeted primarily at a white audience, while the others drew in large crowds of African American urban moviegoers. Historically, African American film audiences have been subject to increased surveillance by studios, theater exhibitors, and the media, as Jane Gaines notes in her discussion of race films of the silent era: "[Race films] had to be historically censored because the black bodies exposed to it could, by means of mimic operations, carry the images they saw into the streets. What was believed was that through the incorporation of the image into the black body, the criminal violence (coupled with taboo sexuality) on the screen would be replicated in the wider society. The black body, in its remarkable capacity to reproduce images, then, is not only the screen but the projector as well" (*Fire and Desire*, 252). The media frenzy following *Boyz N the Hood*'s opening weekend initially convinced twenty-one theaters to drop the film. Ultimately, however, this seemingly negative publicity was a boon to *Boyz N the Hood* and its claim of depicting the "reality" of the contemporary ghetto: after a $10 million opening weekend, more than one hundred theaters across the United States picked the film up for the following weekend (Leland and Foote, "Bad Omen"). *Boys N the Hood* eventually proved to be a box-office success; costing only $6.5 million, it earned more than $57 million domestically.[3] Audiences were drawn in by the aura of danger surrounding the film, which mirrored the danger depicted in the film.

In her article "Screening Race: Responses to Theater Violence at *New Jack City* and *Boyz N the Hood*," Laura Baker convincingly argues that the media's extraordinary reaction to audience violence at these films resulted from "the tension between Hollywood's desire to screen race and many mall multiplexes' desire to screen out nonwhite audiences." In other words, since most theater exhibitors were reluctant to open theater chains in inner cities, city-dwelling gang members had to travel outside their turf to suburban theaters frequented mainly by white middle-class audiences (*Christian Science Monitor*, "'Boyz N the Hood' Boosts Debate"). Gang members, anticipating that gang members from other territories might also be attending the same film, armed themselves accordingly.[4] These young men attended *Boyz N the Hood* expecting violence—and, not surprisingly, violence ensued. Baker contends that Warner Bros. and Columbia Pictures, the studios behind *New Jack City* and *Boyz N the Hood*, tried to defuse any negative press generated by these violent incidents by working to convince audiences that their viewing experiences would be "safe." The studios promised extra security at screenings and provided videos discussing the violence contained in the films. "In contrast to the media's magnification of the incidents of violence, the film industry's response was deliberately reserved," Baker explains. "Neither Warner Bros. (*New Jack City*) nor Columbia (*Boyz N the Hood*) actively exploited the incidents to promote the film" (Baker, "Screening Race"). Baker sees these studio responses as "reserved" and nonexploitative, but my analysis will show that the studios behind *Boyz N the Hood* and a later entry in the ghetto action cycle, *Juice*, sought to exploit, rather than to downplay, their films' potential to incite real-life violence.

But why would studios want to encourage an association between their films and actual violence? Why would they want their films to be viewed as dangerous rather than safe? Simply put, these strategies sought to confirm an image of authentic or realistic "blackness" that the studios wanted to associate with their ghetto action films. Within the marketing discourses and press coverage surrounding these films, "authenticity" was treated as synonymous with aggressive masculinity, random violence, and gang culture in general. Furthermore, the target audiences for these films were white suburban teenage fans of gangsta rap and African American urban moviegoers.[5] These two target audiences were attracted to ghetto action films because they promised to echo, in visual form, the stories these audiences heard in their favorite music: stories of police brutality, drive-by shootings, and drug dealing. This marketing technique—emphasizing violence and antisocial behaviors—is surprising given that most ghetto action films articulated strong antiviolence messages and attempted to paint a portrait of the inner city very different from that found in the news media and in gangsta rap. Hence, what is most interesting about the exploitation of the ghetto action cycle is that it engaged in a kind of doublespeak: the directors' articulations of the purposes and meanings of their films were in conflict with their studios' sensationalistic marketing strategies. Of course, the studios were able to ride the wave of this sensationalism for only so long. Academics lamented what Jacquie Jones termed the "the new ghetto aesthetic" of violent, nihilistic men and hypersexualized women, and even the filmmakers themselves became annoyed with the nation's obsession with stories depicting violent young black males killing and being killed.[6] By 1996, the ghetto action cycle had largely disappeared from the big screen, moving to low-budget direct-to-DVD releases.[7]

To understand how images of "authentic blackness" and the depiction of a "black point of view" were both defined and marketed for audiences in the early 1990s, and to appreciate how the contentious issue of race in America was exploited for the launch of this intergeneric film cycle, I employ, as I did in Chapter 2, Janet Staiger's model of historical reception analysis. This chapter largely bypasses a discussion of these films' content to focus instead on the public discourses surrounding the marketing of two of the most contentious ghetto action films, *Boyz N the Hood* and *Juice*.[8] Using a detailed analysis of movie trailers, posters, studio-issued press kits, director and producer interviews, and editorials, I argue that blackness as an image of violence, masculinity, and urban cool was erroneously conflated with the contemporary, real-world experiences of black youth and with a particular conception of "authenticity." This definition of blackness was central to the eventual success of the ghetto action cycle and also explains why the black film boom of the 1990s, which initially held so much promise, had seemed to disappear by the end of the decade.

"BLAXPLOITATION" OF THE PAST

The ghetto action cycle's marketing campaigns exhibit numerous parallels with previous attempts to make black films for an African American audience, including silent race films of the 1910s and 1920s and blaxploitation films of the 1970s, a comparison highlighting how controversies over race, representation, and the commodification of authenticity have historically led both to the creation of black film cycles and to their destruction.[9] A side-by-side comparison of race films, blaxploitation films, and ghetto action films reveals that most films created for and marketed to the African American community can be categorized as forms of exploitation. In other words, all three cycles rely on the promise (and delivery) of "forbidden spectacle" as their raison d'être (Schaefer, *Bold! Daring! Shocking!*, 75–76). Eric Schaefer defines spectacle as "something presented to fascinate the eye of the spectator" and to elicit "an immediate, affective response" (76). In the case of black film cycles, this forbidden spectacle is the image of the black body.[10] Similar to classic exploitation films like *Mom and Dad* (1944, William Beaudine), black film cycles are sold primarily based on their ability to provide audiences with images not represented in mainstream Hollywood films. The images found in black film cycles do not offer the sort of titillation found in exploitation films (nude bodies, close-ups of diseased genitals, childbirth scenes), but they nevertheless offer their target viewers a glimpse of previously absent images. For example, race films of the 1920s, 1930s, and 1940s differ from studio films containing African American characters, such as *Gone with the Wind* (1939, Victor Fleming), because they place African American actors in central, active, and, often, nonstereotypical roles. Characters in race films live

and work in the present and in settings resembling those most familiar to the target audiences for these films, such as northeastern cities (Massood, *Black City Cinema*, 12).[11] These contemporary urban images were the primary draw of the race film. Therefore "blackness"
was what was being sold to the audience, rather than big-name stars,
directors, or product quality.

The primary difference between classical exploitation films and
black film cycles is that while the audiences for the former were seeking out images of the (alleged) Other—the drug user, the sexually
promiscuous young woman, the syphilis victim—the audiences for
the latter were seeking out images of themselves. I see a strong corre-
lation between these two sets of images: neither market would have
existed if Hollywood had not deemed images of drug-using characters or contemporary African American urban characters unsuitable
material for mainstream (white) consumption. These markets were
created because audiences were denied the opportunity to see some
aspect of their contemporary reality. As Jane Gaines puts it, "Race
movies were an audacious invention that helped to make an audience that most white entrepreneurs did not see, that helped to imagine a separate community into existence" (*Fire and Desire*, 17). The images found in these race films were often sensationalized in ad copy
and other public discourses, such as film reviews and editorials. However, the images targeted at those audiences were often sensationalized in ad copy and other public discourses, like film reviews and
editorials.

For example, the African American director Oscar Micheaux exploited hot-button racial issues in his race films, making them some
of the earliest examples of "blaxploitation."[12] The longevity of Micheaux's career, which spanned thirty years and more than forty
films, can be attributed to his uncanny ability to produce topical films
touching on issues important to African American communities, including lynching, "passing," and prostitution (Nesteby, *Black Images*,
75). He was therefore criticized by white critics who chafed at his depictions of contemporary racial issues, and by African American critics who "had similar objections and were upset because Micheaux often directed critiques toward the black community . . . or practiced
a form of color casting" (Massood, *Black City Cinema*, 40). Many of
these complaints about "appropriate representation" would be taken
up by critics of both the 1970s blaxploitation and 1990s ghetto action
cycles.

One of Micheaux's earliest attempts to exploit images of blackness
in a sensational manner is *Within Our Gates* (1919). In addition to its

The infamous lynching scene from *Within Our Gates* (1920) was intended to be provocative.

outsider mode of production, *Within Our Gates* can be considered an exploitation film in that it caters to an African American audience by focusing on images of contemporary blackness and by centering the film's appeal and marketing strategies on one sensational scene of forbidden imagery: an African American couple being lynched by a mob of angry white townspeople. The film's primary narrative is about a southerner, Sylvia Landry (Evelyn Preer), who ventures north to Boston in order to raise money to save Piney Woods, an all-black school in her hometown. However, the film contains a brief backstory detailing how Sylvia's family members were the victims of a lynching. The inclusion of this brief segment drew intense criticism from African American and white critics alike.[13] Because of the controversial nature of this scene, *Within Our Gates* was banned in numerous cities; authorities feared that the film might cause African American audiences to riot. Other cities allowed the film to play, but only in a heavily edited form (Jane Gaines, *Fire and Desire*, 162).

Paula Massood explains that part of the controversy over the film's depiction of lynching was linked to the racial climate of the time. She cites the "Red Summer of 1919," during which African American residents of Chicago rose up in protest over, among other injustices, the stoning of an African American youth who attempted to cross a racial line on a public beach (*Black City Cinema*, 51). By staging such a controversial scene at a time when race relations were already vexed, Micheaux, like any good exploiter, was providing his target audience with a forbidden spectacle, one absent from mainstream Hollywood films. This is not to say that Micheaux's choice to direct attention to the subject of lynching was purely profit based. Many Americans at this time wanted to pretend that lynching did not exist at all, and Micheaux must have been aware of the important political and social implications of this scene.[14] However, he was also a huckster at heart, and it is likely at least one of his motivations was to generate a healthy profit by stirring up controversy.

Jane Gaines likens Micheaux to the "circus sideshow promoter P. T. Barnum" because of his gift for fast talk, exaggeration, and canny manipulation (*Fire and Desire*, 120). Describing him also as "an instigator and actualizer, someone who not only designs the work but who orchestrates its reception," she locates his rhetorical strategies within the classic exploitation tradition of ballyhoo (123). As discussed in the Introduction, ballyhoo promises audiences a visceral, sensational moviegoing experience, which it does not always deliver. As reflected in the ad copy for the film, Micheaux promised to generate a strong emotional and bodily reaction in his African American audience. For instance, publicity for *Within Our Gates* advertised it as a "Preachment of Race Prejudice and the Glaring Injustices Practiced Upon Our People." He promised also that you, the viewer, would "Grit Your Teeth in Silent Indignation" when watching the film (quoted in Gaines, *Fire and Desire*, 169). This emotion, indignation, is very different from the feelings generated by the classic exploitation film, which aimed at arousal, titillation, disgust, or terror. However, since the spectacle of the exploitation film image aimed to fascinate the eye and to elicit an affective response, Micheaux was clearly participating in that tradition. He expected his viewers to be outraged by the sensational images of racial injustice projected on the theater screen. As Gaines describes the film, "Yes, this is lynching as sensational spectacle" (169). The difference between exploitation films and Micheaux's spectacles, however, lies in the viewer's relation to the on-screen image.

While graphic images of a newborn's head pushing its way out of a woman's vagina in *Mom and Dad* generated disgust through their Otherness or distance from the spectators (only doctors, nurses, and midwives would have been familiar with such images at the time), the images of lynching in *Within Our Gates* generated outrage because of their similarity to the target audiences' personal experiences. Many viewers, particularly those residing in the South, would have recognized these images as a frightening aspect of their reality. And like *Mom and Dad*, the appeal of *Within Our Gates* was not the narrative, the actors, or the production values, but rather a brief scene of sensational imagery intended to fascinate the eye of the spectator. *Within Our Gates* is an important film to mention within the context of the history of black film cycles and their exploitation because it highlights "the way the symbolism of events (inflected as socially dangerous) can become inextricably mixed up with the events themselves, especially during racially sensitive moments in history" (Gaines, *Fire and Desire*, 161). Micheaux's race films routinely addressed such controversial issues, and this controversy helped fill theater seats. Thus, long before directors like John Singleton (*Boyz N the Hood*) and Ernest R. Dickerson (*Juice*) assessed and then targeted the needs of an underserved African American audience with sensational, politically loaded images of urban black existence, Oscar Micheaux understood the value of effectively marketing and exploiting racially and politically charged imagery.

Like race films, the blaxploitation cycle of the 1970s was conceived during a racially sensitive moment in American history. The cycle was also decried as being "socially dangerous" because of its deployment of images of urban blackness and its re-creation of scenes of violence—police brutality, urban uprisings, drive-by shootings—that were occurring in the real world. Furthermore, the African American audience's initial embrace of the blaxploitation cycle was strongly tied to how the films' messages dovetailed with the contemporary audience's political leanings, particularly in their articulation of Black Nationalism. As S. Craig Watkins explains, blaxploitation's "concentration on black heroes defeating corrupt white police officials and Mafia men . . . undoubtedly appealed to a younger generation of African Americans, who experienced the frustrations of urban rebellions, police repression, and a heightened racial backlash" (*Representing*, 94). As with race films, the formation of the blaxploitation cycle was also tied to its ability to supply and exploit images that were absent from mainstream Hollywood productions—namely, images of defiant, sexualized, empowered African American heroes living in a contemporary urban milieu.[15] This cycle consequently relied upon hyperbolic definitions of (primarily masculine) blackness to sell films to the public.

The blaxploitation cycle would not have been able to form if Hollywood had not needed a quick cash infusion. Throughout the 1960s, the major studios lost money at the box office for several interrelated reasons, including, the rising popularity and widespread availability of television, the slow dissolution of the studio system's reigning mode of production, and the studios' investment in a series of expensive flops (Martinez, Martinez, and Chavez, *What It Is*, 59). The urban African American population, which attended the movies in disproportionate numbers, consequently became a coveted demographic (Hartmann, "Trope of Blaxploitation," 382). This population was particularly important because as "white flight" to the suburbs continued throughout the 1950s and 1960s, historic downtown movie palaces in the urban centers of Chicago, New York City, Washington, D.C., and parts of Los Angeles were increasingly empty (Martinez, Martinez, and Chavez, *What It Is*, 59). With the release and consequent success of Melvin Van Peebles's *Sweet Sweetback's Baadasssss Song* in 1971, studios discovered that films centering on African American heroes and appealing to an African American audience could earn a massive box office.[16] Van Peebles's film was a success because he carefully studied his market—the African American urban population—and then determined the best form of ballyhoo for pulling them in. He recalls asking himself, "How am I going to advertise the film if I don't have any money? Okay, Black people like music, I'll write a hit song. . . . I had this whole marketing idea to use music to sell the movie" (quoted in Martinez, Martinez, and Chavez, *What It Is*, 37). Though Van Peebles (erroneously) credits himself with discovering that music could be used to sell films, he did initiate one primary convention of the blaxploitation cycle: the employment of contemporary rhythm and blues (R&B) artists—in this case, Earth, Wind & Fire—to compose or perform the film's sound track.[17] But the biggest draw of *Sweetback* was its political appeal.

Perhaps the most important vehicle for exploiting *Sweetback*'s contemporary racial politics was its posters, which appeared in national newspapers and magazines as well as in the lobbies of downtown theaters. According to Jon Kraszewski, movie posters "frame" movies for spectators, acting not only as a lure, but also as a rubric for reading the film they are about to watch ("Reception of Blaxploitation," 50). The *Sweetback* poster features a close-up of the protagonist's face, partially obscured by shadows, against a black background. He looks directly at the viewer with a confrontational but detached expression. Below this image are a series of line drawings depicting mostly violent vignettes from the film: a white cop holding a gun to the face of a frightened African American woman, another white cop releasing a pack of hunting dogs in a field, and Sweetback raising a handcuffed arm over his head in order to strike something (or someone) that does not appear within the frame. Melvin Van Peebles's defiant stare, coupled with images of police brutality and black empowerment, clearly

The original theatrical poster for *Sweet Sweetback's Baadasssss Song* (1971) invokes tropes of Black Nationalism.

tapped into the tropes of Black Nationalism, which had a strong currency in the urban centers where the film was marketed. This poster is constructed to appeal to the viewer's sense of outrage over racial injustice. Most famously, Huey Newton, the minister of defense for the Black Panthers, described *Sweetback* as "required viewing" for the African American community and offered a detailed analysis of the film in the Black Panther party's newsletter, the *Black Panther* (Hartmann, "Trope of Blaxploitation," 389; Massood, *Black City Cinema*, 94; Guerrero, *Framing Blackness*, 87).[18] The poster's designers used carefully selected images to connote a definition of blackness—persecution by the state, rebellion against racist institutions, and aggressive masculinity—that would draw contemporary African American audiences into theaters.

In interviews in mainstream publications like *Newsweek* and African American–targeted publications like *Jet*, Van Peebles further emphasized the "sensational ploys to ethnic and socio-political fears and fashions" that he used to draw in his target audience (Hartmann, "Trope of Blaxploitation," 384). In his in-depth analysis of *Sweetback*'s reception in the media, Jon Hartmann found that these periodicals "were most easily hypnotized by Van Peebles' claims" and were "reluctant to do more than let Van Peebles' well-rehearsed promotions speak for themselves" (397). In a 1971 *Time* magazine interview, Van

Peebles proclaimed, "Of all the ways we've been exploited by the Man, the most damaging is the way he destroyed our self-image. The message of *Sweetback* is that if you can get it together and stand up to the Man, you can win" (*Time*, "Power to the Peebles"). Here Van Peebles portrays himself as a rogue artist who took on the film industry and won.[19] And in a *Life* magazine interview, he claimed to have made America's "first black revolutionary film" (quoted in Guerrero, *Framing Blackness*, 88).

Like *Sweet Sweetback's Baadasssss Song* and *Within Our Gates*, the formation and success of the ghetto action cycle was tied to its ability to supply and exploit images that were absent from mainstream Hollywood productions. The box-office draw of the ghetto action cycle was based on a "forbidden spectacle"—on the promise of providing audiences with a peek into worlds and lifestyles (the lives of young African American men living in the nation's cities) that mainstream films generally ignored or marginalized. According to S. Craig Watkins: "The menacing specter of ghetto youth culture became *the* exploitative hook that made the production of this particular film cycle timely, sensational and oddly enough, more easily marketable" ("Ghetto Reelness," 238). Moreover, as Eric Schaefer points out, "exploitation films generally follow when discourse on a given issue or problem reached a convulsive state" (*Bold! Daring! Shocking!*, 25), and in the early 1990s, discourses about the inner city, drugs, gang culture, and the implicit association of all these with African American youth pervaded the media. All film cycles are, for the most part, the result of exploitation. But as these examples demonstrate, the history of film cycles targeted at African American audiences is strongly tied to the promotion of sensational, violent, politically controversial imagery as well as appeals to authenticity.

RACIAL SIGNIFIERS AND THE FORMATION OF A FILM CYCLE

Like the blaxploitation cycle of the 1970s, the formation of the ghetto action cycle was partly grounded in its ability to generate profits when studios were in financial crisis. In 1991, industry profits dropped by almost 26 percent from the previous year. As in the 1960s, this recession hit major studios hard, but big independent studios also began to suffer. This decrease in profits was tied to a number of factors, including the Gulf War (1990–1991) and an economic recession (Guerrero, *Framing Blackness*, 164–166). Like the studios' big-budget event pictures of the 1960s, the cinema of the 1980s relied primarily on high-concept, or "tent pole," pictures—those films that can be marketed along with a sound track, product tie-ins, and fast-food deals (Balio, "Hollywood Production Trends," 165).[20] These tent-pole pictures, which were often dependent upon the presence of A-list actors, who demanded ever-increasing paychecks, had to earn large profits if studios were to maintain financial solvency. The box-office failures of a few major productions, including *The Bonfire of the Vanities* (1990, Brian De Palma), *Hook* (1991, Steven Spielberg), and *The Godfather III*, forced studios to turn to less expensive films that targeted specific, identifiable markets. The success of low-budget, African American–directed, African American–targeted films like *She's Gotta Have It* (1986, Spike Lee) and *Hollywood Shuffle* (1987, Robert Townsend) revealed that young African American audiences had once again become a desirable demographic. As in the 1970s, the African American audience, which in the early 1990s made up 12 percent of the population and 25 percent of the moviegoing audience, proved to be an ideal target (Bates, "'They've Gotta Have Us,'" 18). As a result, larger studios began to offer more and more low-budget "specialty" films directed by African Americans, since these films involved little economic risk and provided near-certain profits in an uncertain moviemaking climate (Watkins, *Representing*, 102).

The film historian David Walker argues that the success of Spike Lee's *She's Gotta Have It*, a film set in an urban milieu featuring a wide range of African American characters, proved that audiences were tired of the contemporary depiction of African American movie characters and "were hungry for something other than the Eddie Murphy and Whoopie [*sic*] Goldberg stuff that was being forced upon us" (quoted in Martinez, Martinez, and Chavez, *What It Is*, 61). As with race films and blaxploitation films, the ghetto action cycle fully rejected the conventional, conservative (and infrequent) depictions of African American characters found in mainstream Hollywood films of the previous decade, films like *Stir Crazy* (1980, Sidney Poitier), *Beverly Hills Cop* (1984, Martin Brest), and *Jumpin' Jack Flash* (1986, Penny Marshall). In these popular films, actors like Richard Pryor, Eddie Murphy, and Whoopi Goldberg were placed in all-white environments, a strategy that depicted the African American experience as devoid of a definable context or politics (Guerrero, *Framing Blackness*, 125). The African American audience's desire for a more realistic depiction of blackness, one that seemed to better reflect the experiences of contemporary African Americans, paved the way for the success of the black film boom in general and the ghetto action cycle in particular.

In the 1970s, studios tapped into the politically charged atmosphere created by the Black Power movement, the Vietnam War, second-wave feminism, and the gay rights movement by creating active, aggressive blaxploitation heroes like Coffy (Pam Grier) and Slaughter (Jim Brown). The images of blackness employed to sell the ghetto action cycle, however, were neither tied to nor reflective of any particular political movement (Watkins, *Representing*, 94; Boyd, *Am I Black Enough*, 39). Instead, these films express profound frustration, even rage, over the state of race relations (Guerrero, *Framing Blackness*, 159). Instead of political engagement, the ghetto action cycle capitalized on a particular definition of authentic blackness, which was, according to S. Craig Watkins, aligned with "two elements that commonly arouse popular appetites: sex and violence" ("Ghetto Reelness," 238). In the service of this definition, "young African-American men 'strapped' (armed with guns), 'gangbanging' (killing each other), and 'slingin'' (dealing drugs) became staple images in the ghetto film cycle."

Much as the teenage juvenile delinquent was the object of intense fear, study, and media speculation in the 1950s, the African American urban (usually male) teenage gangsta or gangbanger was an object of fear in the 1980s and early 1990s (Robbins, "Armed, Sophisticated, and Violent"). This fear was the product of several high-profile media events that associated African American youth with crime and violence. In 1991, a videotape depicting the brutal beating of Rodney King, an African American motorist, by officers of the Los Angeles Police Department was released to the media, generating outrage over the department's abuse of power. In April 1992, after the acquittal of the four officers implicated in the incident, a rebellion (or riot, depending on which media source is consulted) began in the South Central neighborhood of Los Angeles and lasted for almost three days (resulting in the deaths of more than fifty people).[21] Of course, the King verdict was not the sole cause of this rebellion or riot. The socioeconomic situation in Los Angeles had been grim for decades: unemployment was exceedingly high, the city was experiencing its worst economic downturn since the Great Depression, the "war on drugs" of the 1980s had turned Los Angeles neighborhoods into war zones, and friction between various racial and ethnic groups, particularly between the relatively new Korean population and the long-established African American population, was growing daily (Mitchell, "Truce Called"; Bernard, "L.A. Rebellion," 40). Nevertheless, the Los Angeles rebellion of 1991 had a profound impact on the way Americans viewed the inner city.

Related to these anxieties about black violence in cities was a growing backlash against rap music. As with the juvenile-delinquent-themed teenpic cycle, the emergence of the ghetto action cycle was strongly tied to a new, deviant musical genre, in this case, gangsta rap. In 1989, the West Coast–based group N.W.A. (Niggas With Attitude) released the first commercially successful gangsta rap album, *Straight Outta Compton*, initiating a style of rap that would dominate the genre for more than a decade.[22] With songs like "Fuck tha Police" and "Dopeman," N.W.A. helped establish the salient characteristics of gangsta rap: angry, antiestablishment lyrics detailing the crime, violence, and desperation of life in the primarily African American, postindustrial, working-class neighborhoods of east Oakland and south-central Los Angeles. The lack of new industries in these neighborhoods in the years following the World War II–era factory boom helped facilitate the crack-cocaine-based economy that eventually caused so much bloodshed in the 1980s and 1990s; some estimates put the unemployment rates for African American youth at more than 40 percent at this time (Neal, "Postindustrial Soul," 369).[23] Gangsta rap songs often focus on re-creating for the listener—in both lyrics and sound effects—the experience of living in the crime-infested neighborhoods of this "new" Los Angeles (Forman, "Race, Space, and Place," 203). For this reason, the subgenre has been characterized as the "voice of black urban poor people" (Lott, "Marooned in America," 79).

Just as entertainment executives had been caught off guard when clean-cut white suburban teenagers fell in love with rock 'n' roll music, which was considered primitive, bestial, and low class, they were likewise surprised when, in the early 1990s, gangsta rap, the "voice of black urban poor people," became extremely popular among white suburbanites. In the early 1990s, many rap industry insiders began to speculate that by the time a rap record sold 500,000 units (that is, was certified as a gold record), white consumers—the crossover market—had accounted for at least 60 percent of that album's sales (Upski, "Words like 'Mackadocious,'" 64). Beyond enjoyment of the music, argues Marc Spiegler, white teens were attracted to hip-hop culture in all of its manifestations because it allowed them to imagine themselves a part of African American ghetto culture: "The attraction . . . is part admiration, part fascination, and part fear" ("Marketing Street Culture," 3). Hank Schocklee, a rap producer, agreed: "If you're a suburban white kid and you want to find out what life is like for a black city teenager, you buy a record by N.W.A. It's like going to an amusement park and getting on a roller coaster ride—records are safe, they're controlled fear, and you always have the choice of turn-

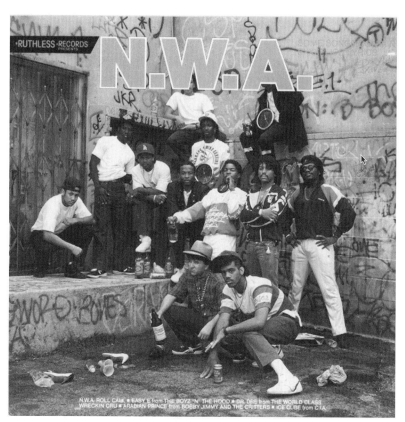

Groups like N.W.A. offered their fans an "authentic" look at life in the ghettos of Los Angeles.

ing it off" (quoted in David Samuels, "Rap on Rap," 153).[24] Like participating in drag racing and chickie runs in the 1950s, listening to gangsta rap in the 1990s offered suburban teenagers (both African American and white) a sense of danger and of transgressing social boundaries.

However, despite its acceptance among teenagers of all races and backgrounds, the adult, primarily white mainstream disapproved strongly of rap music, particularly in its gangsta rap form. Its critics complained that rap lyrics were violent, misogynistic, homophobic, and nihilistic (as is most popular music, including rock 'n' roll, punk, and heavy metal). As a result, the genre was the object of intense scrutiny. Furthermore, a number of events in the late 1980s and early 1990s culminated in the sensationalization of rap music and its presumed effects on its fans. In 1988, an eighteen-year-old was stabbed to death during a rap concert at Nassau Coliseum; in 1989, N.W.A.'s record label, Priority Records, received a letter from Milt Ahlerich, an FBI assistant director, objecting to the content of their popular song "Fuck tha Police" (Pollack, "FBI Hit List," 20); in 1990, an obscenity case over the lyrics to 2 Live Crew's album *As Nasty as They Wanna Be* (1989), was tried in Florida;[25] in 1991, eight young people were trampled to death in New York City at a charity basketball game with rappers (Powell, "Crushed," 52); and in 1994, a series of congressional and senatorial hearings addressed the controversial musical genre (Rose, "Rap Music and Demonization"). Mirroring the mainstream coverage of rock 'n' roll music in the 1950s, the 1990s coverage of rap music both implicitly and explicitly linked it with violence and the African American community. According to Tricia Rose, such media coverage was "part of a long-standing sociologically based discourse that considers black influences a cultural threat to American society" ("Hidden Politics," 241).

The most publicized movement against rap music was Tipper Gore's Parents Music Resource Center (PMRC). The PMRC's original target was rock 'n' roll and heavy metal music in the 1980s, but its focus abruptly shifted to rap music in the late 1980s and early 1990s after rap began to increase its mainstream fan base (Pollack, "FBI Hit List," 20). As part of her antirap crusade, Gore published a now-famous editorial entitled "Hate, Rape and Rap" in the *Washington Post* in 1990, which erroneously connected 2 Live Crew's sexual lyrics to the rape of a jogger in Central Park jogger (Berry, "Redeeming Rap Music," 175).[26] In her editorial, Gore linked urban crime, African American male teenagers, and rap music to suit her censorship agenda. The PMRC campaign was successful primarily because Gore was able to associate urban crime with urban music. This process, which Stanley Cohen describes as a "widening of the net," occurs when ambiguous stimuli (such as rap) are roped into the framework of other pressing but unrelated social problems (rape, the drug problem in inner cities), all of which are believed to be signs of a larger social meltdown (*Folk Devils*, 81–82).

THE GHETTO ACTION CYCLE

Thus, in the late 1980s and early 1990s, the American public became increasingly concerned about the connections between youth, race, inner-city crime, drug abuse, poverty, and gangsta rap. The newly emergent ghetto action cycle tapped into all of these real and media-exacerbated concerns. Contemporary film reviews, one of the first ways in which a film's structures of meaning are communicated to a mass audience, further aided this exploitation process by consistently describing the films of the ghetto action cycle as timely records of an authentic black experience that audiences needed to see. Valerie Smith points out: "Reviewers and certain viewers grant [films made by African American directors] a proximity to and power over real life that is rarely seen in discussions of other types of films" ("Documentary Impulse," 60).[27] Indeed, when *Boyz N the Hood* debuted in 1991, film reviewers and mainstream journalists in national newspapers like the *New York Times, Washington Post,* and *Los Angeles Times,* as well as in black-targeted periodicals like *Jet* and *Essence,* uniformly described the films as authentic and socially significant. Roger Ebert of the *Chicago Sun-Times* wrote in a review: "By the end of *Boyz N the Hood,* I realized I had seen not simply a brilliant directorial debut, but an American film of enormous importance"; Desson Howe of the *Washington Post* told his readers: "If you don't live in or near one of these neighborhoods, just turn to the news at 11 to see" ("It's Murder Out There"). When Ice Cube, one of the film's stars, was interviewed about *Boyz N the Hood* in the *Source,* a magazine created for and marketed to hip-hop fans, he was asked, "Does the movie depict real life?" He responded: "Most definitely! It's not even a movie people can criticize. People should just be happy that they are really getting a look into *our* world" (quoted in Mills, "Gangsta Rapper," 32; emphasis added). And in the academic journal *Cultural Critique,* Michael Eric Dyson declared *Boyz N the Hood* "the most brilliantly executed and fully realized portrait of the coming-of-age odyssey that black boys must undertake in the suffocating conditions of urban decay and civic chaos" ("Apocalypse and Redemption," 122).

Valerie Smith argues that an emphasis on the factual has been a persistent presence throughout the history of black narrative writing, dating back to slave narratives. Ghetto action films constantly work to reassure the viewer that the director is in a position of authority in relation to his or her material: "The techniques and narratives of these films thus conceal their status as mediations and suggest that they occupy an intimate, if not contiguous, relation to an externally verifiable reality" ("Documentary Impulse," 60). We can see this implicit linking of race and authenticity in the discourses surrounding *Boyz N the Hood* and even in John Singleton's own claims about his film. For example, in an *Essence* interview, Singleton explains: "My whole thing is that if I make intelligent street movies for a common audience about common people, my generation will learn something." Singleton felt that in making *Boyz N the Hood,* he was educating "his generation" about the importance of a college education, parental responsibility, and the rejection of gang violence. The interviewer adds that "Singleton's own life mirrors that of the main characters." This autobiographical information, including the fact that Singleton grew up in an area of South Central similar to the one depicted in the film, was emphasized in many of the interviews preceding and following the film's release. In a *Time* profile of Singleton, published shortly before the 1992 Academy Awards ceremony (Singleton was nominated for best director), he explains why he fought to direct his screenplay after it was purchased by Columbia Pictures: "So many bad films had been made about black people, and most of them had been done by people who weren't African American. . . . I wasn't going to let some fool from Encino direct a movie about living in *my neighborhood*" (Simpson, "Not Just One of the Boyz"; emphasis added). And in an interview in *Ebony* in November 1991, Singleton describes his film as a "powerful drama depicting the first realistic portrait of what it's like to be young, Black and American in the '90s" (*Ebony*, "Angry, Assertive, and Aware").

In interviews, Singleton claimed his film was authentic or realistic because it was based on his personal experiences and emphasized community pride and social responsibility. He saw *Boyz N the Hood* as a corrective to previous, unrealistic depictions of African American youth. However, the studio's marketing of *Boyz N the Hood*'s authenticity packaged the film very differently, emphasizing images of threatening African American masculinity, violence, and guns—images mirroring those produced by the news media and by the lyrics of gangsta rap. For example, the theatrical trailer for *Boyz N the Hood* opens with warlike imagery. Over the Columbia Pictures logo come sounds of police sirens as a somber newscaster declares: "Los Angeles, gang capital of the world." The trailer fleshes out the film's coming-of-age narrative by briefly recounting the stories of its three central characters, but concludes with a montage of the film's most violent images, set to the nihilistic Ice Cube single "How to Survive in South Central" (1991).[28] The images used in this montage include drive-by shootings, characters being handcuffed or harassed by the police, and characters fleeing from gun-wielding assailants. The montage culminates in a series of brief images of angry African American males shooting their guns directly at the viewer. This trailer presents *Boyz N the Hood* as a violent but realistic action film about "life on the streets" (*Boyz N the Hood*, trailer). Likewise, the film's teaser trailer begins with a television displaying black-and-white combat footage from Vietnam as a voice-over intones: "Five minutes away from your nice, *safe* neighborhood, there's a war going on." The trailer's opening statement posits *Boyz N the Hood*'s screen violence as an enticement to come to the theater—a challenge (or taunt) to the suburban viewer who might otherwise to be too frightened to leave the confines of his or her "nice, safe neighborhood."

The violent imagery in both versions of *Boyz N the Hood*'s trailer was supported by its studio-issued press kit, which established the film's authenticity by stressing its links with real-life gang culture. For example, the press kit describes how three members of a South Central gang acted as consultants on the film, providing input on the actors' wardrobes, dialect, and dialogue in order to "most accurately reflect current reality." These materials also mention that because many of the locations where the film was being shot overlapped with actual gang territory, the crew required the on-set security of both the Los Angeles Police Department and the Fruits of Islam, the Nation of Islam's security force.[29] The press kit also implies that like the flak-jacket-clad reporters who fly to war zones in order to get their story, Singleton and his crew had risked their own safety in order to make the film: "[*Boyz N the Hood*] aims to give the first true picture of what life is like in the 'LA Hood.' It was not uncommon during production for police helicopters to circle above nearby houses, for gang members to object that actors were wearing an opposing gang's colors or for police cars to speed past the set in high pursuit."[30] The press kit points to the on-set participation of gang members and the crew's proximity to violence as signs of *Boyz N the Hood*'s authenticity. Again, this definition of "authenticity" was very different from the one articulated by Singleton in interviews.

Given this divide between Singleton's prosocial intentions and Columbia Pictures' exploitative marketing approach, it is not surprising that the latter was frequently blamed in the media's coverage of the violence associated with *Boyz N the Hood*'s theatrical premiere. In a 1991 *Ebony* piece entitled "What's behind the Black-on-Black Violence at Movie Theaters," the director Robert Townsend, who also participated in the black film boom, argues that the content of *Boyz N the Hood*'s promotional campaign led to the outbreaks of theater violence: "I think when you have a lot of shooting in your promotional material and the publicity shows a lot of guns and violence, people respond to that. . . . Anytime you talk about gangs, it's going to bring out that element" (quoted in Collier, "Black-on-Black Violence"). And Michael Patrick, the president of Carmike Cinemas, attributed the violence surrounding *Boyz N the Hood* to a mixture of media hype and studio encouragement: "A lot of the problem is coming from the news media discussing the potential of media violence ahead of time. . . . Of course, the marketing is tied into that. One tends to escalate the other" (quoted in Ptacek, "Despite Violence"). Thus, Frank Price, the chairman of Columbia Pictures, was prompted to defend his studio in a *New York Times* letter to the editor: "Our advertising [for *Boyz N the Hood*] promised entertainment and action—in line with the conventions of the motion picture business. But in no way have we sought to exploit or pander to violence." Despite the studio's claims that its original campaign did not exploit violence, Columbia Pictures nevertheless decided to alter the campaign when promoting *Boyz N the Hood*'s release on videocassette and laser disc in March 1992. The original theatrical poster contained the tagline "Once upon a time in South Central L.A. . . . It ain't no fairytale," but the poster for the film's home-video release contained a new tagline: "Increase the Peace." This tagline, appearing after the outbreaks of violence at theaters, attempted to counter criticism that the film sensationalized violence and downplayed prosocial themes.

NOT ONLY
SCREEN BUT
THE PROJECTOR
AS WELL

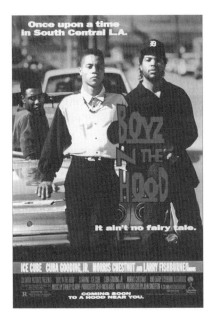

The original theatrical poster for *Boyz N the Hood* (1991) promises that the film is "no fairy tale."

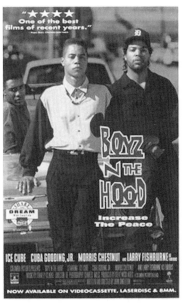

The revised poster for *Boyz N the Hood*'s release on home video urges viewers to "increase the peace."

After the media widely reported on the violence linked with screenings of *Boyz N the Hood*, Columbia Pictures offered to compensate theaters for extra security; theaters in the South Central area of Los Angeles banned gang colors from screenings and gave lectures to audiences before running the film (Leland and Foote, "Bad Omen"). Columbia Pictures' preemptive attempts to manage audiences implied that viewers would be driven to acts of violence if not properly "handled" by the theaters. Indeed, not long after the release of *Boyz N the Hood*, producer-distributor companies began to shift the premieres of "minority-oriented" films from Friday to Wednesday nights, a practice hinging on the belief that "spreading out" a film's premiere would "diffuse" the potential for violence (Surowiecki, "If It's Wednesday"). Was this policing of the crowd necessary, or was it just an updated form of classic exploitation-film ballyhoo? After all, exploitation filmmakers often converted the negative reactions to their films into sensational marketing strategies. One exploiteer of the late 1960s and 1970s, Joe Solomon, describes how he created a media frenzy around his exploitation films: "I'd turn off the ventilation in the theater, or throw some kind of crap into the ventilation, some gas to make them nauseous, and I'd call the local paper to come and get a picture of people fainting. . . . By now we had every guy in town ready to see that picture" (quoted in Betrock, *Teenage Juvenile Delinquent*, 21).

Furthermore, as Eric Schaefer has documented, some classic ballyhoo techniques included restricting particularly licentious films to "adults only" screenings, segregating screenings by gender, and warning audiences about the potentially dangerous effects of watching the sensational imagery contained in the film.[31] Such self-policing measures served two purposes: adults-only shows made the filmmakers and exhibitors appear socially responsible, and, more importantly, they lured in viewers with the promise of images that were deemed too risqué for general or "mixed" audiences or for the weak of heart (Schaefer, *Bold! Daring! Shocking!*, 124). I believe that the sensational reception of *Boyz N the Hood* was consciously encouraged by Columbia Pictures: such a response added to the film's appeals to authenticity, much as filmmakers like Joe Solomon and Oscar Micheaux sensationalized their films by promising viewers that they would faint or "grit their teeth in outrage" in reaction to the on-screen images. While audiences were not in true bodily danger when they went to see *Boyz N the Hood*, the film's ballyhoo lent a sense of danger to that viewing experience and thus made the film more appealing to its target youth audience.

Six months after *Boyz N the Hood*'s premiere, when memories of the theater violence associated with "black" films were still fresh in the public imagination, Ernest R. Dickerson released his ghetto action film *Juice*. Whereas the studio- and director-generated discourses surrounding *Boyz N the Hood* and the more overtly violent *New Jack City* had made claims about the educational value of their films (another tactic employed by the classic exploitation film [Schaefer, *Bold! Daring! Shocking!*, 105]), *Juice*'s marketing campaign focused almost entirely on its sensational, violent aspects (again, despite the fact that the film promotes an antiviolence message). Rather than distance *Juice* from the outbreaks of theater violence that had occurred with previous ghetto action films, Paramount's advertising strategy emphasized the film's potential to *incite* violence. For example, *Juice*'s original theatrical poster features one of the film's protagonists, played by Tupac Shakur, in the foreground of the frame. Shakur, a popular rapper whose persona, by the time of the film's release, was already associated with violence and criminality, holds a small revolver and looks off to the side, as if pursued by an unseen enemy.[32] *Juice*'s other three protagonists appear behind Shakur in diminishing size. This poster confronts the viewer, daring him or her to see the film, with the tagline "Power. Respect. *Juice*. How far will you go to get it?"

The poster proved to be inflammatory, at least in the world of entertainment media. A *Hollywood Reporter* article published on January 10, 1992, quotes Jay St. John, a Los Angeles police detective, who compares the ad to "waving a red flag in front of a bull" (Busch and King, "Paramount Marketing Plan"). In the same story, a studio head who passed on *Juice* explained: "I liked [*Juice*] very much and it's particularly well cast, but I decided it would be hard for me, in good conscience, to distribute a picture solely to exploit a volatile issue to a young black audience." Just three days after the *Hollywood Reporter* piece appeared, it was widely reported that Paramount Pictures had redesigned *Juice*'s original poster. The revolver in Shakur's hand was airbrushed out and replaced with an image of one of his hands cradling the other. The redesigned poster, even without the prominent image of a revolver, retains the same sentiments and taglines as the first poster. Once again, it is significant that the viewer is implicated by the tagline; potential audience members are asked to imagine themselves in the place of the film's protagonists, urban street toughs who may have to do something unsavory to obtain the elusive "juice" to which the poster refers. Likewise, the poster still features Shakur, who plays Bishop, the film's most violent, out-of-control character, as the most prominent figure in the frame. The film's more moderate and peaceful protagonist, Q (Omar Epps)—the only character to denounce Bishop's violent credo at the film's conclusion—is partially obscured by the looming figure of Shakur. This poster visually marginalizes its antiviolence themes while simultaneously promoting its most violent and sensational elements.

In a 1992 article in the *Source* entitled "Crying over Spilled *Juice*," Kierno Mayo points out that the ad campaigns for contemporaneous films like *Rush* (1991, Lili Fini Zanuck) and *Kuffs* (1992, Bruce A. Evans) featured white characters holding guns. The *Kuffs* poster, like the *Juice* poster, directly addresses the viewer with the question "When you have attitude who needs experience?" While Christian Slater is smirking in this poster (*Kuffs* is billed as a comedy), the tagline nevertheless conveys the idea that a large gun, or "attitude," can act as an equalizer in confrontational situations. Despite these similarities with *Juice*'s campaign, neither *Rush*'s nor *Kuffs*' advertising campaign was publicly discussed or altered for fear of inciting violence. Mayo therefore wonders: "A Paramount representative said that the removal of the gun was part of the normal evolution of a movie ad, but how normal is it when the Paramount president issues a statement about the ad's 'evolution' to media across the country?" (15).[33]

Paramount could just as easily have released several different versions of *Juice*'s poster without comment, but these extra, public steps to ensure that screenings of *Juice* did not lead to any incidents of violence appear to be part of a calculated promotional campaign to ensure that audiences would, paradoxically, associate the film with violence and danger. The public discussions of Paramount's ad campaigns exploited the violent undertones of the film, implying that its subject matter was so provocative that even a still image on a poster could ignite volatile behavior. Warrington Hudlin, the cofounder of the Black Filmmaker Foundation, was outraged over how the incident was handled: "There is a general fear of black youth in America. A black with a gun is a nightmare in America. The implication [of having to remove the gun] is chilling to me. It says to me that you can have white people with guns, but can't have black people with guns in [movie] ads" (quoted in Busch and King, "Studios Struggle"). Paramount also recreated the narratives of containment associated with *Boyz N the Hood* in its marketing of *Juice*. Newspapers reported that Paramount would offer free security assistance to urban theaters screening the film and would be "flexible on contract terms with theater chains that elect not to run *Juice* at danger-prone locations" (King, "Ads Stir De-

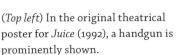

(*Top left*) In the original theatrical poster for *Juice* (1992), a handgun is prominently shown.

(*Top right*) In the revised theatrical poster for *Juice* (1992), the gun is gone.

(*Right*) Neither the original theatrical poster for *Kuffs* (1992), nor the poster for its release on home video (pictured), was revised, despite the presence of a gun.

bate"). Paramount also urged exhibitors to screen the film at later times so that patrons for *Juice* would not be standing in line at the same time as audiences for family films.

Despite, or rather because of, the public precautions taken by both Paramount and various theater chains to police the film's audience, the opening of *Juice* was greeted with sensational headlines linking it with violence at theaters. Gunfire, knife fights, and fistfights were reported at screenings in Boston, New York, Anchorage, Omaha, Lansing, North Little Rock, and Chicago (Lippman, "Outbreaks of Violence"). Although there was no indication that these incidents were directly related to the film's content—in fact, interviews with police on the scene indicated that at least some of the incidents were purely coincidental (Lippman, "Outbreaks of Violence")—newspaper and magazine headlines created direct links between this violence and the exhibition of a black film. The *Washington Post* proclaimed: "Outbreaks of Violence Mar Opening of 'Juice'; Gunfire Outside Theater Kills Chicago Girl" and "Jittery Over 'Juice'; Paramount Steps Up Security for Film," while a headline in the *New Pittsburgh Courier* made the link explicit: "'Juice' Violence: By-Product of Films." A review of *Juice* in the *Chicago Citizen* praises the film for being "definitely antiviolence," but concludes with a brief editorial about the recent epidemic of theater violence (the most publicized of which had occurred in Chicago): "Why young black men continue to talk in a cloud of confusion and show up at such movies with gun in hand and attitude on sleeve continues to amaze me. . . . In the light of recent disturbances all that can be said is pick out a nice theater and be careful" (Boseman, "Bloods Simple"). This article explicitly links theater violence with black male youths and advises readers to seek out a "nice" theater if they wish to view the film safely. Although these alarmist articles warned moviegoers about the potential for violence at screenings of *Juice*, the transgression of racial boundaries promised (and threatened) by the ghetto action film is precisely what drew white suburban audiences into theaters.

I do not believe that Paramount executives desired the violent incidents surrounding the exhibition of *Juice*. Nevertheless, they cultivated an explicitly violent advertising campaign for the film, and this marketing campaign, which made a spectacle of its own potential to incite violence, seems to have been a contributing factor in the violence that did eventually transpire at screenings. As a *Christian Science Monitor* article entitled "Streetwise Film 'Juice' Stirs Up Bad Publicity" acknowledges: "Paramount Pictures managed to spark an extra debate over Juice . . . before it opened anywhere." Here again is the classic exploitation technique of using poster art and ballyhoo in order to promise the audience a certain sensational experience—one dealing with sex, violence, or the taboo in general.[34] The air of danger surrounding the film proved irresistible to audiences. Furthermore, just as Singleton defended his film's promotional campaign by pleading box office, Dickerson offered a similar justification for *Juice*'s media campaign: "You can't expect people to come see [*Juice*] if they feel they're being preached to. In order to really get people to respond to your story, you do have to couch it in a kind of entertainment. . . . I want to reach as wide an audience as possible. Basically because it'll make it easier for me to make my next movie" (quoted in Mills, "Concentrated Juice"). Dickerson's words proved prophetic. The film's box-office success—*Juice* grossed more than $8 million on its opening weekend and made a total of $20 million domestically—brought Dickerson a series of directing projects, including *Surviving the Game* (1994), *Demon Knight* (1995), and *Bulletproof* (1996).

As with blaxploitation films, the skewed definitions of blackness appearing in the ghetto action cycle and the discourses surrounding the films were often collapsed in the mainstream (white) imagination with the contemporary real-world African American experience. Violent, aggressive images of masculinity fit in neatly with how young African American males were being depicted in the mainstream media (Baker, "Screening Race"). Given the media frenzy surrounding these youth in the 1990s, it is not surprising that Columbia and Paramount wanted to capitalize on these images in *Boyz N the Hood*'s and *Juice*'s promotional materials; marketers realized that one specific definition of blackness, corresponding to the mainstream's and the media's prevailing definitions of the term, could generate a considerable box office.³⁵ This marketing approach is especially interesting because only a few scenes in *Boyz N the Hood* and *Juice* contain strong violence. On the whole, both films' narratives stress the significance of family and education in the lives of their young protagonists. But if one paid attention only to print advertisements, trailers, and media coverage, these films would appear to be suffused with violence and tragedy. Furthermore, the moments of violence found in ghetto action films were not the primary factors motivating viewers to shoot and stab one another at theaters; many of these violent incidents took place outside movie theaters *before* screenings of the films (*Christian Science Monitor*, "Streetwise Film"). In other words, it was not the content of these films that generated violence, but rather the ballyhoo surrounding them.

When the ghetto action film *Menace II Society* was slated for release in 1993, exhibitors, fearful that violence might break out in or around their theaters, were nervous about screening the film. In Portland, Oregon, for example, a group of African American leaders requested that the film's opening be moved from areas with large black populations to suburban theaters. And in Los Angeles, the police department asked that exhibitors not show the film in "racially sensitive" areas (Turnquist, "Violent Film Moved"). Given the way that the press discussed *Menace II Society*, these fears were not unwarranted. In an October 1992 interview in the *Source*, Allen Hughes, one of the film's directors, claims that his script initially met with resistance from studio executives because the characters were so unsympathetic: "White people can't relate to us. Period. *Boyz N the Hood* got made 'cause it was 100% street with a sympathetic character. You can't tell no black story without one" (quoted in McCreary, "Hughes' Bad," 24). The implication here is that Singleton had had to somehow appease white studios in order to get his "black story" made, whereas the Hughes brothers had been able to make an uncompromised, and therefore more realistic, vision of black inner-city life. Likewise, in an interview in the *Washington Post*, Hughes defends his film's violence: "No other movie has dealt with the reality of [violence]. *New Jack City* was a comic book look at it. *Juice* was a comic book look at it" (quoted in French, "Brothers Grim"). Again, Hughes accuses previous ghetto action films—precisely those films that were blamed for causing theater violence—of portraying violence simplistically and unrealistically. By contrast, *Menace II Society* provides audiences with "real" violence. According to Hughes, "gangsters" hated *Boyz N the Hood* and called it "Toyz N the Hood" because "it had good guys going through this bad city, on their way to college" (quoted in French, "Brothers Grim"). Only authentic gangsters, Hughes implies, could identify the inauthenticity of a film like *Boyz N the Hood*.

Mainstream critics praising *Menace II Society* often echoed Hughes's statements by distancing his film from earlier ghetto action films. Stephen Holden's review in the *New York Times* claims: "Where earlier films with similar settings, like John Singleton's *Boyz N the Hood* and Matty Rich's *Straight Out of Brooklyn*, have offered a somber, almost elegiac view of inner-city life, *Menace II Society* has a manic energy and at times a lyricism that recall movies like *Mean Streets* and *Bonnie and Clyde*. More acutely than any movie before, it gives cinematic expression to the hot-tempered, defiantly nihilistic ethos that ignites gangster rap." By invoking *Bonnie and Clyde* (1967, Arthur Penn), a film that was widely denounced for its brutal, graphic violence at the time of its release, and *Mean Streets* (1973, Martin Scorsese), famous for its groundbreaking "realistic" depiction of inner-city criminality, Holden reiterates *Menace II Society*'s primary marketing hooks: its over-the-top violence and its perceived authenticity. A writer for the *Buffalo News* praised *Menace II Society* also by denouncing the unrealistic qualities of previous ghetto action films: "In its stark and pitiless veracity, [*Menace II Society*] reveals the commercial calculations and naïve didacticism in the whole school of films that have been torn, usually raw and sometimes bleeding, from the heart of America's ghetto—'Boyz N the Hood,' 'Juice,' 'House Party,' etc." (Simon, "Gripping to the End"). Simon posits earlier ghetto action films as "naïve" in comparison with the "raw," violent realism of *Menace II Society*. And yet one has to wonder: are these film critics experts on the minutiae of life in America's inner cities, or are they simply working under the assumption that the more violent a black film is, the more realistic it must be?

In his review of *Menace II Society* in *Artforum*, Arthur Jafa lauds the film for its "unflinching look at the despair and hopelessness underlying the rage so characteristic of young black male urban reality" and compares it with *Killer of Sheep* (1977, Charles Burnett), a classic neorealist tale of struggle in Watts. He also recounts an anecdote about the Hughes brothers' initial meeting with New Line Cinema: "When this script was compared to *Boyz N the Hood* [the Hughes brothers] shouted, '*Boyz in the Hood* [sic], fuck *Boyz in the Hood*, we'll show you some real violence,' upon which they were quickly signed. I laughed when told this." Though Jafa implies that this story is apocryphal or at least exaggerated, he agrees that *Menace II Society* makes *Boyz N the Hood* "seem like *The Cosby Show*." Jafa implies that *Boyz N the Hood* is a sanitized or diluted vision of inner-city life in comparison with *Menace II Society*'s violent realism. However, if the violent images in those earlier ghetto action films were the (alleged) cause of stabbings, shootings, and rioting, then what kind of chaos would ensue at the *Menace II Society* screenings?

New Line Cinema must have asked itself this very question, because it handled the film's marketing campaign differently from the way Columbia and Paramount had promoted *Boyz N the Hood* and *Juice*. The film's original theatrical trailer contains numerous shots of gun violence, but intercuts these images with shots of families, friends, and lovers embracing. And unlike the aggressive, violent rap music used in the *Boyz N the Hood* trailer, *Menace II Society*'s trailer employs Marvin Gaye's famous 1971 protest song "What's Going On," which laments contemporary political and social problems as well as black-on-black crime. Chris Pula, New Line Cinema's president of theatrical marketing, explains the choice to use Gaye's "untraditional peaceful song" in the film's trailer: "['What's Going On'] broke through the clutter of these past films because you pretty much expect everybody to copy hip-hop, urban contemporary or rap. It really gave a poignancy to some of the tough visuals." Mitchell Goldman, the president of marketing and distribution, adds: "The combination of the tough visuals and a rap score on the trailer would have sent the wrong message about what this movie really is. So a deliberate choice was made by New Line to soften the music" (*Hollywood Reporter*, "'Menace' Marketing"). The final words of the *Menace II Society* trailer belong to the character Mr. Butler (Charles S. Dutton), who serves as a positive mentor figure for the film's protagonist, Caine. He warns Caine, just before the trailer ends: "The hunt is on, and you're the prey." In other words, rather than positioning Caine (Tyrin Turner), the young black male, as the "menace to society" promised by the film's title, the trailer informs us that he is actually the prey of society (YouTube, "*Menace II Society* Theatrical Trailer").

The marketers behind *Boyz N the Hood* and *Juice* believed that the only way to sell their films about the contemporary black experience to a mainstream audience was to promote the films' most violent moments. These marketing campaigns implied that the "truth" of the inner city was not that its residents were grappling daily with the fundamental struggle between right and wrong, between reason and violence, but that they were simply shooting one another in the streets, accompanied by the latest rap sound track. And these marketing campaigns acted as a self-fulfilling prophecy. By contrast, although *Menace II Society* was far more violent than previous entries in the ghetto action cycle, the film was not associated with any theater violence. This counterexample provides further proof that it was not the *content* of the ghetto action films that generated violence but, rather, the way these films were marketed to their audiences. New Line did not exploit the film's violent scenes, and, consequently, screenings of the film did not generate violence.

RACIAL SIGNIFIERS AND THE DEATH OF A CYCLE

The initial backlash against the blaxploitation cycle was grounded in the belief that films like *Sweet Sweetback's Baadasssss Song* and *Superfly* (1972, Gordon Parks, Jr.) presented unrealistic, hyperviolent, hypersexual images of African American masculinity as realistic representations of the contemporary African American community, potentially affecting how mainstream society viewed the community as well as dictating the type of black films that would be produced in the future.[36] The initial backlash against the ghetto action cycle, while also rooted in its stereotyped images of blackness, was somewhat different. As previously mentioned, the general response to early ghetto action films such as *Boyz N the Hood* and *Straight Out of Brooklyn* was that they were a realistic reflection of inner city life (Baker, "Screening Race"). However, to lure in audiences eager for an "authentic" moviegoing experience, the marketers behind the ghetto action cycle cultivated an association between the violent African American males depicted on-screen and the allegedly violent African American males seated in the movie audience. This association between real life and reel life ceased being an asset and became a liability to studios when reporters, film critics, and various "experts" began objecting to the film cycle and the type of audience it presumably attracted to movie theaters. There was a perceptible fear in the media that these images were somehow too realistic, that they were so powerful that audiences—specifically, African American audiences— would be moved to commit violence after seeing the films. In other words, they were fearful that the black body would become not just the "screen" of violence but the "projector" as well (Gaines, *Fire and Desire*, 252). Some critics were also frustrated not just by the violence associated with these films, but also by their overall characterization of the urban African American community as America's number one social problem.

As early as the summer of 1991, a coalition of "diverse mainstream black groups" calling themselves the Coalition Against Media Racism in America initiated a boycott of films like *New Jack City*, *Boyz N the Hood*, *Jungle Fever* (1991, Spike Lee), and others, stating that the recent "spate of violent, stereotypic and inflammatory films may give the summer of 1991 the dubious distinction of launching the second era of Blaxploitation movies" (quoted in Ptacek, "Coalition of Black Groups"). The academic community also echoed these sentiments. In 1991, Jacquie Jones published "The New Ghetto Aesthetic," a scathing critique of what she saw as a dangerous new trend in filmmaking.[37] Her fears were remarkably similar to those that had been expressed by the critics of blaxploitation cinema. She argued that the popularity of the images in these films "may threaten the viability of other types of mainstream Black cinematic expression" (33). She also criticized what she saw as a new trend of objectifying women, particularly African American women, as "bitches" or "hos" (36). Her conclusion was that, as in the 1970s, the black experience was being converted into a commodity—a surface image that had no real engagement with the problems that the ghetto action cycle purported to illuminate.

Jones's concerns circulated within the academic community, but the release of *Juice* in 1992 marked the first time that the mainstream press stopped uniformly praising the cycle and began questioning the images of blackness presented in the ghetto action cycle. It was at this point that the issue of "responsibility" began to pepper public discourses. For example, Charles Richardson, the president of Tri-Ad Communications Group, a company that advises studios and corporations on how to market to African American audiences, offered this opinion on the *Juice* poster controversy: "When I saw the poster I was stunned. This is six to seven months after 'Boyz' and we all saw what happened there. Given a city like New York, there is so much racial tension here. And this ad art is in New York transit areas and in the subways?" (quoted in Busch and King, "Paramount Marketing Plan"). Richardson's implication was that studios had to take care when catering to the African American audience. In the same article in which Richardson was quoted, an African American marketer who wished to remain anonymous explained: "I think that [Paramount] have seized the lowest common denominator to sell tickets. Given the history of films in this genre, I think their approach is exploitative." Studios were initially able to pull viewers into the theaters by exploiting signifiers of racial difference. But comments like these, implying that such exploitation was wrong and even irresponsible, heralded the ghetto action cycle's eventual demise.

Of course, most articles, editorials, and "expert" interviews on this subject made several dangerous assumptions: that the violence in ghetto action films was somehow more dangerous than the violence in contemporaneous "white" action films, that African American audiences relate to violent or aggressive images because these images reflect their experiences, and that, as a result, African American audiences are compelled to imitate the violence they see on-screen. Indeed, a *New York Times* editorial appearing shortly after *Juice*'s release blamed the violence at screenings of the film on its inflammatory ad campaign, but then went on to make a generalized statement about the film's audience: "Similar things could be said of other violent films like *Terminator 2* or the latest installment of *Nightmare on Elm Street*. But those unrealistic films don't draw gun-toting moviegoers. The difference is that *Juice* and its cousins dwell on specific forms of violence that their audiences *know well and even participate in*" (*New York Times*, "Curbing Violence"; emphasis added). Likewise, a short piece in the *New Pittsburgh Courier* quoted Dr. Sharon Nelson-LeGall, a professor of psychology at the University of Pittsburgh: "It's not that there is more violence in these movies; it's that people can relate to what they are seeing on the screen. Some of these inner-city youths might not be gang members or drug dealers, but chances are they probably know someone who is. Being able to relate, sometimes, generates those reactions" (Carlisle, "'Juice' Violence"). Dr. Nelson-LeGall implies that African American audiences—whether involved in the criminal lifestyle or not—cannot watch violent films without feeling the need to re-create what they have watched.

By 1993, the year of *Menace II Society*'s release, the backlash against the ghetto action cycle had reached critical mass. In a 1993 *Washington Post* interview, Albert Hughes addressed this rising criticism: "You know, a lot of [blacks] are screaming and yelling that they want 'positive' movies out there about family life. But they're the first ones out on Memorial Day spending $20 million on a movie about killing people—*Cliffhanger*," while his brother, Allen, added, "We're filmmakers, not politicians" (quoted in French, "Brothers Grim").[38] By 1994, many reviews of black-cast films like *Sugar Hill* (1994, Leon Ichaso), *The Inkwell* (1994, Matty Rich), and *Fresh* were referring to the problematic glut of violent ghetto action films and noting how some of these new releases (*Fresh*, *The Inkwell*) acted as antidotes to previous films, while others (*Sugar Hill*) perpetuated their violent themes.[39] Given this increasingly negative reception, it is not surprising that later entries in the ghetto action cycle failed to resonate with audiences. *Boyz N the Hood* (1991) made more than $10 million on its opening weekend; *Menace II Society* (1993) made $3.8 million; and *Clockers* (1995) made $4.4 million. *New Jersey Drive* (1995), however, pulled in the lowest opening-weekend box office of the ghetto action cycle, with just $1.3 million.[40] Decreasing opening-weekend numbers—the barometer most contemporary studios use to gauge a film's overall commercial success—convinced the producers of ghetto action films that this particular cycle was no longer financially viable. Likewise, public discourses in both predominantly white and predominantly black periodicals expressed an apparent "exhaustion" with films about violence, drugs, and gangs in African American neighborhoods, motivating producers to abandon the ghetto action film formula.[41] This waning interest in the problems of the black ghetto was also likely tied to the mainstream perception that the situation in the nation's cities was somehow improving. A nationwide drop in crime, coupled with a strong economy, generated a "new optimism" in the African American community. A 1999 *Newsweek* article explained: "While drugs, violence and unemployment continued to plague ghetto communities [throughout the late 1990s], the issue lost currency as the perception grew that these were not exclusively Black problems, and that Black youths were no longer without options" (Cose, "Good News about Black America").

In 1996 there was even a parody of these once-serious social problem films entitled *Don't Be a Menace to South Central While Drinking Your Juice in the Hood* (Paris Barclay). The film opens with the statement "1 out of every 10 black males will be forced to sit through at least one 'Growing Up in the 'Hood' movie in their lifetime. At least 1 out of 5 will be shot in the theater while watching the movie." While intended to mock the similar square-up that opened *Boyz N the Hood*, this statement also acknowledges the pervasiveness of the conventions of the ghetto action film in the American cinematic imagination as well as the media-hyped violence surrounding them.[42] While the Wayans brothers (who wrote, coproduced, and starred in the film) are famous for their ability to lampoon popular culture, their film is also a specific attack on the clichés that circulate in and around the ghetto action film, including the welfare mother, the tough young gangsta, and the constant, mindless violence. By placing these floating signifiers of urban menace and tragedy within a comic climate, the film's creators point to the inadequacy of these images to signify the reality of life in the contemporary ghetto. Marlon Wayans, one of the film's stars and cowriters explains: "I think that everyone has their own medicine, and comedy is ours. We come from a place where it's better to laugh at something than cry. *Don't Be a Menace* had a lot of social statements, but we made them with jokes" (Wayans and Wayans, interview). Therefore, in addition to indicating that the images of the ghetto action cycle had fully saturated the mainstream and were ripe for comedic treatment, *Don't Be a Menace* also revealed how these images were incapable of representing the realities of the contemporary African American experience.[43]

CONCLUSION

Much like the Dead End Kids cycle, the ghetto action cycle initially formed in order to capitalize on contemporary concerns about the state of inner-city youth. Stereotypes about urban blackness nurtured by the media as well by gangsta rap neatly dovetailed with stories about outbreaks of theater violence. For nonblack or nonurban audiences, curiosity about those newspaper headlines—and an opportunity not just to see a slice of authentic African American urban life but also to "experience" it in the form of extradiegetic violence—was clearly a draw. For African American audiences, the lure of these films was the opportunity to see black faces on the movie screen after a decade-long drought. In both cases, it was racial politics that drew viewers into movie theaters and made this particular film cycle so successful. The ghetto action cycle stopped being produced for several reasons: negative press, an overabundance of films about "coming of age in the hood," and the feeling that the inner city was no longer the epicenter of a national crisis. However, beyond all these reasons, the ghetto action cycle failed for the same reason that so many films and cycles dedicated to the African American experience fail: they were asked to portray the reality of the black experience, and this reality was ultimately (and unavoidably) unsatisfactory. Much as racial politics motivated the formation of the ghetto action cycle, the same politics also led to its undoing.

Since the days of Oscar Micheaux's race films, African American directors have been criticized for not infusing their films with the "right" politics (Gaines, *Fire and Desire*, 4). Much of the criticism of black filmic representation is based not on the fact that these representations are stereotypes, but that they are the wrong (that is, negative) stereotypes (261). The violent and (allegedly) violence-producing images of drug pushers, gangstas, crack addicts, and welfare mothers populating the ghetto action cycle did not offer a political or revolutionary message, or at least not the message that the cycle's critics desired. Jane Gaines notes that "*wanting something back* from the image has the potential to be one of the most radical demands that has ever been made on the cinema. . . . If the viewer simply wants confirmation of who he or she is, why not just look in the mirror?" (266). Although *Boyz N the Hood* was lauded for being one of the first and only films to truly grapple with the urban African American youth experience, it was precisely its status as the "first" and the "only" that eventually drew the ire of so many viewers and critics. With so few black films in existence, the heavy weight of "responsible," politically correct, and realistic representation—categories that are often collapsed in the discourses surrounding these films—were shouldered by those few texts circulating in the popular culture landscape (Lubiano, "Compared to What?" 106). Black films must portray the reality of the contemporary African American experience, and this reality must somehow account for the range of social, political, and economic differences that characterize the diverse African American population. The strength of this radical demand is what opened the

LOVE, DISDAIN, AND THE FUTURE OF CYCLE STUDIES

Als long as there are audiences willing to pay money to have shit shoveled down their throats, the *Movie*–movie machine will keep rolling out new models. *Spy Movie*, for example, is already slated for a 2009 release, to be followed, I'm guessing, by *Psychological Thriller Movie, Fatal-Disease Domestic Drama Movie, Silent German Expressionism Movie*, and, eventually, *Spoof Movie*, each more cynical and misanthropic than the last, and each a printer of dirty money.

JOSH ROSENBLATT, REVIEW OF DISASTER MOVIE (2008)

FILM CYCLE PARODIES

This book opened with a brief look at some of the earliest examples of film cycles, kissing films and train films, and examined how those two subjects were soon combined as a way to extend the financial viability of each cycle. I conclude here with an examination of some of the more recent manifestations of the film cycle, along with the cycle's place in contemporary film production. The quotation opening this chapter is from a particularly negative review of *Disaster Movie* (2008, Jason Friedberg and Aaron Seltzer), a film that parodies the cycle of disaster films that were released throughout the 2000s, including *The Day After Tomorrow* (2004, Roland Emmerich), *War of the Worlds* (2005, Steven Spielberg), *Poseidon* (2006, Wolfgang Petersen), *Cloverfield* (2008, Matt Reeves), and *2012* (2009, Roland Emmerich). However, *Disaster Film* is itself an entry in a larger, intergeneric cycle of films that parody other, recently successful film cycles. These parodies, which I have labeled the "cycle-parody cycle," have their roots in films like *I'm Gonna Git You Sucka* (1988, Keenen Ivory Wayans), a parody of the 1970s blaxploitation cycle, and *Don't Be a Men-*

ace to South Central While Drinking Your Juice in the Hood, a parody of the 1990s ghetto action cycle.[1] However, the cycle-parody cycle did not pick up steam until after the release and consequent box-office success of *Scary Movie* (2000, Keenen Ivory Wayans), a parody of the self-reflexive teen-slasher-movie cycle of the 1990s.[2] The success of *Scary Movie*, which was made for $19 million and grossed more than $157 million worldwide, prompted the release of a series of cycle parodies, including *Not Another Teen Movie* (2001, Joel Gallen), *Date Movie* (2006, Aaron Seltzer), *Epic Movie* (2007, Jason Friedberg and Aaron Seltzer), *Dance Flick* (2009, Damien Dante Wayans), and *Vampires Suck* (2010, Jason Friedberg and Aaron Seltzer).[3]

As their generic titles indicate, entries in the cycle-parody cycle are released to capitalize on the recent success of another film cycle, lampooning its familiar characters, images, and plots. For example, *Dance Flick* parodies the dance film cycle of *Save the Last Dance* (2001, Thomas Carter), *You Got Served* (2004, Chris Stokes), and *Step Up* (2006, Ann Fletcher), as well as the recent teen-targeted musical cycle of *High School Musical* (2006, Kenny Ortega) and *Hairspray!* (2007, Adam Shankman).[4] While many critics have argued that the appearance of a parody signals that a group of films has reached a point of creative exhaustion and is no longer able to satisfy the needs of its audience, I agree more with Dan Harries's claim that parody both "situates and subverts the viewing experience," facilitating the perpetuation of a film genre or film cycle in a revised form (Harries, "Film Parody," 282). In other words, a parody has the capacity to "weed out" clichéd conventions "in order to allow for the canon's continued healthy growth," thereby forcing a cycle or genre to use its familiar images in new ways (287). This last point is significant. Parodies do not "kill" a cycle; rather, their presence indicates that there is yet something compelling in the text being lampooned. Thus, a film like *Vampires Suck*, released as a parody of Stephanie Meyer's wildly popular *Twilight* series and its filmic adaptations, is not the last word on the subject of vampires. Rather, its release encourages the films and television series that follow it to avoid reusing certain overused tropes, such as the moody vampire hero and a pair of star-crossed human and vampire lovers.

One central characteristic of cycle-parody films is their reliance on stock characters lifted directly from the films being parodied. Many of the actors in these films are cast because of their resemblance to other, iconic stars. Thus, in the credits for *Epic Movie*, several characters are not given names and are instead listed as "Ashton Kutcher Look-Alike," "Samuel Jackson Look-Alike," or "Paris Hilton Look-

Epic Movie (2007) features actors who resemble either characters from other successful film cycles or contemporary popular-culture icons.

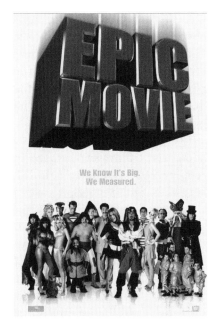

Alike." Such casting decisions are useful, since many of the jokes in cycle parodies bank on the audience's ability recognize the similarities (and differences) between the original film and its comic counterfeit. As Dan Harries explains: "Film parody functions by taking preestablished and fairly stable semiotic structures (such as a genre, or the work of a director, or even a widely viewed single film) and recontextualising the structure through oscillation between similarity to and difference from the targeted texts" ("Film Parody," 282).

Another distinguishing trait of the films in the cycle-parody cycle is that their plots lack plausible cause-and-effect relationships. Instead, the films' narratives are structured around a series of visual gags. *Epic Movie* pulls characters from previous films like *Nacho Libre* (2006, Jared Hess) and *X-Men* (2000, Bryan Singer) and then has them enter the plots of other films, like *Charlie and the Chocolate Factory* (2005, Tim Burton) and *The Chronicles of Narnia: The Lion, the Witch, and the Wardrobe* (2005, Andrew Adamson). Because audiences are already familiar with the plots of these films, the importance of cause and effect—or what happens next—falls away. Instead, these preestablished characters and plots serve as the backdrop for a series of sight gags.[5] In *The Chronicles of Narnia*, for example, Aslan the Lion (Liam Neeson) is a noble protector and benevolent guide for the children in the film; in *Epic Movie*, this same character, now called

Aslo the Lion (Fred Willard), agrees to help the children only in exchange for sexual favors. Just as the syntax of the social problem film dropped away when the images of the original Dead End Kids cycle were placed in the comic frame of the East Side Kids cycle, cycle parodies generally abandon the parodied films' syntax in order to make comedy from the incongruous use of their most iconic semantic elements.

Cycle parodies are also extremely topical, both because they lampoon recent films and because they are rife with references to recent events in popular culture. *Meet the Spartans* (Jason Friedberg and Aaron Seltzer), released in 2008, contains jokes about such then-topical events as Britney Spears shaving her head (from February 2007), the resulting YouTube video of a young man named Chris Crocker tearfully begging society to "leave Britney alone!" (September 2007), and Paris Hilton's lack of chastity (a joke in circulation ever since a sex tape featuring the heiress was released in 2004).[6] Given their ephemeral cultural relevance, many of these jokes will not make sense five or ten years after the parody's release. This comedic strategy signals that cycle parodies are not interested in longevity. These are products to enjoy now, preferably in a crowded movie theater filled with boisterous patrons, before their jokes become too dated. This strategy makes sense, since the primary material being parodied—recent film cycles—likewise have a fleeting cultural cachet.

One final characteristic of this cycle, which should be clear from the sampling of reviews quoted so far, is that they are almost universally lambasted by critics.[7] Though the criticisms launched against these films are numerous, they can be boiled down to one general sentiment: cycle parodies lack originality. In his review of *Date Movie*, Ben Kenigsberg writes, "with few exceptions, [the movies parodied in the film] are reprocessed so minimally that it's easy to feel cheated— it takes a certain gall to pass off mere references as jokes." Critics like Kenigsberg argue that cycle parodies are lazy—they simply recycle the images, characters, and plots of previous films without adding their own creative signature.[8] In the opinions of most critics, films that copy the plots, characters, and jokes of other successful films do not deserve the audience's hard-earned money. Why should the audience reward derivative filmmaking? In his review of *Disaster Movie*, Josh Rosenblatt goes so far as to label its directors, Jason Friedberg and Aaron Seltzer, "a plague on our cinematic landscape, a national shame, a danger to our culture, a typhoon-sized natural disaster disguised as a filmmaking team, a Hollywood monster wreaking havoc on the minds of America's youth and setting civilization back thousands of years. . . . They degrade, and we pay—like a bunch of saps getting fleeced at a carnival." This review shifts from merely criticizing the film's poor quality to criticizing its creators, Jason Friedberg and Aaron Seltzer, and their perceived negative impact on society. Friedberg and Seltzer have had a hand in writing or directing most of the entries in the cycle-parody cycle, including *Scary Movie, Scary Movie 2, Scary Movie 3, Scary Movie 4, Date Movie, Epic Movie, Meet the Spartans*, and *Vampires Suck*. Rosenblatt therefore characterizes them as a "danger" to our culture and as a "plague" infecting the cinema. These men are cunning exploiteers, and American moviegoing audiences are their willing marks. Indeed, this critic seems especially frustrated with the audience that not only accepts this standard of filmmaking but is willing to pay for it also.

Rosenblatt's rhetoric is hyperbolic, but not unprecedented. Throughout film history, the interlinked tropes of artlessness, contamination, and exploitation have been prevalent in the public discourses surrounding film cycles. In 1940, Bosley Crowther described the Dead End Kids cycle as a dying serpent with a minute brain (review of *East Side Kids*); a 1957 *Time* magazine review of *I Was a Teenage Werewolf* lamented that the new cycle of juvenile-delinquent-teenpic–horror-film hybrids was "the next step in low, lowbrow cinema" (*Time*, "Shock Around the Clock"); and in the 1990s, Jacquie Jones saw the ghetto action cycle as a real threat to the viability of mainstream African American cinematic expression ("New Ghetto Aesthetic," 33). Film cycles, more so than any other production strategy, are credited with the ability to threaten the artistic viability and the very dignity of the cinema. Furthermore, because so many film cycles deal with sensational topics, such as gangsters, juvenile delinquency, hot-rod racing, inner-city violence, and gang culture, critics see them as exploiting the worst tendencies of our society.

The success of these film cycles may befuddle their critics, but their appeal is clear to those who love them. As the title to the introduction of this book states, film cycles represent a case of "love at first sight." Audiences are drawn to film cycles because they repeat something— a character, a series of conventions, a style of humor—that they enjoyed in a previous film. Film cycles are like the perfect lover—constantly aiming to please the audience by giving them exactly what they want and then disappearing not long after the audience tires of them. However, theatrically released film cycles, the topic of this book, are not the only film cycles currently performing this function for audiences. Another thriving arena for the contemporary film cycle is the much-maligned direct-to-video market, now known as direct-to-DVD releases.

DIRECT-TO-DVD CYCLES

In *More Than Night* (1998), James Naremore argues that the campy, highly sexual, direct-to-video mystery thrillers of the 1990s were financially successful because they catered to the desires of their target audience, which wanted to see more pornography and less narrative (162). Direct-to-DVD releases currently perform the same function. They provide their audiences with more of the product they hunger for—a product not supplied by mainstream theatrical releases. Direct-to-DVD releases are films that are never shown in movie theaters (or else have a small, limited run) and thus receive their primary exposure to audiences through the DVD format. According to the Motion Picture Association of America, the cost of making prints of a film and advertising its theatrical release add an average of $34.4 million to a production (Arnold, "Coming Back for Seconds"). Consequently, it is often more profitable for a studio to release a film directly to DVD if it appears that a theatrical release will not generate a box office large enough to recoup production costs. Furthermore, according to the National Endowment for the Arts' 2008 Survey of Public Participation in the Arts, between 2002 and 2008, attendance at theatrically released films dropped from 60 percent to 53.3 percent of adults age eighteen and older (Italie, "Arts Survey"). Given this drop in theater attendance, it makes financial sense for studios to release some of their products directly to DVD. Indeed, the direct-to-DVD industry has become extremely profitable in recent years. Since 2005, the number of direct-to-DVD films has risen 36 percent, and it is estimated that the direct-to-DVD industry currently accounts for $1 billion in annual sales (Barnes, "Direct-to-DVD Releases"). Nevertheless, despite their proliferation and profitability in recent years, direct-to-DVD films are rarely reviewed in mainstream publications, and they are almost wholly absent from academic discourse.[9]

Direct-to-DVD releases are stigmatized because they have typically been the provinces of two film categories that seldom receive serious critical attention: sequels to children's movies and pornography. As Linda Ruth Williams argues: "The VCR amplifies and individualizes the association of movies with sex" because the very concept of the home video or DVD implies a solitary, possibly illicit viewing situation (*Erotic Thriller*, 255). Direct-to-DVD releases are also stigma-

Originally conceived as a theatrical release, *Major Movie Star* was repackaged as the direct-to-DVD release *Private Valentine: Blonde and Dangerous* (2008).

tized because of their low-budget status. Unlike theatrical releases, whose makers are presumed to have taken time and care in their production, the direct-to-DVD release is associated with a low-budget aesthetic: simple sets, unknown actors and directors, recycled plots, and poor writing. Occasionally, films produced for theatrical release are shuttled to the direct-to-DVD market if the studio feels the finished product is not going to recoup its investment as a theatrical release. The Jessica Simpson vehicle *Major Movie Star* (2009, Steve Miner), to name one example, was originally conceived as a theatrical release. But because of Simpson's waning star power and the unflattering coverage of her acting ability and personal life in the tabloids, the film was repackaged as the direct-to-DVD release *Private Valentine: Blonde and Dangerous*. The decision to repackage a theatrical release as a direct-to-DVD release often prompts derisive press coverage of the film's stars and their careers, indicating that the industry still carries a stigma.[10]

The reputation of direct-to-DVD releases is starting to improve, however, as studios discover the benefits of this untapped market. First, studios are profiting from extending the life of lucrative franchises. For example, the teenpic comedy *American Pie* (1999, Paul Weitz) generated two theatrically released sequels, *American Pie 2* (2001, J. B. Rogers) and *American Wedding* (2003, Jesse Dylan). These sequels retained most of *American Pie*'s original cast members and had similar productions values. Universal then revived the *American Pie* franchise in 2005 with the direct-to-DVD releases *American Pie Presents: Band Camp* (2005, Steve Rash), *American Pie Presents: The Naked Mile* (2006, Joe Nussbaum), *American Pie Presents: Beta House* (2007, Andrew Waller), and *American Pie Presents: Book of Love* (2009, John Putch). With the exception of Eugene Levy, none of the original cast members appear in these sequels. However, the use of the "American Pie" name and its recognizable logo on the DVD cover signals to audiences that these films will be similar in content and tone. The studio's choice to renew the *American Pie* franchise in the direct-to-DVD market is based on the fact that such releases do not need to pull in large audiences in order to make a profit. Rather than abandon a previously successful story property, "studios have realized that the power of the DVD market gives them another option," according to Brooks Barnes, who adds: "They drop everything but the franchise concepts and the titles, and hire cheaper acting talent" ("Direct-to-DVD Releases"). In the past, making a film that appealed only to a small segment of the audience would have been financially risky, but direct-to-DVD releases are built for such micro-audiences (Barnes, "Direct-to-DVD Releases").

"Parallel content" is another way for studios to make money with direct-to-DVD releases. When employing this strategy, studios produce a film for theatrical release and simultaneously release a film with parallel content for the direct-to-DVD market (Swanson, "Direct-to-DVD"). Ten days after Warner Bros. released *Get Smart* (2008, Peter Segal) in theaters in the summer of 2008, Warner Premiere released a parallel-content film about two of *Get Smart*'s supporting characters, entitled *Get Smart's Bruce and Lloyd Out of Control* (2008, Gil Junger). This film's tagline, "Loved Get Smart? Get More!" does not promise a novel viewing experience. Rather, fans of *Get Smart* are promised a similar viewing experience, only without the film's A-list stars. As Linda Ruth Williams argues, direct-to-DVD and direct-to-TV films are the "supreme American genre product: recognisable instances of alike substitutions, repetitions which ring a few character and plot changes but retain a brand identity. They offer the safety of the known, the reassurance of the typical, but promise a modicum of differentiation and variety" (*Erotic Thriller*, 366). Direct-to-DVD films bank on fans' willingness—or rather, their desire—to watch the same characters, plots, and settings over and over again.

As with the exploitation film and the B film, the direct-to-DVD release must compensate for the poverty of its images and the stigma of its downscale market through some other exploitable hook. The

The direct-to-DVD release *Get Smart's Bruce and Lloyd Out of Control* (2008) offers a viewing experience similar to the one provided by *Get Smart* (2008).

direct-to-DVD film's primary hook is the promise of sensation, particularly sex, gore, violence, or perversity. Too much of any of these things would turn off a mainstream audience and limit the box-office returns of a theatrical release. However, as I mentioned, direct-to-DVD releases can afford to limit their audiences. Indeed, Lionsgate, a studio dealing in both theatrical and direct-to-DVD releases, describes its direct-to-DVD horror films as "too graphic, too disturbing and too shocking for general audiences" (quoted in Barnes, "Direct-to-DVD Releases"). To snag an R rating, the original *American Pie* films titillated their teenage audiences with partial nudity—such as a topless Shannon Elizabeth—but avoided repeated displays of full-frontal nudity. Too much nudity would have resulted in an NC-17 rating, which would have limited the franchise's chance of being seen by its target theatrical audience of teenagers under the age of seventeen. However, direct-to-DVD films can revel in unlimited sex and violence because they are "not required to meet the same rating standards as theatrical releases" (Barnes, "Direct-to-DVD Releases"). Therefore, in the direct-to-DVD branch of the *American Pie* franchise, full-frontal nudity is part of a film's appeal and ensures its success with a teenage audience that is not subject to ratings restrictions.

Direct-to-DVD releases' other exploitable hook is their ability to cater to a specific demographic. These films are made quickly on small budgets: most direct-to-DVD films cost between $75,000 and $2 mil-

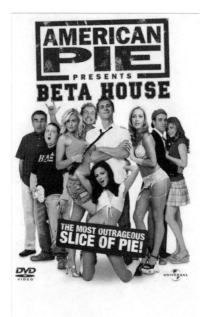

The direct-to-DVD release *American Pie Presents: Beta House* (2007) promises to be even more outrageous than the original *American Pie* (1999).

lion to produce (Littlejohn, "Black Directors"). As a result, these re-leases are able to target a niche audience that remains underserved by the majority of theatrical releases. For example, direct-to-DVD is the primary mode of distribution for queer cinema; distributors like Wolfe Video, Picture This! Entertainment, Water Bearer Films, TLA Releasing, Strand Releasing, and Ariztical Entertainment are devoted exclusively to the production of gay- and lesbian-themed films. These companies distribute new direct-to-DVD titles in a multitude of genres, including slasher films (*Fraternity Massacre at Hell Island* [2010, Mark Goshorn Jones]), comedies (*Homewrecker* [2010, Paul Hart]), and ac-tion-adventure films (*Hit Parade* [2010, Joe Casey]). They also distrib-ute theatrically released titles, such as the Oscar-nominated *A Single Man* (2009, Tom Ford), that are of interest to fans of queer cinema.[11]

African American moviegoers are another prominent example of a niche audience currently being courted by studios. Production com-panies like Maverick Entertainment and the Simmons Lathan Media Group have created entire "urban" departments, the term direct-to-DVD producers have euphemistically applied to the films they market to African American audiences. Many major studios, such as MGM, are also targeting African American audiences by creating smaller production units devoted to these so-called urban films (Hettrick, "MGM Homevideo").

Films made for the historically neglected African American audience (as well as foreign markets) "were among the first to prove the [direct-to-DVD] market was more than a dumping ground, and they have subsequently paved the way for other genres traditionally shut out of theaters" (Littlejohn, "Black Directors"). Furthermore, like the B films of the East Side Kids cycle, the direct-to-DVD urban films are capable of exploiting contemporary trends and interests by attaching the same characters, images, settings, and themes to more viable genres and film cycles. For example, *Hood of tha Living Dead* (2004, Ed Quiroz) repeats many of the semantic and syntactic elements of the original ghetto action cycle—a formula that ceased to be financially viable in theatrical markets in 1996—and marries these elements to a more successful cycle—the zombie cycle of the 2000s.[12] *Hood of tha Living Dead* tells the story of an aspiring scientist, Ricky (Carl Washington), and his younger brother, Jermaine (Brandon Daniels), who live in a dangerous section of Oakland. Ricky worries about Jermaine, who is hanging around with gang members, and vows to move them to a safer neighborhood. Thus, *Hood of tha Living Dead* ensures its success with its target urban audience by including one of the basic plot formulas of the ghetto action cycle: a hardworking young man who wants a better life for his family outside of the 'hood. However, before the brothers can move, Jermaine is killed in a drive-by shooting. The grief-stricken Ricky decides to test an experimental formula he has just developed, which regenerates dead cells, on his dead brother. The formula works, but it has the unfortunate side effect of turning Jermaine into a flesh-eating monster. Here the film shifts from ghetto action film to zombie film, ensuring that the film will appeal to fans of both cycles.

Another example of this generic mixing occurs in *Leprechaun 5: Leprechaun in the Hood* (2000, Rob Spera). Although *Leprechaun 5*'s subtitle indicates that it is intended for the urban market, the film uses the semantics of several film genres and cycles, a tactic that allows the film to appeal to a wider audience. First, as its title, suggests, *Leprechaun 5* is part of the popular *Leprechaun* franchise.[13] The film is therefore meant to appeal to fans of the campy horror series as well as fans of horror films in general. To that end, the film contains numerous gory set pieces and moments of suspense. *Leprechaun 5* also opens with an extended reference to the blaxploitation cycle: Mack Daddy (Ice-T), a music producer and thug, heads to an abandoned subway track with a companion, where they search for a mysterious treasure. We know this scene is set in the 1970s because blaxploitation-style funk music is playing and the men are sporting enormous afros, platform shoes, and bright polyester suits, despite the fact that these outfits are wildly inappropriate for a day of breaking up concrete walls and digging through rubble in an abandoned subway tunnel. When the men accidentally awaken the Leprechaun (Warwick Davis), who has been trapped in a state of suspended animation, they fight over his magic flute. In a visual quote of *Coffy* (1973, Jack Hill) and *Foxy Brown* (1974, Jack Hill), Mack Daddy pulls increasingly larger weapons out of his afro, including a gun and a baseball bat.

Leprechaun 5 also contains a plot lifted directly from the social problem films of the 1930s. Three African American teenagers, Postmaster P (Anthony Montgomery), Stray Bullet (Rashaan Nall), and Butch (Red Grant), dream of creating positive rap music, despite the fact that Mack Daddy, the most successful person in the neighborhood, built his music empire on gangsta rap. The teens therefore face the difficult choice of either making easy money by rapping about violence and misogyny or staying poor but maintaining their ideals, a choice the Dead End Kids face in many of their films from the 1930s and 1940s (substitute petty crime for violent gangsta rap). *Leprechaun 5* employs prominent semantic elements of the ghetto action film: the presence of Ice-T, a veteran of *New Jack City* (1991, Mario Van Peebles) and numerous low-budget ghetto action films;[14] an emphasis on the deteriorating mise-en-scène of the ghetto; an antagonistic Korean store clerk; disapproving, church-going adults; and buffoonish, exploitative white characters.

One significant difference between *Leprechaun 5* and other ghetto action films, however, is that the protagonists' main antagonist is not poverty, racism, or the brutality of the streets. Instead, the bloodthirsty Leprechaun, who terrorizes the neighborhood in search of his magic flute, represents the insidious forces of the ghetto environment, which seduce the boys and keep them from pursuing their goal of making positive rap music and getting "out of the 'hood." Early in the film, we hear the boys perform their prosocial rap music, with lyrics like "The crew and me, we all got unity / We keep the crowd hyped, *pos-i-tive-ly*!" However, after the boys get their hands on the Leprechaun's magic flute (an instrument bringing success and glory to its owner), their music changes from themes of "saving the 'hood" to violent lyrics about gunplay and gangstas. This performance sequence is filmed with frantic handheld cameras; rapid, MTV-style editing; close-ups of the boys' angry faces; and plenty of low-angle shots, all in a style mimicking the aesthetics of a conventional gangsta rap video. Although the boys originally reject Mack Daddy's offer to join his label because it would require them to abandon their dream of creating positive music, the Leprechaun's magic flute hypnotizes them

When two franchises collide: the Leprechaun (Warwick Davis) smokes
marijuana with Mack Daddy (Ice-T) in *Leprechaun 5: Leprechaun in the Hood*
(2000).

into valuing money and power over morality and social responsibility. And this decision to take the easy, immoral way out of their difficult living situation leads to each boy's demise, just as Doughboy's
decision to perpetuate the cycle of violence in *Boyz N the Hood* is posited as the reason for his death at the end of the film. *Leprechaun 5*
thus takes up the social problem film's syntax by offering harsh consequences (death) for poor choices. However, it is difficult to detect
this social-problem-film message, since it is buried within the conventions of the horror film; the boys' primary antagonist is a super-
natural force masquerading as the debilitating socioeconomic conditions of the ghetto.

Even while mixing together so many genres and cycles, *Leprechaun 5* retains its urban flavor by coding the film's eponymous monster as a "gangsta": he disposes of his enemies with violence and inspires fear in those around him, loves rap music and engages in a rap
battle, has a trio of "zombie fly girls," and loves to smoke marijuana
"blunts." Furthermore, when he is first freed from his inanimate state
at the beginning of the film, the Leprechaun proclaims, "Free at last!
Free at last! Thank God Almighty, free at last!" By quoting Martin Lu-
ther King's "I Have a Dream" speech, the Leprechaun allies his own
imprisonment with the African American community's struggle for
equal rights. It is well known that leprechauns hail from Ireland, and
the Leprechaun speaks with an Irish accent throughout the film, so it
is curious that the character identifies with African American youth

cultures throughout the film. But by claiming this franchise character as distinctly urban, the film's producers found a way to tap into the African American market while still providing a product for fans of the *Leprechaun* franchise.

Despite (or perhaps because of) its status as a campy low-budget farce, *Leprechaun 5* has generated a surprising amount of viewer discussion on the Internet Movie Database's message boards and comment sections. According to their posts, viewers chose to watch the film because of their devotion to low-budget films, the *Leprechaun* franchise, or ghetto action films. One viewer writes: "Don't listen to the pundits who criticize the excesses and outright incongruities common to all straight-to-video camp. . . . This movie shows how dangerous it can be when two totally different worlds crash straight into each other" (Nemtuskii, "This Is What They Mean"). This viewer is enthusiastic about the incongruities of the characters and conventions from the *Leprechaun* franchise mixing with those found in the ghetto action cycle. However, this type of generic mixing is also what ruined the film for other fans: "As a huge supporter of the *Leprechaun* series, and especially of *Leprechaun 4: In Space* (who cares how he got into space?), I was extremely excited to see Part 5. However, it seemed to be more of an afterschool [*sic*] special on gang warfare, the glories of church, and the ever-important 'be true to yourself' theme, with a leprechaun thrown in instead of a true vehicle of Leprechaunisms" (Sptbgjen, "Boring Tripe"). For this viewer, the injection of syntax from ghetto action films—the "message with a capital M"—into the basic *Leprechaun* plot was an awkward and unwelcome addition to the franchise.

These responses to *Leprechaun 5*, both positive and negative, illustrate why producers continue to create these films. By mixing together several genres and cycles, each targeting a seemingly different demographic, producers can continue to exploit the semantics of a cycle whose films are no longer viable as theatrical releases. And because they cost so little to make, these films can afford to appeal to a niche audience; in the case of *Leprechaun 5*, the ideal viewer is someone who loves horror films, ghetto action films, rap music, and low-budget releases. Thus, like their theatrically released counterparts, direct-to-DVD cycles are tailored to meet the specific needs of their audiences, only on a much smaller scale. By examining direct-to-DVD titles aimed at niche audiences, we can better understand how production companies envision and construct particular racial, ethnic, sexual, religious, and social groups.[15] I see a study of direct-to-DVD film cycles as the next logical step in a comprehensive understanding of contemporary film genres and cycles.

CONCLUSION

Film cycles—an industrial strategy dating back to the origins of cinema—are a valuable subject of inquiry both within and outside the discipline of film studies. Studying film cycles is analogous to studying fossils: because they retain the marks of their historical, economic, and generic contexts, they are poised to reveal much about the state of contemporary politics, prevalent social ideologies, aesthetic trends, popular desires, and anxieties. They are also crucial to our understanding of the complex relations between film studios, audiences, and popular culture; an analysis of film cycles reveals how and why studios choose their film projects and why these projects succeed or fail. Cycle studies highlights cinema's ability to translate the zeitgeist into popular entertainment, as well as popular entertainment's ability to affect the zeitgeist. Some film cycles have become part of the public discourse on race relations, and some are so interwoven into the popular imagination that their images and themes can, in hindsight, stand in for reality. I believe that the study of film cycles offers new ways of understanding how the popular imagination interprets moments of social and cultural anxiety, and how the film, television, music, and media industries seek to both shape and capitalize on these interpretations.

The study of film cycles is also central to a comprehensive understanding of contemporary genre studies. A cyclical approach to film genres does not privilege one group of texts as being the most central in a genre's corpus; instead, it views each cycle within that genre as an attempt to attend to the changing needs of the audience and the film industry. Furthermore, the study of how film cycles grow and change over time reveals that cycles do not move straightforwardly from serious text to parody and that evolution rarely ends in the "death" of a cycle. Rather, the images of a successful cycle continue to circulate in various texts over the course of film history. Of course, by championing the validity and use of cycle studies, my goal is not to abandon or supplant traditional approaches to genre study. Those approaches examine how and why a group of films come to share a similar semantics and syntax. Cycle studies complements this approach by analyzing other shared elements, including industrial conditions, marketing approaches, target audiences, and cultural influences. Cycle studies thus offers an alternative, more user-based understanding of individual films, revealing how genres and cycles are "site[s] of struggle and co-operation among multiple users" (Altman, *Film/Genre*, 211). I hope that this book serves as the opening statement, rather than the final word, on cycle studies.

AMERICAN
FILM CYCLES

This book is focused on the American film cycle and the American moviegoing audience. Therefore, with the exception of the silent films listed under "The Kissing Cycle," this filmography contains only those film cycles produced by American studios and made for American audiences. Furthermore, while the filmographies listed for some cycles, like the Dead End Kids cycle, are complete, others, like the juvenile-delinquent-themed teenpic cycle, are simply too vast to list in their entirety. In these cases, entries were selected to reflect the cycle's diversity and life span. The following cycles are listed in the order in which they are discussed in the text.

THE KISSING CYCLE

The John C. Rice–May Irwin Kiss (1896, William Heise)
The Soldier's Courtship (1896, Alfred Moul and Robert W. Paul)
Hanging Out the Clothes (1897, G. A. Smith)
The Amorous Guardsman (1898, British Mutascope and Biograph Company)
Tommy Atkins in the Park (1898, Robert W. Paul)
The Kiss in the Tunnel (1899, G. A. Smith)
The Kiss in the Tunnel (1899, James Banforth)
Love in a Railroad Train (1902, S. Lubin)
What Happened in the Tunnel (1903, Edwin S. Porter)
Nervy Nat Kisses the Bride (1904, Edwin S. Porter)

THE TORTURE PORN CYCLE

Saw (2004, James Wan)
Hostel (2005, Eli Roth)
Saw II (2005, Darren Lynn Bousman)
Wolf Creek (2005, Greg McLean)
The Devil's Rejects (2005, Rob Zombie)
The Hills Have Eyes (2006, Alexandre Aja)
Saw III (2006, Darren Lynn Bousman)
The Texas Chainsaw Massacre: The Beginning (2006, Jonathan Liebesman)
Turistas (2006, John Stockwell)
Captivity (2007, Roland Joffé)
Saw IV (2007, Darren Lynn Bousman)
Hostel II (2007, Eli Roth)
Saw V (2008, David Hackl)
Last House on the Left (2009, Dennis Iliadis)
Saw VI (2009, Kevin Greutert)
Saw 3-D (2010, Kevin Greutert)
The Human Centipede (2010, Tom Six)

THE CLASSICAL GANGSTER CYCLE

Little Caesar (1930, Mervyn LeRoy)
The Public Enemy (1931, William Wellman)
Scarface (1932, Howard Hawks)

THE MELODRAMATIC GANGSTER FILM CYCLE

The Musketeers of Pig Alley (1912, D. W. Griffith)
The Gangsters of New York (1914, James Kirkwood)
Regeneration (1915, Raoul Walsh)
The Penalty (1920, Wallace Worsley)
Big Brother (1923, Alan Dwan)
Fool's Highway (1924, Irving Cummings)
Underworld (1927, Josef von Sternberg)
Me, Gangster (1928, Raoul Walsh)
Alias Jimmy Valentine (1928, Jack Conway)
Thunderbolt (1929, Josef von Sternberg)
Ladies Love Brutes (1930, Rowland V. Lee)
The Doorway to Hell (1930, Archie Mayo)
The Big House (1930, George Hill)
Born Reckless (1930, John Ford)
A Free Soul (1931, Clarence Brown)
Manhattan Melodrama (1934, W. S. Van Dyke)
The Last Gangster (1937, Edward Ludwig)
Angels with Dirty Faces (1938, Michael Curtiz)
The Roaring Twenties (1939, Raoul Walsh)
Each Dawn I Die (1939, William Keighley)
High Sierra (1941, Raoul Walsh)
Lucky Jordan (1942, Frank Tuttle)
The Big Shot (1942, Lewis Seiler)
Kiss of Death (1947, Henry Hathaway)
Force of Evil (1948, Abraham Polonsky)

THE DEAD END KIDS CYCLE (WARNER BROS.)

Dead End (1937, William Wyler)*
Crime School (1938, Lewis Seiler)
Angels with Dirty Faces (1938, Michael Curtiz)
They Made Me a Criminal (1939, Busby Berkeley)
Hell's Kitchen (1939, Lewis Seiler)
Angels Wash Their Faces (1939, Ray Enright)
On Dress Parade (1939, William Clemens)

*The first film in this cycle was distributed by United Artists.

THE DEAD END KIDS AND LITTLE TOUGH GUYS CYCLE (UNIVERSAL)

Little Tough Guy (1938, Harold Young)
Little Tough Guys in Society (1938, Erle C. Kenton)
Newsboys' Home (1938, Harold Young)
Code of the Streets (1939, Harold Young)
Call a Messenger (1939, Arthur Lubin)
You're Not So Tough (1940, Joe May)
Junior G-Men (1940, Ford Beebe and John Rawlins)
Give Us Wings (1940, Charles Lamont)
Hit the Road (1941, Joe May)
Sea Raiders (1941, Ford Beebe and John Rawlins)
Mob Town (1941, William Nigh)
Junior G-Men of the Air (1942, Lewis D. Collins and Ray Taylor)
Tough as They Come (1942, William Nigh)
Mug Town (1943, Ray Taylor)
Keep 'Em Slugging (1943, Christy Cabanne)

THE EAST SIDE KIDS CYCLE (MONOGRAM PICTURES)

East Side Kids (1940, Robert F. Hill)
Boys of the City (1940, Joseph H. Lewis)
That Gang of Mine (1940, Joseph H. Lewis)
Pride of the Bowery (1941, Joseph H. Lewis)
Flying Wild (1941, William West)
Bowery Blitzkrieg (1941, Wallace Fox)
Spooks Run Wild (1941, Phil Rosen)
Mr. Wise Guy (1942, William Nigh)
Let's Get Tough! (1942, Wallace Fox)
Smart Alecks (1942, Wallace Fox)
'Neath Brooklyn Bridge (1942, Wallace Fox)
Kid Dynamite (1943, Wallace Fox)
Clancy Street Boys (1943, William Beaudine)
Ghosts on the Loose (1943, William Beaudine)
Mr. Muggs Steps Out (1943, William Beaudine)
Million Dollar Kid (1944, Wallace Fox)
Follow the Leader (1944, William Beaudine)
Block Busters (1944, Wallace Fox)
Bowery Champs (1944, William Beaudine)
Docks of New York (1945, Wallace Fox)
Mr. Muggs Rides Again (1945, Wallace Fox)
Come Out Fighting (1945, William Beaudine)

IMITATORS OF THE ORIGINAL DEAD END KIDS CYCLE

Boys of the Streets (1938, William Nigh), Monogram Pictures
Boys' Reformatory (1939, Howard Bretherton), Columbia
Boys' Town (1938, Norman Taurog), MGM
Beloved Brat (1938, Arthur Lubin), Warner Bros.
Girls on Probation (1938, William C. McGann), Warner Bros.
Streets of New York (1939, William Nigh), Monogram Pictures
Prison Bait (aka *Reform School*) (1939, Leo C. Popkin), Million Dollar Productions
Boy Slaves (1939, P. J. Wolfson), RKO
Take My Life (1942, Harry M. Popkin), Goldseal Productions

THE BOWERY BOYS CYCLE (MONOGRAM PICTURES)

Live Wires (1946, Phil Karlson)
In Fast Company (1946, Del Lord)
Bowery Bombshell (1946, Phil Karlson)
Spook Busters (1946, William Beaudine)
Mr. Hex (1946, William Beaudine)
Hard Boiled Mahoney (1947, William Beaudine)
News Hounds (1947, William Beaudine)
Bowery Buckaroos (1947, William Beaudine)
Angels' Alley (1948, William Beaudine)
Jinx Money (1948, William Beaudine)
Smugglers' Cove (1948, William Beaudine)
Trouble Makers (1948, Reginald LeBorg)
Fighting Fools (1949, Reginald LeBorg)
Hold That Baby! (1949, Reginald LeBorg)
Angels in Disguise (1949, Jean Yarbrough)
Master Minds (1949, Jean Yarbrough)
Blonde Dynamite (1950, William Beaudine)
Lucky Losers (1950, William Beaudine)
Triple Trouble (1950, Jean Yarbrough)
Blues Busters (1950, William Beaudine)
Bowery Battalion (1950, William Beaudine)
Ghost Chasers (1951, William Beaudine)
Let's Go Navy! (1951, William Beaudine)
Crazy Over Horses (1951, William Beaudine)
Hold That Line (1952, William Beaudine)
Here Come the Marines (1952, William Beaudine)
Feudin' Fools (1952, William Beaudine)
No Holds Barred (1952, William Beaudine)
Jalopy (1953, William Beaudine)
Loose in London (1953, Edward Bernds)
Clipped Wings (1953, Edward Bernds)

Private Eyes (1953, Edward Bernds)
Paris Playboys (1954, William Beaudine)
Jungle Gents (1954, Edward Bernds)
Bowery to Bagdad (1955, Edward Bernds)
High Society (1955, William Beaudine)
Spy Chasers (1955, Edward Bernds)
Jail Busters (1955, William Beaudine)
Dig That Uranium (1956, Edward Bernds)
Crashing Las Vegas (1956, Jean Yarbrough)
Fighting Trouble (1956, George Blair)
Hot Shots (1956, Jean Yarbrough)
Hold That Hypnotist (1957, Austen Jewell)
Spook Chasers (1957, George Blair)
Looking for Danger (1957, Austen Jewell)
Up in Smoke (1957, William Beaudine)
In the Money (1958, William Beaudine)

THE JUVENILE-DELINQUENT-THEMED TEENPIC CYCLE

City Across the River (1949, Maxwell Shane)
Bad Boy (1949, Kurt Nuemann)
Knock on Any Door (1949, Nicholas Ray)
The Wild One (1953, Laslo Benedek)
Blackboard Jungle (1955, Richard Brooks)
Teenage Crime Wave (1955, Fred F. Sears)
Rebel without a Cause (1955, Nicholas Ray)
Crime in the Streets (1956, Don Siegel)
Hot Rod Girl (1956, Leslie Martinson)
Rock, Pretty Baby (1956, Richard Bartlett)
The Violent Years (1956, William Morgan)
Rock Around the Clock (1956, Fred F. Sears)
Shake, Rattle, and Rock! (1956, Edward L. Cahn)
Rock, Rock, Rock (1956, Will Price)
Dino (1957, Thomas Carr)
I Was a Teenage Werewolf (1957, Gene Fowler, Jr.)
The Delinquents (1957, Robert Altman)
Hot Rod Rumble (1957, Leslie Martinson)
Teenage Thunder (1957, Georg Tressler)
Dragstrip Girl (1957, Lou Rusoff)
Teenage Monster (1957, Jacques Marquette)
I Was a Teenage Frankenstein (1957, Herbert L. Strock)
Teenage Doll (1957, Roger Corman)
No Time to Be Young (1957, David L. Rich)
Reform School Girl (1957, Edward Bernds)
Rock All Night (1957, Roger Corman)

High School Confidential! (1958, Jack Arnold)
Dragstrip Riot (1958, David Bradley)
Hot Car Girl (1958, Bernard Kowalksi)
Hot Rod Gang (1958, Lew Landers)
Joy Ride (1958, Edward Bernds)
The Cool and the Crazy (1958, William Witney)
Girls on the Loose (1958, Paul Henreid)
Dangerous Youth (1958, Herbert Wilcox)
Teenage Caveman (1958, Roger Corman)
Unwed Mother (1958, William A. Doniger)
High School Hellcats (1958, Edward Bernds)
Live Fast, Die Young (1958, Paul Henreid)
Go, Johnny, Go! (1959, Paul Landres)
The Beat Generation (1959, Charles Haas)
Blue Denim (1959, Phillip Dunne)
Cry Tough! (1959, Paul Stanley)
Teenagers from Outer Space (1959, Tom Graeff)
Ghost of Dragstrip Hollow (1959, Lou Rusoff)
Teenage Zombies (1960, Jerry Warren)
Date Bait (1960, O. Dale Ireland)
High School Caesar (1960, O. Dale Ireland)
Platinum High School (1960, Charles Haas)
This Rebel Breed (1960, Richard L. Bare)
The Young Savages (1961, John Frankenheimer)
The Sadist (1963, James Landis)
Kitten with a Whip (1964, Douglas Heyes)
The Incredibly Strange Creatures Who Stopped Living and Became Crazy Mixed-Up Zombies (1964, Ray Dennis Steckler)
Village of the Giants (1965, Bert I. Gordon)
Teenage Gang Debs (1966, Sande Johnson)
Teen-Age Strangler (1968, Ben Parker)

THE BLAXPLOITATION CYCLE

Cotton Comes to Harlem (1971, Ossie Davis)
Sweet Sweetback's Baadasssss Song (1971, Melvin Van Peebles)
Shaft (1971, Gordon Parks)
Superfly (1972, Gordon Parks, Jr.)
Blacula (1972, William Crane)
Slaughter (1972, Jack Starrett)
Trick Baby (1972, Larry Yust)
Come Back, Charleston Blue (1972, Mark Warren)
The Legend of Nigger Charley (1972, Martin Goldman)
Coffy (1973, Jack Hill)
Black Caesar (1973, Larry Cohen)

Hell Up in Harlem (1973, Larry Cohen)
The Mack (1973, Michael Campus)
Cleopatra Jones (1973, Jack Starrett)
Five on the Black Hand Side (1973, Oscar Williams)
Ganja and Hess (1973, Bill Gunn)
Foxy Brown (1974, Samuel Z. Arkoff)
Sugar Hill (1974, Paul Maslansky)
Truck Turner (1974, Jonathan Kaplan)
Willie Dynamite (1974, Gilbert Moses)
Dolemite (1975, D'Urville Martin)
Mandingo (1975, Richard Fleischer)
Sheba, Baby (1975, William Girdler)
Dr. Black, Mr. Hyde (1976, William Crane)
J. D.'s Revenge (1976, Arthur Marks)

THE GHETTO ACTION CYCLE

New Jack City (1991, Mario Van Peebles)
Boyz N the Hood (1991, John Singleton)
Straight Out of Brooklyn (1991, Matty Rich)
Juice (1992, Ernest R. Dickerson)
South Central (1992, Steve Anderson)
Menace II Society (1993, Allen and Albert Hughes)
CB4 (1993, Tamra Davis)
Fresh (1994, Boaz Yakin)
Fear of a Black Hat (1994, Rusty Cundieff)
Dangerous Minds (1995, John N. Smith)
Tales from the Hood (1995, Rusty Cundieff)
Friday (1995, F. Gary Gray)
Clockers (1995, Spike Lee)
New Jersey Drive (1995, Nick Gomez)
Original Gangstas (1996, Larry Cohen)
Set It Off (1996, F. Gary Gray)
Don't Be a Menace to South Central While Drinking Your Juice in the Hood (1996, Paris Barclay)

THE CYCLE-PARODY CYCLE

Scary Movie (2000, Keenen Ivory Wayans)
Scary Movie II (2001, Keenen Ivory Wayans)
Not Another Teen Movie (2001, Joel Gallen)
Scary Movie 3 (2003, David Zucker)
Scary Movie 4 (2006, David Zucker)
Date Movie (2006, Aaron Seltzer)
Walk Hard: The Dewey Cox Story (2007, Jake Kasdan)

Epic Movie (2007, Jason Friedberg and Aaron Seltzer)
Meet the Spartans (2008, Jason Friedberg and Aaron Seltzer)
Disaster Movie (2008, Jason Friedberg and Aaron Seltzer)
Superhero Movie (2008, Craig Mazin)
Dance Flick (2009, Damien Dante Wayans)
Vampires Suck (2010, Jason Friedberg and Aaron Seltzer)

THE URBAN DIRECT-TO-DVD CYCLE

I'm Bout It (1997, Moon Jones)
Da Last Don (1998, Michael Martin)
Hot Boyz (1999, Master P)
Urban Menace (1999, Albert Pyun)
The Horrible Dr. Bonz (2000, Ted Nicolaou)
Leprechaun 5: Leprechaun in the Hood (2000, Rob Spera)
Streetwise (2002, Bruce Brown)
Gangster Party (2002, Ryan Combs)
Leprechaun 6: Back 2 tha Hood (2003, Steve Ayromlooi)
Jack Movez (2003, Eduardo and Jose Quiroz)
Gang of Roses (2003, Jean-Claude La Marre)
Do or Die (2003, Jason Young)
Cutthroat Alley (2003, Timothy Wayne Fulsome)
Kickin' It High (2003, Juney Smith)
Real Hustla (2003, Tony Manshino)
Drug Lordz (2003, Eduardo and Jose Quiroz)
Hood of tha Living Dead (2004, Ed Quiroz)
Brothas in Arms (2005, Jean-Claude La Marre)
Ride or Die (2005, Jean-Claude La Marre)
Death of a G (2006, Larry Gardiner)
Endz (2006, Curtis J. Schultz)
Gang Girl (2010, Damian Bailey)

INTRODUCTION

1. John C. Rice and May Irwin were the stars of the popular stage play *The Widow Jones* (1895). The kiss portrayed in the Edison film is from the final act of the play.

2. The Edison catalogue description for *The Kiss* explains: "They get ready to kiss, begin to kiss, and kiss and kiss and kiss in a way that brings down the house every time" (quoted in Gray, *"Kiss in the Tunnel,"* 60).

3. See Gunning, "Aesthetic of Astonishment," for a detailed discussion of early train films and modernity.

4. See Lawrence, *Blaxploitation Films*; Seate, *Two Wheels on Two Reels*; and Middleton, *Dying for a Laugh.*

5. In Chapter 2, I disprove Altman's claim that film cycles are bound to a single studio.

6. Hoberman and Rosenbaum argue: "The fleeting evanescence of cinema as a medium has been both its blessing and its curse—establishing at once the grounds for its loftiest claims to transcendence and some of its sleazier business transactions" (*Midnight Movies*, 16).

7. See Cawelti, *Six-Gun Mystique*; Warshow, "Gangster as Tragic Hero"; Will Wright, *Sixguns and Society*; and Kaminsky, *American Film Genres.*

8. Kaminsky recommends this approach to the study of genres: "Genre in film, if it is to have meaning, must have a limited scope, a limited definition . . . a narrowing of definition" (*American Film Genres*, 7).

9. For example, the blaxploitation cycle contains westerns (*Boss Nigger* [1975, Jack Arnold]), gangster films (*Black Caesar* [1973, Larry Cohen]), and horror films (*Blacula*, [1972 William Crain]).

10. For example, Andy Warhol's films undercut even the most basic audience expectations. *Sleep* (1963) is composed of six hours of footage of a sleeping man. Even the director was bored by the footage. When asked why he left during the screening of this film, Warhol replied, "Sometimes I like to be bored, and sometimes I don't" (quoted in Hoberman and Rosenbaum, *Midnight Movies*, 58).

11. Earlier adult-targeted social problem films like *Knock on Any Door* (1949, Nicholas Ray) and *The City Across the River* (1949, Maxwell Shane) also warned of the dangers of juvenile delinquency, but these films did not capture the youth imagination (Doherty, *Teenagers and Teenpics*, 121).

12. All box-office figures cited in this chapter are taken from www.boxoffice mojo.com.

13. Here it is worth noting that later films in a cycle are often advertised as "sequels" to an earlier, more successful film, even if the cast, directors, or writers used in the sequel are different from those used in the original film. *Saw II* (2005, Darren Lynn Bousman) was advertised as a sequel to *Saw* but employed a different director and a different cast from the original film (which makes sense, since almost every character dies in the first film), retaining only the premise of

the Jigsaw Killer. Audiences did not seem to mind this change, since *Saw II* made even more money ($87 million) than the original.

14. See for example, Edelstein, "Now Playing at Your Local Multiplex"; Cochrane, "For Your Entertainment"; and Ouellette, "Reclaiming Our Space."

15. See Soloway, "Remove the Rating for *Captivity*"; Lopez, "Billboard's 'Captivity' Audience Disgusted"; and the blog *Remove the Rating* (http://removethe rating.blogspot.com/).

16. See Chapter 5 for a more detailed discussion of cycle parodies.

17. Although film cycles live for a short period of time in order to capitalize on the public's interest in a particular topic, select film cycles also recur periodically throughout film history. For example, disaster film cycles appeared in the 1970s (*Airport* [1970, George Seaton], *The Poseidon Adventure* [1972, Ronald Neame], *The Towering Inferno* [1974, John Guillermin and Irwin Allen]) and in the 2000s (*The Day after Tomorrow* [2004, Roland Emmerich], *Poseidon* [2006, Wolfgang Petersen], *2012* [2009, Roland Emmerich]). Disaster films address audience anxieties about the stability of the world, so it makes sense that these cycles appeared in the 1970s and in the 2000s, which coincided with U.S. involvement in "quagmires" like Vietnam and Iraq and with rising concerns over the human impact on the environment.

18. Gustave LeBon first proposed these theories in *The Crowd*.

19. See Guerrero, *Framing Blackness*; S. Craig Watkins, *Representing*; Massood, *Black City Cinema*; Harris, *Boys, Boyz, Bois*; and Fisher, *Black on Black*.

CHAPTER 1

1. According to Stephen Prince, the gangster film was a major target of the PCA: "Perhaps because their violence belonged to a recognizably real world of urban streets, rather than ancient castles in Europe or uncharted tropical islands, the gangster films ignited a level of controversy that surpassed what surrounded the horror films" (*Classical Film Violence*, 87).

2. For example, in *Scarface* (1932), the chief of police warns the gangster hero, Tony Camonte (Paul Muni), "You've come into this town and you think you're headed somewhere, don't you? You think you're gonna get there with a gun, but you're not. Get me? You know why? Because you've got thousand-dollar bills pasted right across your eyes. And someday you're gonna stumble and fall down in the gutter, right where the horses have been standing, right where you belong."

3. In his discussion of Italian American gangsters, Fred L. Gardaphé explains that "Italian masculinity is typically expected to be displayed through actions rather than words. 'Le parole sono feminine,' goes an Italian saying, 'Words are feminine'; but 'I fatti sono maschi,' 'actions are masculine'" (*Wiseguys to Wise Men*, 16).

4. I borrow the idea of the border text from Altman's discussion of "marginalized adjectives": "All genre formation, I have suggested, begins with a process of cycle-making creolization, combining gypsy adjectives with established, land-

owning generic substantives. Only when those previously marginalized adjectives plant their flag in the centre of the world are they transmuted into substantival genres, thus putting them on the map, as it were, while simultaneously opening them up to new adjectival settlements and an eventual squatter take over" (*Film/Genre*, 199).

5. Ryall argues that the very act of assigning a film to a genre limits its meanings: "When we suggest that a certain film is a Western, we are really positing that a particular range of meanings will be available in the film, and not others. We are defining the limits of a genre's significance" ("Teaching through Genre," 27–28). Thus, even though the lens of genre opens up certain hidden meanings, once a generic label is applied to a text, other possible meanings are simultaneously shut down (Berger, *Popular Culture Genres*, 45).

6. Tudor argues that the paradox of beginning a genre study is that the body of films composing a generic corpus "can only be isolated on the basis of the 'principal characteristics,' which can only be discovered from the films themselves after they have been isolated" (*Theories of Film*, 138). This quandary highlights the often arbitrary nature of defining genres.

7. The following works use the classical cycle to partly or fully define the genre's central traits: McArthur, *Underworld USA*; Schatz, *Hollywood Genres*; Yaquinto, *Pump 'Em Full of Lead*; Clarens, *Crime Movies*; Rafter, *Shots in the Mirror*; and Shadoian, *Dreams and Dead Ends*.

8. See McArthur, *Underworld USA*, 35; Rosow, *Born to Lose*, 27; Munby, *Public Enemies*, 43–44; Yaquinto, *Pump 'Em Full of Lead*, 25; Clarens, *Crime Movies*, 53; and Mason, *American Gangster Cinema*, 6.

9. By the late 1920s, the gangster was understood to be a criminal working within an organized, hierarchical structure. Criminal activities like bootlegging required a group of people working together in order to succeed (Ruth, *Inventing the Public Enemy*, 45).

10. Other prominent examples of films written by Hecht include *His Girl Friday* (1940, Howard Hawks) and *Twentieth Century* (1934, Howard Hawks).

11. This definition of melodrama has not remained consistent throughout film history. In *Genre and Hollywood*, Steve Neale carefully examines how and why the term "melodrama" has been used in industry discourse since the early 1900s. Historically, the term "melodrama" was used to refer to stories that were suspenseful, thrilling, action packed, and even "realistic" (180–185). In studio memos and film reviews, melodramas were defined as action films emphasizing seedy characters, events, and settings, such as prisons, crime syndicates, and the wild, wild West, and implied that a film *lacked* sentiment, romance, or female characters.

12. Esther Sonnet identifies 1930s "society melodramas" as another significant production cycle of the gangster film. This cycle, which includes titles like *Ladies Love Brutes* (1930, Rowland V. Lee) and *A Free Soul* (1931, Clarence Brown), "dramatizes not only personal and emotional entanglements but also ones that register most forcefully as often irreparable infractions of social norms and codes. It is a narrative form that centers on the usually doomed consequences of

illicit liaisons between lovers and intended partners ill-matched by birth, class or wealth" ("Ladies Love Brutes," 97–98). This production cycle has some overlap with the films I am identifying, particularly *The Racketeer*.

13. For more on the relationship between cinema and the Progressive movement, see Chapter 2.

CHAPTER 2

1. Although *East Side Kids* is technically the first entry in the East Side Kids cycle, it does not star any of the actors who would later become the core cast of the series.

2. As discussed in the Introduction, Steve Neale describes "systemization" as the repetition and exploitation of a film's most marketable elements (*Genre and Hollywood*, 51).

3. Throughout the remainder of this chapter, I will use the word "original" to designate the cycle of films initiated by United Artists' *Dead End* and continued by Warner Bros. (1938–1939). I use the label "Dead End Kids cycles" to collectively refer to the original cycle and its three spin-off cycles, including Universal's Dead End Kids and Little Tough Guys (1938–1943) and Monogram's East Side Kids (1940–1945) and the Bowery Boys (1946–1958). This chapter does not examine the Bowery Boys cycle, since that group of films is almost entirely divorced from its origins in the original Dead End Kids cycle. The adult protagonists of this cycle, Slip (Leo Gorcey) and Sach (Huntz Hall), are clearly modeled on the success of other slapstick duos like Abbott and Costello. The cycle is significant however, in that with forty-eight entries, it is the longest-running cycle in American film history.

4. The Dead End Kids films also inspired a parody entitled *The Lemon Grove Kids Meet the Monsters* (1965, Peter Balakoff and Ray Dennis Steckler). This film, composed of three 16 mm short films (*The Lemon Grove Kids, Lemon Grove Kids Meet the Green Grasshopper and the Vampire Lady from Outerspace,* and *Lemon Grove Kids Go Hollywood*) has acquired cult-film status.

5. "Whaddya" instead of "what do you," "mudder" for "mother," "poifect" for "perfect," "moider" for "murder," etc.

6. See Chapter 3 for a detailed discussion of the rise of the teenager as a cultural force in the 1950s.

7. There are exceptions to this rule. Films like *I Am a Fugitive from a Chain Gang* and *Dead End* are examples of social problem films ending on a note of ambiguity rather than resolution.

8. According to Leonard Getz, Warner Bros. was not pleased with the final cut of *Crime School* and temporarily dropped the Kids' contracts. Universal quickly signed the cast to make the film *Little Tough Guy*, the first entry in the Dead End Kids and Little Tough Guys cycle.

9. *Boy of the Streets* (1937) was pitched as being even "grittier" than Dead End: "Dead End without clothes; Dead End without any make up" (quoted in Hayes and Walker, *Bowery Boys*, 223).

10. The Harlem Tuff Kids generated only two titles: *Prison Bait* (aka, *Reform School*; 1939, Leo C. Popkin) and *Take My Life* (1942, Harry M. Popkin). Thus, the Harlem Tuff Kids cannot be considered a film cycle.

11. In his seminal 1953 essay "Some Ideas on the Cinema," Cesare Zavattini explains why the use of unknown or nonprofessional actors helps create an aura of realism: "In neorealism, as I intend it, everyone must be his own actor. To want one person to play another implies a calculated plot, the fable, and not 'things' happening" (59–60).

12. This cycle starred four of the original Dead End Kids—Bobby Jordan, Leo Gorcey, Huntz Hall, and Gabriel Dell—plus several other youths, including an African American character played by "Sunshine" Sammy Morrison.

13. Muggs always wears a porkpie hat; Glimpy wears a turned-up baseball cap; Danny wears a snug-fitting T-shirt tucked into belted khakis; and Scruno dons a painter's cap and a button-down shirt.

14. This exclusion is not surprising; until World War II, most Hollywood studio films either omitted African American characters altogether or placed them in the roles of domestic servants and happy slaves (Mammy [Hattie McDaniel] in *Gone with the Wind* [1939, Victor Fleming]), obedient sidekicks (Sam [Dooley Wilson] in *Casablanca* [1942, Michael Curtiz]), or entertainers (Lena Horne in anything).

15. I want to thank my colleague Molly Brown for making this connection.

16. In the period leading up to and during U.S. involvement in World War II, many African Americans became increasingly frustrated by the apparent contradictions in America regarding racial discrimination. As Wendell Willkie, the Republican Party chairman, noted, "Our very proclamations of what we are fighting for have rendered our own inequalities self-evident" (quoted in Nickel, "African American Men," 25).

17. Films like *We've Never Been Licked* (1943, John Rawlins) and *Betrayal from the East* (1945, William A. Berke), among others, implied that Japanese Americans were aware of the plot to bomb Pearl Harbor (Dick, *Star-Spangled Screen*, 230–232).

18. Several East Side Kids regulars, including Sammy Morrison, Bobby Jordan, and Gabriel Dell, had to leave the series briefly because of the draft (Getz, *Broadway to the Bowery*, 309, 323, 340).

19. See Chapter 3 for a discussion of the juvenile-delinquent-themed teenpic and Chapter 4 for a discussion of the ghetto action cycle.

CHAPTER 3

1. *I Was a Teenage Werewolf* cost an estimated $82,000 to produce and grossed $2 million (www.imdb.com). It also spawned a cycle of "teenagers as monsters" pictures, including *I Was a Teenage Frankenstein* (1957, Herbert L. Strock), *Teenagers from Outer Space* (1959, Tom Graeff), and *Teenage Zombies* (1960, Jerry Warren).

2. For a discussion of "confrontation dressing," see Hebdige, *Subculture*, 107.

3. See, for example, Jarrett, "Rock & Roll"; Marchant, "Micro-Macro Gap"; and Stahl, "Renovating Subcultural Theory."

4. Stanley Cohen cautions about putting too much value on the academic interpretation of subcultural symbols. He suggests that scholars of youth culture take their cues from anthropologists, who compile three levels of data: the observable external form, the "indigenous exegetics" offered by ritual specialists or laymen, and the social scientists' interpretation (*Folk Devils*, xv). When possible, I use all three levels of data in this chapter.

5. See Chapter 2 for a detailed discussion of the Dead End Kids cycle and its spin-off cycles.

6. *Youth in Crisis*, a brief, Oscar-nominated documentary, argues that postwar culture, created by absent fathers, working mothers, and disposable teen incomes, created a subversive teenage culture. It posits several prosocial solutions to the "teenage problem," including urging teenagers to sell war bonds or join 4-H clubs.

7. A 1956 poll conducted by the Gilbert Youth Research Organization found that the average weekly allowance or earnings for a teenage boy was $8.96 (up from $2.41 approximately twelve years before). The poll found that "in some cases, the youngsters have more uncommitted pocket money than their parents" (*Time*, "Bobby-Soxers' Gallup").

8. For early examples of films concerned with the problem of the young, see the trilogy *Our Dancing Daughters* (1928, Harry Beaumont), *Our Modern Maidens* (1929, Jack Conway), and *Our Blushing Brides* (1930, Harry Beaumont), which formed a popular film cycle addressing contemporary anxieties about "jazz babies" in the 1920s. Furthermore, the earliest citation for the word "teenager" in the *Oxford English Dictionary* is from a 1941 article in *Popular Science*. The term gained broader circulation after it appeared in Elliot E. Cohen's 1945 *New York Times Magazine* article "A Teen-Age Bill of Rights" (Doherty, *Teenagers and Teenpics*, 67).

9. *'Teen Life* explained in its first issue that the editorial staff was composed of "young people" and that some were even "teens like yourself" ("Editor's Letter," 5).

10. The film is based on an incident that occurred in 1947 in the town of Hollister, California (McGee and Robertson, *JD Films*, 20).

11. Until the mid-1950s, *Billboard* kept two different charts for popular music, one for white "pop" and one for African American "R & B" (Doherty, *Teenagers and Teenpics*, 54).

12. Economics also played a role in the recording industry's negative reaction to the new musical subgenre, since rock 'n' roll's success with small, independent record companies initially threatened major recording labels (Hill, "Enemy Within," 62). Likewise, many rock 'n' roll artists composed their own music and lyrics, endangering the monopoly held by the American Society of Composers, Authors and Publishers (ASCAP) (Szatmary, *Rockin' in Time*, 22–24).

13. A 1956 survey found that *Blackboard Jungle* was the favorite film of high school students (Doherty, *Teenagers and Teenpics*, 76).

14. Some studies of teen films, including Doherty's *Teenagers and Teenpics*

and Tropiano's *Rebels and Chicks*, place 1950s teenpics centering on rock 'n' roll and teenpics centering on delinquent youth into separate categories. However, other studies, like Shary's *Generation Multiplex*, categorize rock 'n' roll teenpics as juvenile delinquent films, since these texts treat rock 'n' roll as a primary cause and marker of teenage delinquency. This chapter follows Shary's lead in categorizing listening to rock 'n' roll as a delinquent behavior.

15. Until the early 1950s the automobile was primarily a utilitarian vehicle. However, several factors, including the growth of the suburbs, President Eisenhower's aggressive push for highway construction, the establishment of the Big Three carmakers (General Motors, Ford, and Chrysler), and an increase in televised advertisements for bigger, flashier, faster cars, led to America's fetishization of cars and car culture. See *Wheels, Tail Fins, and Drive-ins* (1996, no director listed) for a detailed account of America's postwar obsession with cars.

16. See, for example, the October 1959 issue of *Modern Teen*, which offered teens a way to customize their cars on the cheap ("Cool Scallops," 40–41).

17. Thornton's term "subcultural capital" is a play on Pierre Bourdieu's concept of "cultural capital," positioning "hipness" as a currency traded among members of a subculture.

18. In his 1955 study of contemporary youth, *1,000,000 Delinquents*, journalist Benjamin Fine described juvenile delinquency in a similar fashion: "a national epidemic, a serious epidemic" that "can go on spreading and contaminate many good cells in our society" (26, 27–28).

19. Although many JD teenpics address issues of class difference, remarkably few touch on the issue of race, ethnicity, and delinquency. *Teenage Doll* indicates that Squirrel's family members are Mexican immigrants, but her ethnicity is not explicitly addressed in the diegesis. *This Rebel Breed* (1960, Richard L. Bare) is one of the few JD teenpics to include nonwhite characters and to explicitly recognize that 1950s teenagers, like their adult counterparts, were participants in America's racial and ethnic conflicts.

CHAPTER 4

1. See the documentary *Sisters in Cinema* (2003, Yvonne Welbon) for a detailed account of the struggles of African American female directors to find funding and support for their projects in Hollywood.

2. *New Jack City*, press kit, 1991.

3. All box-office figures are taken from www.boxofficemojo.com.

4. As one Hollywood insider reasoned, "Clearly, when a film draws kids in gangs, rival gangs will show up at the theater, and tension will result" (Leach, letter to the editor).

5. In a 1991 letter to the editor of the *New York Times*, the chairman of Columbia Pictures, Frank Price, describes the target audience for *Boyz N the Hood*: "Our marketing campaign sought primarily to reach a young black audience. . . . We also identified a secondary audience we believed would respond to *Boyz N the Hood*. Among them were (1) young white, primarily those who listen to music

like that in the film; (2) older white and black, who would respond to the themes and the reviews we received."

6. In 1991, Jones published "The New Ghetto Aesthetic," a critique of this new film cycle, which I will discuss later in this chapter.

7. See the Conclusion to this book for a more detailed discussion of direct-to-DVD ghetto action films.

8. Although *New Jack City* is the first entry in the ghetto action cycle as well as the first entry to be associated with theater violence, I have excluded it from this analysis since I do not think Warner Bros. was yet aware of the usefulness of exploiting the violence surrounding the film in order to promote it. I argue that *Boyz N the Hood*, released four months after the violence surrounding *New Jack City*'s initial screening, was the first ghetto action film to knowingly incorporate the promise of danger into its marketing campaign.

9. Race films were feature films released concurrently with mainstream, white-cast Hollywood fare, but starring casts composed of African American actors and, usually, helmed by African American directors. Many producers of race movies were motivated to enter the field of filmmaking in order to take control of how African Americans were depicted in the cinema; however, they also saw race movies as an opportunity to exploit a previously untapped market: African American moviegoers.

10. Eric Schaefer argues that silent race films diverge from the classic exploitation film in that they do not rely on the promise (and delivery) of "forbidden spectacle" as their raison d'être (*Bold! Daring! Shocking!*, 75–76). I am arguing that race films do offer their viewers a forbidden spectacle.

11. As mentioned in Chapter 2, the Great Migration (1910–1930) greatly increased the black populations in northeastern cities (Massood, *Black City Cinema*, 12).

12. For more on the history of early black cinema, see Massood, *Black City Cinema*; Bogle, *Toms, Coons, Mulattoes*; Cripps, *Black Film as Genre*; Stewart, *Migrating to the Movies*; Nesteby, *Black Images*; and Antonio, *African American Cinema*.

13. African American ministers also objected to the film because of Micheaux's unflattering depiction of the clergy. Their objections convinced some African American theater owners to not book the film (Siomopoulos, "Birth of a Black Cinema," 114).

14. Between 1882 and 1968, 4,743 lynchings were recorded throughout the United States (Lockard, review).

15. Throughout the 1950s and 1960s, the majority of films that centered on black characters or that took a black point of view were social problem films or "message movies" emphasizing racial oppression and the need for social equality; see, for example, *Nothing But a Man* (1964, Michael Roemer), *A Raisin in the Sun* (1961, Daniel Petrie), and *Guess Who's Coming to Dinner* (1967, Stanley Kramer). While these films illuminated racial issues similar to those later addressed by the blaxploitation cycle, in general, "the portrait of the African American male

painted by the problem pictures was asexual, middle-class, and more rural or suburban than urban" (Massood, *Black City Cinema*, 80). The blaxploitation cycle therefore offered an antidote to these images.

16. *Sweetback*'s estimated production cost was $150,000, and its box-office gross was $15,180,000 (Martinez, Martinez, and Chavez, *What It Is*, 58).

17. The use of hit songs as a marketing technique dates back to at least the 1950s with films like *Rock Around the Clock*.

18. Huey Newton later changed his mind on the subject of blaxploitation films. In a July 1972 article in *Newsweek*, Newton complains that these films "leave revolution out or, if it's in, they make it look stupid and naïve. I think it's part of a conspiracy" (quoted in Michener, "Black Movies," 77).

19. Van Peebles is known for his hyperbolic self-promotion. In an interview published in *What It Is . . . What It Was*, Van Peebles claims: "[*Sweetback*] was so successful that everybody jumped on the bandwagon. The original *Shaft* was a white guy. So when I made all this money, they threw in a couple of 'mother fucks,' found a Black guy, and made themselves a Black detective. That's what happened" (Martinez, Martinez, and Chavez, *What It Is*, 38).

20. A "tent pole" picture is a film that makes enough money to support the rest of a studio's operations, much as a tent pole supports a tent.

21. In his article "The L.A. Rebellion," James Bernard explains: "This was no riot. It was a rebellion" (39).

22. According to most accounts, the year 1989 is when gangsta rap became a widely known subgenre of rap music. However, Robin D. G. Kelley argues that "gangsta lyrics and style" were present from the moment of hip-hop's origins in the South Bronx in the mid-1970s (*Race Rebels*, 186).

23. See Kelley, *Race Rebels*, for a detailed discussion of the socioeconomic factors influencing gangsta rap.

24. Schoolly D, credited with being one of the first gangsta rappers, opined about the suburban teenager's attraction to rap music in a 1990 interview: "It's teenage rebellion. They've got to get something out of their system. Their mom told 'em they got to mow the lawn, and they want to be mad, so they go listen to Eazy-E and get it out of their system" (quoted in Mills, "Gangsta Rapper," 39).

25. In 1990, the *New York Times* printed more than ninety stories on 2 Live Crew, including ones headlined "Shock Greets Banning of a Rap Album" (McFadden) and "An Album is Judged Obscene; Rap: Slick, Violent, Nasty and, Maybe Hopeful" (Pareles). There was also extended coverage in the *Village Voice*, *Time*, *Newsweek*, and Florida-based papers like the *Miami News Times* and the *Ft. Lauderdale Sun-Sentinel* (*Source*, "The Luke Trial," 22).

26. According to many reports, this rape was inspired by the lyrics of Tone-Lōc's sexually charged 1989 single "Wild Thing"; one of the alleged rapists sang the song just after he was arrested.

27. See also, Mermin, "'Searing Portraits': The Persistence of Realism in Black Urban Cinema."

28. The lyrics to "How to Survive in South Central" are as follows:

Rule number one: get yourself a gun
A nine in your ass'll be fine
Keep it in your glove compartment
'Cause jackers (yo) they love to start shit . . .
Rule number two: don't trust nobody
Especially a bitch, with a hooker's body
'Cause it ain't nuttin but a trap
And females'll get jacked and kidnapped . . .
Rule number three: don't get caught up
'Cause niggaz aren't doing anything that's thought up
And they got a vice
On everything from dope, to stolen merchandise.

29. It was believed that the Fruits of Islam's authority was more likely to be respected by the local African American community.

30. *Boyz N the Hood*, press kit, 1991.

31. For example, the theatrical poster for the exploitation film *Because of Eve* (1948, Howard Bretherton) includes a list of screening times that are broken down according to gender and age (Nourmand and Marsh, *Exploitation Poster Art*, 109).

32. In 1991, Shakur's first solo album, *2Pacalypse Now*, gained notoriety when a Texas teenager claimed that the album incited him to shoot and kill a Texas state trooper. Vice President Dan Quayle subsequently made a public statement that the album had "no place in our society" (Phillips, "Music to Kill Cops By?").

33. George Jackson, a coproducer of *New Jack City*, expressed outrage over what he saw as a double standard in how Paramount handled the *Juice* campaign: "I think this is a little unfair, and it's an issue which I think is borderline racism" (quoted in King, "Ads Stir Debate").

34. See also Maslin, "Making a Movie Take the Rap for the Violence That It Attracts."

35. When Fine Line studios was deciding on a release date for *Hangin' with the Homeboys* (1991, Joseph B. Vasquez), a coming-of-age film centering on the lives of African American and Puerto Rican teenagers, it agreed to wait until the hype surrounding *Boyz N the Hood* had died down. Studio executives were fearful that *Hangin' with the Homeboys*, because of its cast and subject matter, would be negatively associated with the allegedly violence-inducing ghetto action cycle. Fine Line's president, Ira Deutchman, explained: "The marketplace is too crowded with films going to black audiences. . . . [*Hangin'*] is really an entirely different kind of film that needs to stand on its own merit" (quoted in Toumarkine, "Release Pushed Back"). In this particular case, being associated with a successful film cycle was a liability rather than an asset.

36. For a sampling of negative contemporary receptions of blaxploitation films, see Riley, "Shaft Can Do Everything"; Griffin, "Black Movie Boom"; Canby, "Does It Exploit Injustice?"; Bennett, "Emancipation Orgasm"; and Ward, *Cultural Condemnation*.

37. Jones's piece appeared in a special issue of the film journal *Wide Angle* devoted the black film boom of the early 1990s.

38. Carol Speed noticed a similar hypocrisy in the reception of the blaxploitation cycle: "[The NAACP, CORE, and the SCLC] came in and said 'Look at what you're doing to our people.' But they never said anything to Clint Eastwood, with his big guns and his 'make my day.' Eastwood was making violent films that Black kids were going to see and nobody said a word to him about it" (quoted in Martinez, Martinez, and Chavez, *What It Is*, 171).

39. See Bournea, "What's the Buzz?"; Sinclair, "Same Old Story"; Mitchell, "Revolution Just May Be Televised"; Rule, "Young Black Film Makers"; and Rogers, "Well-Acted Ghetto Film."

40. All box-office figures are taken from www.boxofficemojo.com.

41. See Hinson, "'Drive' Takes Familiar Route"; Arlinda Smith, "John Singleton Doesn't Mince Words When He Talks to the Press."

42. *Boyz N the Hood* opens with the following titles: "One out of every 21 Black American males will be murdered in their lifetime. Most will die at the hands of another Black male."

43. For more on the process of cycle evolution, see Chapter 2.

CONCLUSION

1. An earlier cycle of film parodies starring Leslie Nielsen and lampooning a variety of film genres and individual blockbusters was popular throughout the 1980s and 1990s. Titles in this cycle include: *Airplane!* (1980, Jim Abrahams and David Zucker), *Airplane II: The Sequel* (1982, Ken Finkleman), *The Naked Gun: From the Files of Police Squad!* (1988, David Zucker), *The Naked Gun 2½: The Smell of Fear* (1991, David Zucker), *Dracula: Dead and Loving It* (1995, Mel Brooks), *Wrongfully Accused* (1998, Pat Proft), and *2001: A Space Travesty* (2000, Alan A. Goldstein).

2. The self-reflexive teen-slasher-movie cycle of the 1990s includes *Scream* (1996, Wes Craven), *Scream 2* (1997, Wes Craven), *I Know What You Did Last Summer* (1997, Jim Gillespie), and *I Still Know What You Did Last Summer* (1998, Danny Cannon).

3. Box-office figures are taken from www.boxofficemojo.com.

4. In his article "Film Parody and the Resuscitation of Genre," Dan Harries offers a broad definition of the contemporary film parody, which includes entries like *Austin Powers: The Spy Who Shagged Me* (1999, Jay Roach), *Galaxy Quest* (1995, Dean Parisot), and *Toy Story* (1995, John Lasseter). While all these films meet Harries's detailed definition of parody, I exclude them from my cycle-parody cycle because these films were not released to capitalize on the popularity of recent film cycles: *Austin Powers* parodies the long-running spy film genre, while *Galaxy Quest* pokes fun at science fiction films. Furthermore, these films are stylistically different from the films I include in the film-cycle-parody cycle in that they generally involve high-profile actors and larger budgets.

5. For this reason, A. O. Scott criticized the plot of *Scary Movie* for being a

"slapdash piece of scaffolding on which to hang bits of humor that are annoying less for their vulgarity than for their tiredness" ("Not Quite a Scream"). Salon .com's Charles Taylor agrees: "*Scary Movie* doesn't offer twists or variations on the plot of *Scream* or *I Know What You Did Last Summer*. It just reproduces scenes from those movies and adds gags, and not terribly good ones, either."

6. By November 2010, Crocker's YouTube video had been viewed more than 35 million times and had received more than 560,000 viewer comments.

7. See Gates, "Romance as Comic Montage"; Holden, "Step Up but Stand Clear of the Guy in the Fat Suit"; LaSalle, "'Epic Movie''s Tries at Satire Fail on Grand Scale"; and Lee "Chipmunks with Rabies? That Is So LL Not Cool J."

8. One notable exception to this rule is the musical-biopic-cycle parody *Walk Hard* (2007, Jake Kasdan). *Walk Hard*'s critical success (of the 135 film reviews considered by the website Rotten Tomatoes, 101 were positive) stems from the fact that the film is not simply a parody of the most iconic moments from *Walk the Line* (2005, James Mangold), *Ray* (2004, Taylor Hackford), and *Beyond the Sea* (2004, Kevin Spacey). Instead, the protagonist, Dewey Cox (John C. Reilly), is a defined character who grows and changes over the course of the film, allowing audiences to see him as a real character rather than a one-dimensional joke. As Roger Ebert explains in his review of the film: "Instead of sending everything over the top at high energy, like *Top Secret!* or *Airplane!*, [the writers] allow Reilly to more or less actually *play* the character, so that, against all expectations, some scenes actually approach real sentiment."

9. With the exception of a few pages in James Naremore's *More than Night* and Aaron Barlow's *The DVD Revolution: Movies, Culture, and Technology*, and one chapter in Linda Ruth Williams's *The Erotic Thriller in Contemporary Cinema*, there is no sustained academic discussion of direct-to-DVD releases. However, there are an increasing number of Internet sites devoted to direct-to-DVD films, including Your Video Store Shelf and Bad Cinema Diary.

10. When Simpson's film was repackaged as a direct-to-DVD release, *US Weekly* and other media outlets covered the story. These accounts generally commented on the box-office failure of Simpson's previous films and questioned the viability of her acting career.

11. I thank Hollis Griffin for drawing these films to my attention.

12. Films in this cycle include *28 Days Later* (2002, Danny Boyle), *Dawn of the Dead* (2004, Zack Snyder), *Resident Evil: Apocalypse* (2004, Alexander Witt), and *Land of the Dead* (2005, George Romero), among others.

13. Its predecessors are *Leprechaun* (1993, Mark Jones), *Leprechaun 2* (1994, Rodman Flender), *Leprechaun 3* (1995, Brian Trenchard-Smith), and *Leprechaun 4: In Space* (1997, Brian Trenchard-Smith).

14. Ice-T appeared in low-budget ghetto action films like *Trespass* (1992, Walter Hill), *Surviving the Game* (1994, Ernest R. Dickerson), *The Wrecking Crew* (1999, Albert Pyun), and *Gangland* (2000, Art Camacho).

15. Maverick Entertainment has its "Spirit" line, a series of Christian uplift films. And many studios, including Lionsgate and Maverick, have created lines of direct-to-DVD films targeted at the Latino market.

Abbott and Costello Meet Frankenstein. Directed by Charles Barton. With Bud Abbott and Lou Costello. 1948. Westlake Entertainment, Inc., 2007. DVD.

Adler, J., and J. Foote. "The Rap Attitude." *Newsweek*, 19 Mar. 1990, 56–59.

Altman, Rick. *Film/Genre*. London: British Film Institute, 1999.

———. *The American Film Musical*. Bloomington: Indiana Univ. Press, 1987.

———. "A Semantic/Syntactic Approach to Film Genre." In Grant, *Film Genre Reader III*, 27–41.

Angels with Dirty Faces. Directed by Michael Curtiz. With James Cagney and Pat O'Brien. 1938. Warner Home Video, 2005. DVD.

Antonio, Sheril. *Contemporary African American Cinema*. New York: Peter Lang, 2002.

Arnold, Thomas K. "Coming Back for Seconds, Thirds." *USA Today* 26 Sept. 2005. 24 July 2009.

Asbury, Edith Evans. "Rock 'n' Roll Teen-Agers Tie Up the Times Square Area." *New York Times*, 23 Feb. 1957.

Aquila, Richard. *That Old-Time Rock n' Roll: A Chronicle of an Era, 1954–63*. Urbana-Champaign: Univ. of Illinois Press, 2000.

Auerbach, Jonathan. "A Valentine's Day Feature: The May Irwin Kiss." 12 Jan. 2009. Available at http://www.newsdesk.umd.edu/culture/release.cfm?ArticleID=1815.

Baker, Laura. "Screening Race: Responses to Theater Violence at *New Jack City* and *Boyz N the Hood*." *Velvet Light Trap* 44 (1999): 4–19. Available at http://www.highbeam.com/doc/1G1-90190337.html.

Balio, Tino. "Hollywood Production Trends in the Era of Globalisation, 1990–99." In *Genre and Contemporary Hollywood*, edited by Steve Neale, 165–184. London: British Film Institute, 2002.

Barlow, Aaron. *The DVD Revolution: Movies, Culture, and Technology*. Westport, Conn.: Praeger, 2005.

Barnes, Brooks. "Direct-to-DVD Releases Shed Their Loser Label." *New York Times*, 28 Jan. 2008. http://www.nytimes.com/2008/01/28/business/media/28dvd.html.

Bates, Karen Grigsby. "'They've Gotta Have Us': Hollywood's Black Directors." *New York Times Magazine*, 14 July 1991, 15–19, 38, 40, 44.

Baudrillard, Jean. *Selected Writings*. 2nd ed. Edited by Mark Poster. Stanford, Calif.: Stanford Univ. Press, 2001.

Baxter, John. "The Gangster Film." In *The Gangster Film Reader*, edited by James Ursini and Alain Silver, 29–38. Pompton Plains, N.J.: Limelight, 2007.

Beatles. *Sgt. Pepper's Lonely Hearts Club Band*. Parlophone/Capitol, 1967. CD.

Because of Eve. Theatrical poster. In Nourmand and Marsh, *Exploitation Poster Art*, 109.

Benjamin, Walter. "On Some Motifs in Baudelaire." In *Illuminations: Essays and Reflections*, 155–200. Edited by Hannah Arendt. Translated by Harry Zohn. New York: Schocken, 1968.

Bennett, Lerone. "The Emancipation Orgasm: Sweetback in Wonderland." *Ebony*, Sept. 1971, 106–116.

Berger, Arthur Asa. *Popular Culture Genres: Theories and Texts*. Vol. 2. Newbury Park, Calif.: Sage, 1992.

Berland, Jody. "Sound, Image and Social Space: Music Video and Media Reconstruction." In *Sound and Vision: The Music Video Reader*, edited by Simon Frith, Andrew Goodwin, and Lawrence Grossberg, 25–43. London: Routledge, 1993.

Bernard, James. "Media Watch." *Source*, May 1990, 14.

———. "The L.A. Rebellion." *Source*, Aug. 1992, 38–42, 45–46, 48.

Berry, Venise. "Redeeming the Rap Music Experience." In Epstein, *Adolescents and Their Music*, 165–187.

Betrock, Alan. *The I Was a Teenage Juvenile Delinquent Rock n' Roll Horror Beach Party Movie Book: A Complete Guide to the Teen Exploitation Film, 1954–1969*. New York: St. Martin's, 1986.

Bogle, Donald. *Toms, Coons, Mulattoes, Mammies, and Bucks: An Interpretive History of Blacks in American Films*. New York: Continuum, 1993.

Boseman, Keith. "Bloods Simple." *Chicago Citizen*, 26 Jan. 1992.

Bourdieu, Pierre. *Distinction: A Social Critique of the Judgment of Taste*. Translated by Richard Nice. Cambridge, Mass.: Harvard Univ. Press, 1984.

Bourget, Jean-Loup. "Social Implications in Hollywood Genres." In Grant, *Film Genre Reader III*, 12–26.

Bournea, R. C. "What's the Buzz? Lights, Camera, Talk, but No Action." *Cincinnati Call and Post*, 21 Oct. 1993.

Bowles, Scott. "'Saw 3D' Will Be Final Cut for Horror Franchise." *USA Today*, 22 July 2010.

Box Office Mojo. *Boyz N the Hood*. Accessed 22 Nov. 2005. http://boxofficemojo .com/movies/?id=boyznthehood.htm.

———. *Clockers*. Accessed 22 Nov. 2005. http://boxofficemojo.com/movies/?id =clockers.htm.

———. *Don't Be a Menace to South Central while Drinking Your Juice in the Hood*. Accessed 29 May 2007. http://boxofficemojo.com/movies/?id=dontbea menacetosouthcentral.htm.

———. *Juice*. Accessed 12 June 2007. http://boxofficemojo.com/movies/?id =juice.htm.

———. *Menace II Society*. Accessed 22 Nov. 2005. http://boxofficemojo.com/ movies/?id=menaceiisociety.htm.

———. *New Jack City*. Accessed 22 Nov. 2005. http://boxofficemojo.com/movies/ ?id=newjackcity.htm.

———. *New Jersey Drive*. Accessed 22 Nov. 2005. http://boxofficemojo.com/ movies/?id=newjerseydrive.htm.

———. *Saw*. Accessed 19 June 2007. http://boxofficemojo.com/movies/?id=saw .htm.

———. *Saw II*. Accessed 19 June 2007. http://boxofficemojo.com/movies/?id =saw2.htm.

———. *Scary Movie*. Accessed 24 July 2009. http://boxofficemojo.com/movies/ ?id=scarymovie.htm.

Boyd, Todd. *Am I Black Enough For You? Popular Culture from the Hood and Beyond*. Bloomington: Indiana Univ. Press, 1997.

————. "Check Yo Self Before You Wreck Yo Self: The Death of Politics in Rap Music and Popular Culture." In Forman and Neal, *That's the Joint!* 325–340.

Boys Town. Directed by Norman Taurog. With Spencer Tracy and Mickey Rooney. 1938. Warner Home Video, 2005. DVD.

Boyz N the Hood. Press Kit, Columbia Pictures, 1991.

Boyz N the Hood. Trailer. 1991. Directed by John Singleton. With Cuba Gooding, Jr., Ice Cube, and Morris Chestnut. TriStar Home Video, 1998. DVD.

Bracker, Milton. "Experts Propose Study of 'Craze.'" *New York Times* 23 Feb. 1957.

Brode, Douglas. *Money, Women, and Guns: Crime Movies from Bonnie and Clyde to the Present*. New York: Carol, 1995.

Bromley, Mary. "It's Your Turn." Letter to the editor. *Ingenue*, Sept. 1960, 9.

Brooks, Karen. "Nothing like Sells like Teen Spirit: The Commodification of Youth Culture." In *Youth Cultures: Texts, Images, and Identities*, edited by Kerry Mallan and Sharyn Pearce, 1–16. Westport, Conn.: Praeger, 2003.

Brooks, Peter. *The Melodramatic Imagination: Balzac, Henry James, Melodrama, and the Mode of Excess*. New York: Columbia Univ. Press, 1985.

Browne, Nick. Preface to *Refiguring American Film Genres: Theory and History*, edited by Nick Browne, xi-xiv. Berkeley and Los Angeles: Univ. of California Press, 1998.

Burton, Jeffery F., et al. *Confinement and Ethnicity: An Overview of World War II Japanese American Relocation Sites*. Seattle: Univ. of Washington Press, 2002.

Busch, Anita, and Andrea King. "Studios Struggle with Urban Marketing." *Hollywood Reporter*, 13 Jan. 1992.

————. "Paramount Marketing Plan for 'Juice' Comes Under Fire." *Hollywood Reporter*, 10 Jan. 1992.

Buscombe, Edward. "The Idea of Genre in the American Cinema." Grant, *Film Genre Reader III*, 12–26.

Canby, Vincent. "'Sweetback': Does it Exploit Injustice?" *New York Times*, 9 May 1971.

Carlisle, Anthony T. "'Juice' Violence: By-Product of Films." *New Pittsburgh Courier*, 1 Feb. 1992.

Carroll, Noel. "Horror and Humor." *Journal of Aesthetics and Art Criticism* 57, no. 2 (1999): 145–160.

Cavell, Stanley. *The World Viewed: Reflections in the Ontology of Film*. New York: Viking, 1971.

Cawelti, John. "*Chinatown* and Generic Transformation in Recent American Films." In Grant, *Film Genre Reader III*, 243–261.

————. *The Six-Gun Mystique*. Bowling Green, Ohio: Bowling Green Univ. Popular Press, 1975.

Christian Science Monitor. "'Boyz N the Hood' Boosts Debate on Urban Violence." 22 July 1991.

————. "Streetwise Film 'Juice' Stirs Up Bad Publicity." 11 Feb. 1992.

Cinema Arts. "Dead End." Sept. 1937, 51–52.

Clarens, Carlos. *Crime Movies: An Illustrated History*. Toronto: McLeod, 1980.

Clarke, Gary. "Defending Ski Jumpers: A Critique of Theories of Youth Subcultures." In *The Subcultures Reader*, edited by Ken Gelder and Sarah Thornton, 169–174. London: Routledge, 1997.

Clarke, John. "Style." In *Resistance through Rituals: Youth Subcultures in Post-war Britain*, edited by Stuart Hall and Tony Jefferson, 175–191. London: Hutchinson, 1975.

Cleveland, Al, Marvin Gaye, and Renaldo "Obie" Benson. "What's Going On." Vocal performance by Marvin Gaye. *What's Going On*. Tamla TS-310, 1971, 33F1/3 rpm.

Cochrane, Kira. "For Your Entertainment." *Guardian*, 1 May 2007. http://www .guardian.co.uk/film/2007/may/01/gender.world.

Crocker, Chris. "Leave Britney Alone!" *YouTube*, 10 Sept. 2007. Accessed 24 July 2009. http://www.youtube.com/watch?v=kHmvkRoEowc&feature=fvwrel.

Cohen, Stanley. *Folk Devils and Moral Panics: The Creation of Mods and Rockers*. New York: St. Martin's, 1980.

Collier, Aldore. "What's behind the Black-on-Black Violence at Movie Theaters." *Ebony*, Oct. 1991. Accessed 14 Dec. 2005. Available at http://findarticles.com/ p/articles/mi_m1077/is_n12_v46/ai_11315786/.

Collins, Jim. "Genericity in the Nineties." In *Film Theory Goes to the Movies*, edited by Jim Collins, Hilary Radner, and Ava Preacher Collins, 242–262. New York: Routledge, 1992.

Cormack, Mike. *Ideology and Cinematography in Hollywood, 1930–1939*. New York: St. Martin's, 1994.

Cose, Ellis. "The Good News about Black America." *Newsweek*, 7 June 1999. http://www.newsweek.com/1999/06/06/the-good-news-about-black-america .html.

Cripps, Thomas. *Black Film as Genre*. Bloomington: Indiana Univ. Press, 1978.

Crouch, Stanley. "Menace, Anyone?" *Washington Post*, 27 June 1993.

Crowther, Bosley. Review of *Angels Wash Their Faces*, directed by Ray Enright. *New York Times*, 4 Sept. 1939.

———. Review of *Blackboard Jungle*, directed by Richard Brooks. *New York Times*, 21 Mar. 1955.

———. "Gnashing of Teeth: Here Are a Few of the Things to Which This Column Took Exception This Year." *New York Times*, 7 Dec. 1941.

———. Review of *East Side Kids*, directed by Bob Hill. *New York Times*, 19 Feb. 1940.

———. Review of *Hell's Kitchen*, directed by Lewis Seiler. *New York Times*, 3 July 1939.

———. Review of *Frankenstein Meets the Wolf Man*, directed by Roy William Neil. *New York Times*, 6 Mar. 1943.

Dead End. Directed by William Wyler. With Humphrey Bogart, Sylvia Sidney, and Joel McCrea. 1937. MGM Home Entertainment, 2005. DVD.

Debord, Guy. *Society of the Spectacle*. Translated by Donald Nicholson-Smith. New York: Zone, 1995.

Dick, Bernard F. *The Star-Spangled Screen: The American World War II Film*. Lexington: Univ. Press of Kentucky, 1985.

Dig! "Has 'Rhythm of Death' Invaded America? 'Voodoo Beat' Blamed for Teen Age Riots Coast to Coast as Music-Maddened Maniacs Maul Many!" Nov. 1956, 39. Reprint of an article originally published in a newspaper.

———. "Letters to the Janitor." Nov. 1956, 4.

———. "Picture Is Excellent . . . Advertising Is Really Rank!" Nov. 1956, 10.

Dirks, Tim. Review of *The Wild One*, directed by Laslo Benedek. Filmsite.org. Accessed 24 Apr. 2007. http://www.filmsite.org/wild.html.

Doane, Mary Ann. *The Desire to Desire: The Women's Film of the 1940s*. Bloomington: Indiana Univ. Press, 1987.

Doherty, Thomas. *Teenagers and Teenpics: The Juvenilization of American Movies in the 1950s*. Boston: Unwin Hyman, 1988.

Dotter, Daniel. "Rock n' Roll Is Here to Stray: Youth Subculture, Deviance, and Social Typing in Rock's Early Years." In Epstein, *Adolescents and Their Music*, 87–114.

Dyson, Michael Eric. "Between Apocalypse and Redemption: John Singleton's *Boyz N the Hood*." *Cultural Critique* 21 (1992): 121–141.

Easton, Nina J. "New Black Films, New Insights." *Los Angeles Times*, 3 May 1991.

Ebert, Roger. Review of *Boyz N the Hood*, directed by John Singleton. *Chicago Sun-Times Online*, 12 July 1991. http://rogerebert.suntimes.com/apps/pbcs .dll/article?AID=/19910712/REVIEWS/107120302/1023.

———. Review of *Fear of a Black Hat*, directed by Rusty Cundieff. *Chicago Sun-Times Online*, 17 June 1994. http://rogerebert.suntimes.com/apps/pbcs .dll/article?AID=/19940617/REVIEWS/406170301/1023.

———. Review of *South Central*, directed by Steve Anderson. *Chicago Sun-Times Online*, 18 Sept. 1992. http://rogerebert.suntimes.com/apps/pbcs. dll/article?AID=/19920918/REVIEWS/209180304/1023.

———. Review of *Walk Hard: The Dewey Cox Story*, directed by Jake Kasdan. *Chicago Sun-Times Online*, 21 Dec. 2007. http://rogerebert.suntimes.com/apps/ pbcs.dll/article?AID=/20071220/REVIEWS/712200306.

Ebony. "Angry, Assertive, and Aware—Young Black Filmmakers." Nov. 1991. Accessed 14 Dec. 2005. http://findarticles.com/p/articles/mi_m1077/is_n1_v47/ ai_11415826/.

Edelstein, David. "Now Playing at Your Local Multiplex: Torture Porn." *New York Magazine*, 28 Jan. 2006. http://nymag.com/movies/features/15622/.

Elsaesser, Thomas. "Tales of Sound and Fury: Observations on the Family Melodrama." In Grant, *Film Genre Reader III*, 366–395.

Encyclopedia.com. "Civilian Conservation Corps." Originally published in the *Dictionary of American History*, 2003. Accessed 22 Nov. 2005. http://www .encyclopedia.com/doc/1G2-3401800850.html.

Epstein, Jonathon S., ed. *Adolescents and Their Music: If It's Too Loud, You're Too Old*. New York: Garland, 1994.

Feuer, Jane. *The Hollywood Musical*. 2nd ed. Bloomington: Indiana Univ. Press, 1993.

Fine, Benjamin. *1,000,000 Delinquents*. New York: World, 1955.

Fischer, Craig. "*Beyond the Valley of the Dolls* and the Exploitation Genre." *Velvet Light Trap* 30 (1992): 18–33.

Fisher, Celeste A. *Black on Black: Urban Youth Films and the Multicultural Audience.* Lanham, Md.: Scarecrow, 2006.

Flynn, Charles. "The Schlock/Kitsch/Hack Movies." In *King of the Bs: Working within the Hollywood System*, edited by Todd McCarthy and Charles Flynn, 3–12. New York: Dutton, 1975.

Focillon, Henri. *The Life of Forms in Art.* 2nd ed. New York: Wittenborn, 1948.

Ford, Andrea. "Slain Girl Was Not Stealing Juice, Police Say." *Los Angeles Times*, 19 Mar. 1991.

Forman, Murray "'Represent': Race, Space, and Place in Rap Music." In Forman and Neal, *That's the Joint!* 201–222.

Forman, Murray, and Mark Anthony Neal, eds. *That's the Joint! The Hip-Hop Studies Reader.* New York: Routledge, 2004.

Franchey, John R. "Victims of Café Society." *New York Times*, 21 Jan. 1940.

Freedman, Max, and James E. Myers. "Rock Around the Clock." Vocal performance by Bill Haley. Decca Records, 1954, 45 rpm.

French, Mary Ann. "The Brothers Grim; 'Menace's' Masterminds: Their 'Specialty' Is Violence." *Washington Post*, 27 June 1993.

Friedlander, Paul. *Rock and Roll: A Social History.* Boulder, Colo.: Westview, 1996.

Fristoe, Roger. Review of *Hell's Kitchen*. Turner Classic Movies. Accessed 22 Nov. 2005. http://www.tcm.com/thismonth/article.jsp?cid=18628&mainArticleId =218460.

Gaines, Donna. "The Local Economies of Suburban Scenes." In Epstein, *Adolescents and Their Music*, 47–66.

Gaines, Jane M. *Fire and Desire: Mixed-Race Movies in the Silent Era.* Chicago: Univ. of Chicago Press, 2001.

Gallagher, Tag. "Shoot Out at the Genre Corral." In Grant, *Film Genre Reader III*, 262–276.

Gardaphé, Fred L. *From Wiseguys to Wise Men: The Gangster and Italian American Masculinities.* New York: Routledge, 2006.

Gates, Anita. "Romance as Comic Montage." Review of *Date Movie*, directed by Aaron Seltzer. *New York Times*, 18 Feb. 2008. http://movies.nytimes.com/ 2006/02/18/movies/18date.html.

Gehring, Wes D. "Comedy Genres." In *Handbook of American Film Genres*, edited by Wes D. Gehring, 105–208. New York: Greenwood, 1988.

Getz, Leonard. *From Broadway to the Bowery: A History and Filmography of the Dead End Kids, Little Tough Guys, East Side Kids and Bowery Boys Films, with Cast Biographies.* Jefferson, N.C.: McFarland, 2004.

Gilbert, James. *A Cycle of Outrage: America's Reaction to the Juvenile Delinquent in the 1950s.* New York: Oxford Univ. Press, 1986.

Gilman, Sander L. *Difference and Pathology: Stereotypes of Sexuality, Race, and Madness.* Ithaca, N.Y.: Cornell Univ. Press, 1985.

Gledhill, Christine. "The Melodramatic Field: An Investigation." In *Home Is*

Where the Heart Is: Studies in Melodrama and the Woman's Film, edited by Christine Gledhill, 5–39. London: British Film Institute, 1987.

Glieberman, Owen. Review of *South Central*, directed by Steve Anderson. EntertainmentWeekly.com, 30 Oct. 1992. http://www.ew.com/ew/article/0,,312191 ,00.html.

Grant, Barry Keith, ed. *Film Genre Reader III*. Austin: Univ. of Texas Press, 2007.

Grant, Barry Keith. Introduction to Grant, *Film Genre Reader III*, xv–xx.

Gray, Frank. "*The Kiss in the Tunnel* (1899), G. A. Smith and the Emergence of the Edited Film in England." In *The Silent Cinema Reader*, edited by Lee Grieveson and Peter Kramer, 51–62. New York: Routledge, 2004.

Grieveson, Lee, Esther Sonnet, and Peter Stanfield. Introduction to *Mob Culture: Hidden Histories of the American Gangster Film*, edited by Lee Grieveson, Esther Sonnet, and Peter Stanfield, 1–11. New Brunswick, N.J.: Rutgers Univ. Press, 2005.

Grieveson, Lee. "Gangsters and Governance in the Silent Era." In Grieveson, Sonnet, and Stanfield, *Mob Culture*, 13–40.

———. "The Thaw-White Scandal, *The Unwritten Law*, and the Scandal of Cinema." In *Headline Hollywood: A Century of Film Scandal*, edited by Adrienne McLean and David A. Cook, 27–51. New Brunswick, N.J.: Rutgers Univ. Press, 2001.

Griffin, Junius. "Black Movie Boom—Good or Bad?" *New York Times* 17 Dec. 1972.

Grossberg, Lawrence. "The Political Status of Youth and Youth Culture." In Epstein, *Adolescents and Their Music*, 25–46.

Guerrero, Ed. *Framing Blackness: The African American Image in Film*. Philadelphia: Temple Univ. Press, 1993.

Gunning, Tom. "An Aesthetic of Astonishment: Early Film and the (In)Credulous Spectator." In *Viewing Positions: Ways of Seeing Film*, edited by Linda Williams, 114–133. New Brunswick, N.J.: Rutgers Univ. Press, 1997.

Hall, Carla. "Jittery Over 'Juice'; Paramount Steps Up Security for Film." *Washington Post* 16 Jan. 1992.

Hall, Stuart, and Tony Jefferson. Introduction to *Resistance through Rituals: Youth Subcultures in Post-war Britain*, edited by Stuart Hall and Tony Jefferson, 5–86. London: Hutchinson, 1975.

Hallam, Julia, and Margaret Marshment. *Realism and Popular Cinema*. Manchester, UK: Manchester Univ. Press, 2000.

Hansen, Miriam. *Babel and Babylon: Spectatorship in American Silent Film*. Cambridge, Mass.: Harvard Univ. Press, 1991.

Harries, Dan. "Film Parody and the Resuscitation of Genre." In *Genre and Contemporary Hollywood*, edited by Steve Neale, 281–293. London: British Film Institute, 2002.

Harris, Keith. *Boys, Boyz, Bois: The Ethics of Black Masculinity in Film and Popular Media*. New York: Routledge, 2006.

Harrison, Sandi. Letter to the editor ("A Definition of a Teenager"). *'Teen Magazine*, May 1958, 7.

Hartmann, Jon. "The Trope of Blaxploitation in Critical Responses to *Sweetback*." *Film History* 6 (1994): 382–404.

Hayes, David, and Brent Walker. *The Films of the Bowery Boys: A Pictorial History of the Dead End Kids*. Secaucus, N.J.: Citadel, 1984.

Hazlett, Courtney. "Jessica Simpson is No 'Major Movie Star.'" MSNBC.com, 16 Dec. 2007. http://today.msnbc.msn.com/id/22288063.

Heath, Stephen. *Questions of Cinema*. Bloomington: Indiana Univ. Press, 1981.

Hebdige, Dick. "Posing . . . Threats, Striking . . . Poses: Youth Surveillance and Display." In *The Subcultures Reader*, edited by Ken Gelder and Sarah Thornton, 393–405. London: Routledge, 1997.

———. *Subculture: The Meaning of Style*. London: Methuen, 1979.

Hendershot, Cyndy. "Monster at the Soda Shop: Teenagers and Fifties Horror Films." *Images: A Journal of Film and Popular Culture*, issue 10, Mar. 2001. http://www.imagesjournal.com/issue10/features/monster/.

Hettrick, Scott. "MGM Homevideo to Jibe with Vibe." Variety.com, 6 Apr. 2005. http://www.variety.com/index.asp?layout=awardcentral&jump=news&articleid=VR1117920627&cs=1&query=hettrick.

High School Confidential! Directed by Jack Arnold. With Russ Tamblyn and Jan Sterling. 1958. Lions Gate Home Entertainment, 2004. DVD.

Hill, Trent. "The Enemy Within: Censorship in Rock Music in the 1950s." In *Present Tense: Rock and Roll Culture*, edited by Anthony DeCurtis, 39–71. Durham, N.C.: Duke Univ. Press, 1992.

Hinson, Hal. "A Director's 'Fresh' Start: Boaz Yakin's Startling, Gritty Debut." Review of *Fresh*, directed by Boaz Yakin. *Washington Post*, 31 Aug. 1994.

———. "'Drive' Takes Familiar Route." Review of *New Jersey Drive*, directed by Nick Gomez. *Washington Post*, 19 Apr. 1995.

Hoberman, J., and Jonathan Rosenbaum. *Midnight Movies*. New York: Da Capo, 1983.

Holden, Stephen. "Teen-Agers Living under the Gun." Review of *Menace II Society*, directed by Allen and Albert Hughes. *New York Times*, 26 May 1993. http://www.nytimes.com/1993/05/26/movies/review-film-teen-agers-living-under-the-gun.html.

———. "Step Up but Stand Clear of the Guy in the Fat Suit." Review of *Dance Flick*, directed by Damien Dante Wayans. *New York Times*, 22 May 2009. http://movies.nytimes.com/2009/05/22/movies/22flic.html.

Hollywood Reporter. "'Menace' Marketing Pays off for New Line." 4 June 1993.

Howe, Desson. "It's Murder Out There." Review of *Boyz N the Hood*, directed by John Singleton. *Washington Post*, 12 July 1991.

Hutchings, Peter. "Genre Theory and Criticism." In *Approaches to Popular Film*, edited by Joanne Hollows and Mark Jancovich, 59–78. Manchester, UK: Manchester Univ. Press, 1995.

I Was a Teenage Werewolf. Directed by Gene Fowler, Jr. With Michael Landon and Yvonne Lime. 1957. The Video Beat. DVD.

Ice Cube. "How to Survive in South Central." Vocal performance by Ice Cube. *Death Certificate*. Priority Records, 1991. Audiocassette. The song was not included on the original album, but was added to later, remastered pressings.

Imitation of Life. Directed by Douglas Sirk. With Lana Turner and John Gavin. 1959. Universal Studios, 2003. DVD.

IMP [Internet Movie Poster] Awards. *Boyz N the Hood*. http://www.impawards.com/1991/boyz_n_the_hood.html. Accessed 20 Dec. 2010.

Internet Movie Database. "*I Was a Teenage Werewolf*." Accessed 10 Aug 2009. http://www.imdb.com/title/tt0050530/.

Italie, Hillel. "Arts Survey Finds Drop in Movie, Museum Attendance." Associated Press, 10 Dec. 2009. Accessed 4 Aug. 2010. Available at http://www.artdaily.com/index.asp?int_sec=2&int_new=34853.

Jafa, Arthur. "Like Rashomon but Different: The New Black Cinema." *Artforum* 31, no. 10 (1993): 10–11. Available at http://findarticles.com/p/articles/mi_m0268/is_n10_v31/ai_14156108/.

Jarrett, Michael. "Concerning the Progress of Rock & Roll." In *Present Tense: Rock and Roll Culture*, edited by Anthony DeCurtis, 167–182. Durham, N.C.: Duke Univ. Press, 1992.

Jet. "Lee Counters Actor's Claim He and Singleton Are to Blame for L.A. Rioting." 1 June 1992, 56.

———. "Who Should Be Blamed for the Violence at Movie Theaters?" 1 Apr. 1991, 57–58.

———. "Why Are Rap Stars So Appealing as Actors?" 31 July 1995. Available at http://findarticles.com/p/articles/mi_m1355/is_n12_v88/ai_17361576/.

JoBlo.com. *Kuffs* poster. Accessed 20 Dec. 2010. http://www.joblo.com/posters/view-poster.php?id=22362.

Jones, Jacquie. "The Accusatory Space." In *Black Popular Culture*, edited by Gina Dent, 95–98. Seattle: Bay Press, 1992.

———. "The New Ghetto Aesthetic." *Wide Angle* 13, nos. 3–4 (1991): 32–43.

Junior G-Men of the Air. Directed by Ray Taylor and Lewis D. Collins. With Billy Halop and Huntz Hall. 1942. Alpha Video Distributors, 2003. DVD.

Kaminsky, Stewart. *American Film Genres: Approaches to a Critical Theory of Popular Film*. 2nd ed. Chicago: Nelson-Hall, 1985.

Kelley, Robin D. G. "Looking for the 'Real' Nigga: Social Scientists Construct the Ghetto." In Forman and Neal, *That's the Joint!* 119–136.

———. *Race Rebels: Culture, Politics, and the Black Working Class*. New York: Free Press, 1994.

Kempley, Rita. "At the Root of the Rage." *Washington Post*, 21 July 1991.

Kenigsberg, Ben. Review of *Date Movie*, directed by Aaron Seltzer. *Village Voice*, 14 Feb. 2006. http://www.villagevoice.com/2006-02-14/film/date-movie/.

Kid Dynamite. Directed by Wallace Fox. With Leo Gorcey and Bobby Jordan. 1943. Alpha Video Distributors, 2002. DVD.

King, Thomas R. "New Black-Youth Film's Ads Stir Debate over Inciting Violence." *Wall Street Journal*, 13 Jan. 1992.

Kisner, Ronald E. "What Films Are Doing to Image of Black Women." *Jet*, 29 June 1972, 56–61.

Kraszewski, Jon. "Recontextualizing the Historical Reception of Blaxploitation: Articulations of Class, Black Nationalism, and Anxiety in the Genre's Advertisements." *Velvet Light Trap* 50 (2002): 48–61.

Lacayo, Richard, Jerome Cramer, and Don Winbush. "The Rap against a Rap Group." *Time*, 25 June 1990. http://www.time.com/time/magazine/article/0,9171,970482,00.html.

Landy, Marcia. *Genres: Cinema and Society, 1930–1960.* Princeton, N.J.: Princeton Univ. Press, 1991.

LaSalle, Mick "'Epic Movie"s Tries at Satire Fail on Grand Scale." Review of *Epic Movie*, directed by Jason Friedberg and Aaron Seltzer. *San Francisco Chronicle*, 29 Jan. 2007. 15 July 2009.

Lawrence, Novotny. *Blaxploitation Films of the 1970s: Blackness and Genre.* New York: Routledge, 2008.

Leach, Sharon J. Letter to the editor. *New York Times*, 21 Feb. 1992.

LeBon, Gustave. *The Crowd: A Study of the Popular Mind.* Mineola, N.Y.: Dover, 2002.

Lee, Nathan. "Chipmunks with Rabies? That Is So LL Not Cool J." Review of *Disaster Movie*, directed by Jason Friedberg and Aaron Seltzer. *New York Times*, 30 Aug. 2008. http://movies.nytimes.com/2008/08/30/movies/30disa.html.

Leitch, Thomas. *Crime Films.* Cambridge: Cambridge Univ. Press, 2002.

Leland, John. "New Jack Cinema Enters Screening." *Newsweek*, 10 June 1991. http://www.newsweek.com/1991/06/09/new-jack-cinema-enters-screening.html.

Leland, John, and Donna Foote. "A Bad Omen for Black Movies?" *Newsweek*, 29 July 1991. http://www.newsweek.com/1991/07/28/a-bad-omen-for-black-movies-mr.html.

Leprechaun 5: Leprechaun in the Hood. Directed by Rob Spera. With Warwick Davis and Ice-T. Trimark Pictures, 2000. DVD.

Lévi-Strauss, Claude. *The Savage Mind.* Edited by Julian Pitt-Rivers and Ernest Gellner. Translated by John Weightman and Doreen Weightman. Chicago: Univ. of Chicago Press, 1968.

Lewis, Jon. *American Film: A History.* New York: Norton, 2008.

———. *The Road to Romance and Ruin: Teens and Youth Culture.* New York: Routledge, 1992.

Life. "Teen-Agers: They Are Still Changing Their Customs to Suit Themselves." Dec. 1948, 67–75.

Lipman, Joanne. "Advertising: Suit Raises Issues of Ad Link to Violence." *Wall Street Journal*, 27 Apr. 1992.

Lippman, Thomas W. "Outbreaks of Violence Mar Opening of 'Juice'; Gunfire Outside Theater Kills Chicago Girl." *Washington Post*, 19 Jan. 1992.

Littlejohn, Janice Rhoshalle. "Black Directors Using DVD to Their Advantage." Associated Press, 19 Jan. 2004. Available at http://articles.latimes.com/2004/jan/19/business/fi-blackfilms19.

Lockard, Joe. Review of *Without Sanctuary: Lynching Photography in America. Bad Subjects*, 7 Apr. 2000. http://bad.eserver.org/reviews/2000/2000-4-7-7.53PM.html.

Lopez, Steve. "Billboard's 'Captivity' Audience Disgusted." *Los Angeles Times*, 18 Mar. 2007. http://articles.latimes.com/2007/mar/18/local/me-lopez18.

Lott, Eric. "Marooned in America: Black Urban Youth Culture and Social Pathology." In *The Underclass Question*, edited by Bill E. Lawson, 71–89. Philadelphia: Temple Univ. Press, 1992.

Lowery, Mark, and Nadirah Z. Sabir. "The Making of 'Hollyhood.'" *Black Enterprise*, Dec. 1994. Accessed 21 Mar. 2006. Available at http://findarticles .com/p/articles/mi_m1365/is_n5_v25/ai_15953347/.

Lubiano, Wahneema. "But Compared to What? Reading Realism, Representation, and Essentialism in *School Daze*, *Do the Right Thing*, and the Spike Lee Discourse." In *Representing Blackness: Issues in Film and Video*, edited by Valerie Smith, 97–122. New Brunswick, N.J.: Rutgers Univ. Press, 1997.

Lynd, Robert, and Helen Lynd. *Middletown: A Study in Modern American Culture*. New York: Harcourt, Brace, Jovanovich, 1956.

Macy, Dick. "Leave Us Alone." *Dig!* Nov. 1956, 22.

Males, Mike. *The Scapegoat Generation: America's War on Adolescents*. Monroe, Me.: Common Courage, 1996.

Maltby, Richard. "The Spectacle of Criminality." In *Violence and American Cinema*, edited by J. David Slocum, 117–147. New York: Routledge, 2001.

———. "Why Boys Go Wrong: Gangsters, Hoodlums, and the Natural History of Delinquent Careers." In Grieveson, Sonnet, and Stanfield, *Mob Culture*, 41–66.

Manhattan Melodrama. Directed by W. S. Van Dyke. With Clark Gable, Myrna Loy, and William Powell. 1934. Warner Home Video, 2007. DVD.

Marchant, Oliver. "Bridging the Micro-Macro Gap: Is There Such a Thing as a Post-subcultural Politics?" In *The Post-Subcultures Reader*, edited by David Muggleton and Rupert Weinzierl, 83–97. Oxford: Berg, 2003.

Markson, Stephen L. "Claims-Making, Quasi-Theories, and the Social Construction of the Rock 'n' Roll Menace." In *Marginal Conventions: Popular Culture, Mass Media, and Social Deviance*, edited by Clinton Sanders, 29–40. Bowling Green, Ohio: Bowling Green State Univ. Popular Press, 1990.

Martinez, Gerald, Diana Martinez, and Andres Chavez. *What It Is . . . What It Was! The Black Film Explosion of the '70s in Words and Pictures*. New York: Hyperion, 1998.

Maslin, Janet. "Making a Movie Take the Rap for the Violence That It Attracts." *New York Times*, 22 Jan. 1992.

Mason, Fran. *American Gangster Cinema: From "Little Caesar" to "Pulp Fiction."* Houndmills, UK: Palgrave MacMillan, 2002.

Massood, Paula. *Black City Cinema: African American Urban Experiences in Film*. Philadelphia: Temple Univ. Press, 2003.

Mast, Gerald. *The Comic Mind: Comedy and the Movies*. Chicago: Univ. of Chicago Press, 1979.

Mayland, Charles. "The Social Problem Film." In *Handbook of American Film Genres*, edited by Wes D. Gehring. New York: Greenwood, 1988.

Mayo, Kierno. "Crying over Spilled *Juice*." *Source*, Apr. 1992, 15.

McArthur, Colin. *Underworld USA*. New York: Viking, 1972.

McCarty, John. *Hollywood Gangland: The Movies' Love Affair with the Mob*. New York: St. Martin's, 1993.

McCreary, Judi. "Hughes' Bad." *Source*, Oct. 1992, 24.

McFadden, Robert D. "Shock Greets Banning of a Rap Album." *New York Times*, 8 June 1990, A10.

McGee, Mark Thomas, and R. J. Robertson. *The JD Films: Juvenile Delinquency in the Movies*. Jefferson, N.C.: McFarland, 1982.

McManus, John T. Review of *Dead End*, directed by William Wyler. *New York Times*, 25 Aug. 1937. http://movies.nytimes.com/movie/review?res=EE05E7 DF1738E467BC4D51DFBE66838C629EDE.

Mermin, Elizabeth. "'Searing Portraits': The Persistence of Realism in Black Urban Cinema." *Third Text* 34 (1996): 3–14.

Merritt, Russell. "Melodrama: Postmortem for a Phantom Genre." *Wide Angle* 5, no. 3 (1983): 26.

Michener, Charles. "Black Movies." *Newsweek*, 23 Oct. 1972, 74, 77–78, 80–81.

Middleton, Ken Feil. *Dying for a Laugh: Disaster Movies and the Camp Imagination*. Middletown, Conn.: Wesleyan Univ. Press, 2005.

Mills, David. "'Boyz' and the Breakthrough; The Violent Birth of Hip Hop Cinema." *Washington Post*, 21 July 1991.

———. "Concentrated Juice; Ernest Dickerson, Emerging from Spike Lee's Shadow." *Washington Post*, 17 Jan. 1992.

———. "The Gangsta Rapper: Violent Hero or Negative Role Model?" *Source*, Dec. 1990, 31–34, 36, 39–40.

Mitchell, Marsha. "Truce Called in Black-Korean Conflict." *Los Angeles Sentinel*, 17 Oct. 1991.

———. "The Revolution Just May be Televised." *Los Angeles Sentinel*, 28 Apr. 1994.

Modern Teen. "Cool Scallops." Oct. 1959, 40–41.

———. Letter to the editor. Oct. 1959, 50.

———. "Uncensored Opinions." Oct. 1959, 24.

Molden, David. "African Americans in Hollywood: A Black-on-Black Shame." *Black Issues in Higher Education*, 11 Jan. 1996. Accessed 12 Dec. 2005. Available at http://findarticles.com/p/articles/mi_moDXK/is_n23_v12/ai_18184081/.

Mulvey, Laura. "Notes on Sirk and Melodrama." In *Home Is Where the Heart Is: Studies in Melodrama and the Woman's Film*, edited by Christine Gledhill, 75–112. London: British Film Institute, 1987.

Munby, Jonathan. *Public Enemies, Public Heroes: Screening the Gangster from "Little Caesar" to "Touch of Evil."* Chicago: Univ. of Chicago Press, 1999.

Murphy, William T. "The United States Government and the Use of Motion Pictures during World War II." In *The Japan/America Film Wars: World War II Propaganda and Its Cultural Contexts*, edited by Abé Mark Nornes and Fukushima Yukio, 59–67. Chur, Switzerland: Harwood Academic, 1994.

Musketeers of Pig Alley, The. Directed by D. W. Griffith. With Lillian Gish and Elmer Booth. Biograph, 1912. Disc 1. *D. W. Griffith: Years of Discovery, 1909–1913*. Image Entertainment, 2002. DVD.

Musser, Charles. *Before the Nickelodeon: Edwin S. Porter and the Edison Manufacturing Company*. Berkeley, and Los Angeles: Univ. of California Press, 1991.

Naremore, James. *More than Night: Film Noir in its Contexts*. Berkeley: University of California Press, 1998.

Neal, Mark Anthony. "Postindustrial Soul: Black Popular Music at the Cross-roads." In Forman and Neal, *That's the Joint!* 363–387.

Neale, Steve. *Genre*. London: British Film Institute, 1980.

———. *Genre and Hollywood*. London: Routledge, 2000.

———. "Melodrama and Tears." *Screen* 27.6 (1986): 6–22.

Nelson, Rob. "It's Only a Movie?" *City Pages*, 12 June 2007. http://blogs.citypages.com/gimmenoise/2007/06/its_only_a_movie.php.

Nemtuskii. "This Is What They Mean by 'Black Humor.'" Internet Movie Database, 31 Mar. 2000. Accessed 16 May 2007. http://www.imdb.com/user/ur0590032/comments.

Nervy Nat Kisses the Bride. Directed by Edwin S. Porter. 1904. *Edison: The Invention of the Movies*. Kino Video, 2005. DVD.

Nesteby, James B. *Black Images in American Films, 1896–1954: The Interplay between Civil Rights and Film Culture*. Washington, D.C.: Univ. Press of America, 1983.

New Jack City. Press kit. Warner Bros., 1991.

Newsweek. "Blacks vs. Shaft." 28 Aug. 1972, 88.

Newton, Huey, "He Won't Bleed Me: A Revolutionary Analysis of 'Sweet Sweetback's Baadasssss Song'." *Black Panther* 6 (1971): A-L.

New York Times. "Curbing Violence in Films." 4 Feb. 1992.

———. "Gas Ends Rock n' Roll Riot." 4 Nov. 1956.

———. "Mrs. Luce Upheld on Film Festival." 4 Sept. 1955.

———. "Princeton Suspends 4." 21 May 1955.

———. "Rock 'n' Roll Fight Hospitalizes Youth." 15 Apr. 1957.

———. "Segregationist Wants Ban on 'Rock and Roll.'" 30 Mar. 1956.

———. "Six Dallas Youths Hurt." 17 July 1957.

———. "Youth Crime Rise Is Held Magnified." 12 Aug. 1957.

———. "Youth Killed on Line to See Movie on Gangs." 25 Apr. 1988.

Nickel, John. "Disabling African American Men: Liberalism and Race Message Movies." *Cinema Journal* 44, no. 1 (2004): 25–48.

Nochimson, Martha P. *Dying to Belong: Gangster Movies in Hollywood and Hong Kong*. Malden, UK: Blackwell, 2007.

Nourmand, Tony, and Graham Marsh. *Exploitation Poster Art*. London: Aurum, 2005.

Nugent, Frank S. Review of *Crime School*, directed by Lewis Seiler. *New York Times*, 11 May 1938.

N.W.A. "Dopeman." Vocal performance by Dr. Dre, Eazy-E, Ice Cube. *Straight Outta Compton*. Ruthless, 1988. Audiocassette.

———. "Fuck Tha Police." Vocal performance by Eazy-E, Ice Cube, and MC Ren. *Straight Outta Compton*. Ruthless, 1988. Audiocassette.

———. *Straight Outta Compton*. Ruthless, 1988. Audiocassette.

Osgerby, Bill. *Youth Media*. London: Routledge, 2004.

Ouellette, Jennifer. "Reclaiming Our Space." *Huffington Post*, 21 June 2007. http://www.huffingtonpost.com/jennifer-ouellette/reclaiming-our-space_b_53161.html.

Palladino, Grace. *Teenagers: An American History*. New York: Basic Books, 1996.

Patterson, Martha. *Beyond the Gibson Girl: Reimagining the American New Woman*. Urbana: Univ. of Illinois Press, 2005.

Pareles, John. "An Album Is Judged Obscene; Rap: Slick, Violent, Nasty and, Maybe, Hopeful." *New York Times*, 17 June 1990.

Parker, Trudy. Letter to the editor. *'Teen Magazine*, May 1958, 6.

Peary, Gerald, "*Little Caesar* Takes Over the Screen." In *Little Caesar*, edited by Gerald Peary, 9–28. Madison: Univ. of Wisconsin Press, 1981.

Pelath, Mike. Letter to the editor. *Dig!* Nov. 1956, 5.

Penalty, The. Directed by Wallace Worsley. With Lon Chaney and Ethel Grey Terry. 1920. Kino International Corp., 2001. DVD.

Phillips, Chuck. "Music to Kill Cops By? Rap Song Blamed in Texas Trooper's Death." *Washington Post*, 20 Sept. 1992.

Photoplay. Review of *Crime School*, directed by Lewis Seiler. Sept. 1938, 6.

———. Review of *Hell's Kitchen*, directed by Lewis Seiler. Oct. 1939, 86.

———. Review of *Little Tough Guy*, directed by Harold Young. Sept. 1938, 70.

———. Review of *Streets of New York*, directed by William Nigh. Oct. 1939, 8.

Pileggi, Nicholas. *Wiseguys: Life in a Mafia Family*. New York: Pocket, 1985.

Piott, Steven L. *American Reformers, 1870–1920: Progressives in Word and Deed*. Lanham, Md.: Rowman and Littlefield, 2006.

Pollack, Phyllis. "FBI Hit List Saprize Part II: Are These Seven Rap Artists under F.B.I. Investigation?" *Source*, Sept. 1990, 18–20.

Powell, Kevin. "Crushed." *Source*, Mar. 1992, 52–53.

Price, Frank. Letter to the editor. *New York Times*, 2 Aug. 1991.

Prince, Stephen. *Classical Film Violence: Designing and Regulating Brutality in Hollywood Cinema, 1930–1968*. New Brunswick, N.J.: Rutgers Univ. Press, 2003.

Pryor, Thomas M. "Local Boys Make Good in Films." *New York Times*, 22 Aug. 1937.

Ptacek, Greg. "Coalition of Black Groups Plans 'Fever,' 'Boyz,' Boycott." *Hollywood Reporter*, 2 July 1991.

———. "Despite Violence, Exhibs Laud 'Boyz.'" *Hollywood Reporter*, 16 July 1991.

Public Enemy, The. Directed by William A. Wellman. With James Cagney and Jean Harlow. 1931. Warner Home Video, 2005. DVD.

Rafter, Nicole Hahn. *Shots in the Mirror: Crime Films and Society*. Oxford: Oxford Univ. Press, 2000.

Rebel without a Cause. Directed by Nicholas Ray. With James Dean and Natalie Wood. 1955. Warner Home Video, 2005. DVD.

Regeneration. Directed by Raoul Walsh. With Rockliffe Fellowes and Anna Q. Nilsson. 1915. Film Preservation Associates, 2001. DVD.

Reid, Mark A. "New Wave Black Cinema in the 1990s." In *Film Genre 2000: New Critical Essays*, edited by Wheeler Winston Dixon, 13–26. Albany: State Univ. of New York Press, 2000.

Reinhold, Robert. "Police Deployed to Curb Gangs in Los Angeles." *New York Times*, 9 Apr. 1988.

Renov, Michael. "Warring Images: Stereotype and American Representations of the Japanese, 1941–1991." *The Japan/America Film Wars: World War II Propa-*

ganda and its Cultural Contexts, edited by Abé Mark Nornes and Fukushima Yukio, 95–118. Chur, Switzerland: Harwood Academic, 1994.

Riley, Clayton. "Shaft Can Do Everything—I Can Do Nothing." *New York Times*, 13 Aug. 1972.

———. "What Makes Sweetback Run?" *New York Times*, 9 May 1971.

Roaring Twenties, The. Directed by Raoul Walsh. With James Cagney and Humphrey Bogart. 1939. Warner Home Video, 2005. DVD.

Robbins, William. "Armed, Sophisticated and Violent, Two Drug Gangs Blanket Nation." *New York Times*, 25 Nov. 1988.

Rock Around the Clock. Directed by Fred F. Sears. With Johnny Johnston and Alix Talton. 1956. Sony Pictures Home Entertainment, 2006. DVD.

Roffman, Peter, and Jim Purdy. *The Hollywood Social Problem Film: Madness, Despair, and Politics from the Depression to the Fifties*. Bloomington: Indiana Univ. Press, 1981.

Rogers, Charles E. "'Fresh': Disturbing, Powerful, Well-Acted Ghetto Film." *New York Amsterdam News*, 27 Aug. 1994.

Rose, Tricia. *Black Noise: Rap Music and Black Culture in Contemporary America*. Hanover, N.H.: Wesleyan Univ. Press/Univ. Press of New England, 1994.

———. "Hidden Politics: Discursive and Institutional Policing of Rap Music." In *Droppin' Science: Critical Essays on Rap Music and Hip Hop Culture*, edited by William Eric Perkins, 236–257. Philadelphia: Temple Univ. Press, 1996.

———. "Rap Music and the Demonization of Young Black Males." *USA Today Magazine*, May 1994. Accessed 18 June 2007. Available at http://findarticles.com/p/articles/mi_m1272/is_n2588_v122/ai_15282517/.

Rosenblatt, Josh. Review of *Disaster Movie*, directed by Jason Friedberg and Aaron Seltzer. *Austin Chronicle*, 5 Sept. 2008. http://www.austinchronicle.com/gyrobase/Calendar/Film?Film=oid%3A664798.

Ross, Steven. *Working Class Hollywood: Silent Film and the Shaping of Class in America*. Princeton, N.J.: Princeton Univ. Press, 1998.

Rosow, Eugene. *Born to Lose: The Gangster Film in America*. New York: Oxford Univ. Press, 1978.

Rotten Tomatoes. *Walk Hard*. Accessed 10 Aug. 2009. http://www.rottentomatoes.com/m/walk_hard/.

Rule, Sheila. "Young Black Film Makers Face the Aftermath of Success." *New York Times*, 11 Aug. 1994.

Ruth, David E. *Inventing the Public Enemy: The Gangster in American Culture, 1918–1934*. Chicago: Univ. of Chicago Press, 1996.

Ryall, Tom. "Teaching through Genre." *Screen Education* 17 (1975–1976): 27–35.

Samuels, David. "The Rap on Rap: The 'Black Music' That Isn't Either." In Forman and Neal, *That's the Joint!* 147–153.

Samuels, Gertrude. "Why They Rock 'n' Roll—And Should They?" *New York Times*, 12 Jan. 1958.

Sarris, Andrew. "Big Funerals: The Hollywood Gangster, 1927–1933." In *The Gangster Film Reader*, edited by James Ursini and Alain Silver, 85–96. Pompton Plains, N.J.: Limelight, 2007.

Scarface. Directed by Howard Hawks. With Paul Muni and Ann Dvorak. 1932. Universal Studios, 2003. DVD.

Schaefer, Eric. *"Bold! Daring! Shocking! True!": A History of Exploitation Films, 1919–1959*. Durham, N.C.: Duke Univ. Press, 1999.

———. "Of Hygiene and Hollywood: Origins of the Exploitation Film." *Velvet Light Trap* 30 (1992): 34–47.

Schatz, Thomas. *Hollywood Genres: Formulas, Filmmaking, and the Studio System*. New York: Random House, 1981.

———. "The Structural Influence: New Directions in Film Genre Study." In Grant, *Film Genre Reader III*, 91–101.

Sconce, Jeffery. "Trashing the Academy: Taste, Excess, and an Emerging Politics of Cinematic Style." *Screen* 36, no. 4 (1995): 371–393.

Scott, A. O. "It's Not Quite a Scream and Not Quite a Spoof." Review of *Scary Movie*, directed by Keenen Ivory Wayans. *New York Times*, 7 July 2000. http://movies.nytimes.com/movie/review?res=9C02EFDB1F39F934A35754C0A966 9C8B63.

Seate, Mike. *Two Wheels on Two Reels: A History of Biker Movies*. North Conway, N.H.: Whitehorse, 2000.

Shadoian, Jack. *Dreams and Dead Ends: The American Gangster/Crime Film*. Cambridge, Mass.: MIT Press, 1977.

Shary, Timothy. *Generation Multiplex: The Image of Youth in Contemporary American Cinema*. Austin: Univ. of Texas Press, 2002.

Simon, Jeff. "'Menace,' Gripping to the End." *Buffalo News*, 5 June 1993.

Simpson, Janice. "Not Just One of the Boyz." *Time*, 23 Mar. 1992. http://www.time.com/time/magazine/article/0,9171,975139-1,00.html.

Sinclair, Abiola. "'Sugar Hill': Same Old Story to Take Your Money, Honey." *New York Amsterdam News*, 5 Mar. 1994.

Singer, Ben. "Female Power in the Serial-Queen Melodrama: The Etiology of an Anomaly." *Camera Obscura* 22 (1990): 90–129.

Singleton, John. Interview by Benilde Little. "John Singleton—Afro-American Filmmaker." *Essence*, Sept. 1991.

Siomopoulos, Anna. "The Birth of a Black Cinema: Race, Reception, and Oscar Micheaux's *Within Our Gates*." *Moving Image* 6, no. 2 (2006): 111–118.

Sisters in Cinema. Directed by Yvonne Welbon. With Maya Angelou, Julie Dash, and Cheryl Dunye. 2003. Our Film Works, 2003. DVD.

Sklar, Robert. *Film: An International History of the Medium*. 2nd ed. Upper Saddle River, N.J.: Prentice Hall, 2001.

Smart Alecks. Directed by Wallace Fox. With Leo Gorcey and Bobby Jordan. 1942. Alpha Video Distributors, 2002. DVD.

Smith, Arlinda. "John Singleton Doesn't Mince Words When He Talks to the Press." *Afro-American Red Star*, 7 Aug. 1993.

Smith, Valerie. "The Documentary Impulse in Contemporary U.S. African-American Film." In *Black Popular Culture*, edited by Gina Dent, 56–64. Seattle: Bay Press, 1992.

Smith-Shomade, Beretta E. "'Rock-a-Bye, Baby!': Black Women Disrupting Gangs and Constructing Hip-Hop Gangsta Films." *Cinema Journal* 42, no. 2 (2003): 25–40.

Snead, James. *White Screens/Black Images*. New York: Routledge, 1994.

Sobchack, Thomas "Genre Film: A Classical Experience." In Grant, *Film Genre Reader III*, 103–114.

Soloway, Jill, et al. "Action Letter." *Remove the Rating* (blog). 22 Mar 2007. http://www.removetherating.blogspot.com/.

———. "Remove the Rating for *Captivity*." *Huffington Post*. 27 Mar. 2007. http://www.huffingtonpost.com/jill-soloway/remove-the-rating-for-cap_b_44404.html.

Sonnet, Esther. "Ladies Love Brutes: Reclaiming Female Pleasures in the Lost History of Hollywood Gangster Cycles, 1929–1931." In Grieveson, Sonnet, and Stanfield, *Mob Culture*, 93–119.

Sonnet, Esther, and Peter Stanfield. "'Good Evening Gentlemen; Can I Check Your Hats Please?': Masculinity, Dress, and the Retro Gangster Cycles of the 1990s." In Grieveson, Sonnet, and Stanfield, *Mob Culture*, 163–184.

Source. "The Luke Trial." Jan. 1991, 22.

South Central. Press kit. Warner Bros. Pictures, 1992.

Sparber, Max. "L.A. Story: A Few Helpful Tips on How Not to Get Beaten Up in a Race Riot." *City Pages*, 13 Feb. 2002. http://www.citypages.com/2002-02-13/arts/l-a-story/.

Spiegler, Marc. "Marketing Street Culture: Bringing Hip Hop Style to the Mainstream." *American Demographics*, Nov. 1996. *Find Articles*. Accessed 17 Sept. 2004. Available at http://findarticles.com/p/articles/mi_m4021/is_n11_v18/ai_18819521/.

Sptbgjen. "Boring Tripe." *Internet Movie Database*, 2 Nov. 2000. Accessed 16 May 2007. http://www.imdb.com/user/ur0708063/comments.

Stagecoach. Directed by John Ford. With John Wayne and Claire Trevor. 1939. Warner Home Video, 2007. DVD.

Stahl, Geoff. "Tastefully Renovating Subcultural Theory: Making Space for a New Model." In *The Post-Subcultures Reader*, edited by David Muggleton and Rupert Weinzierl, 27–40. Oxford: Berg, 2003.

Staiger, Janet. *Perverse Spectators: The Practices of Film Reception*. New York: New York Univ. Press, 2000.

———. "Taboos and Totems: Cultural Meanings of *The Silence of the Lambs*." In *Film Theory Goes to the Movies*, edited by Jim Collins, Hillary Radner, and Ava Collins, 142–183. New York: Routledge, 1993.

Stead, Peter. *Film and the Working Class: The Feature Film in British and American Society*. London: Routledge, 1989.

Stewart, Jacqueline Najuma. *Migrating to the Movies: Cinema and Black Urban Modernity*. Berkeley and Los Angeles: University of California Press, 2005.

Surowiecki, James. "If It's Wednesday, a Black Film Must be Opening." Salon.com, 13 Aug. 1997. http://www.salon.com/aug97/media/media970813.html.

Swanson, Tim. "Direct-to-DVD: H'wood's New Boom Biz." Portfolio.com, 20 Apr. 2007. http://www.portfolio.com/views/blogs/the-hollywood-deal/2007/04/20/direct-to-dvd-hwoods-new-boom-biz/.

Sweet Sweetback's Baadasssss Song. Press kit. Cinemation Industries, 1971.

———. Theatrical poster. In Nourmand and Marsh, *Exploitation Poster Art*, 118.

Szatmary, David P. *Rockin' in Time: A Social History of Rock-and-Roll.* 3rd ed. Upper Saddle River, N.J.: Prentice Hall, 1987.

Taves, Brian. "The B Film: Hollywood's Other Half." In *Grand Design: Hollywood as a Modern Business Enterprise, 1930–1939,* edited by Tino Balio, 313–350. New York: Scribner's, 1993.

Taylor, Charles. Review of *Scary Movie,* directed by Keenen Ivory Wayans. Salon.com, 7 July 2000. http://dir.salon.com/ent/movies/review/2000/07/07/scary_movie/index.html.

'Teen. "Editor's Letter." June 1957, 1.

———. "Editor's Letter." May 1958, 7.

Teenage Doll. Directed by Roger Corman. With June Kenney and Fay Spain. 1957. Image Entertainment, 2000. DVD.

'Teen Life. "Editor's Letter." Apr. 1957, 5.

Teens Today. Letter to the editor ("He Looks Like a Hood"). Mar. 1961, 5.

Thatcher, Mary Anne. *Immigrants and the 1930's: Ethnicity and Alienage in Depression and On-Coming War.* New York: Garland, 1990.

Thompson, Dave. *Black and White and Blue: Adult Cinema from the Victorian Age to the VCR.* Toronto: ECW, 2007.

Thompson, Richard. "Sam Katzman: Jungle Sam, or the Return of 'Poetic Justice, I'd Say' (1969)." In *King of the Bs: Working within the Hollywood System,* edited by Todd McCarthy and Charles Flynn, 71–80. New York: Dutton, 1975.

Thornton, Sarah. "The Social Logic of Subcultural Capital." In *The Subcultures Reader,* edited by Ken Gelder and Sarah Thornton, 200–212. London: Routledge, 1997.

Time. "Bobby-Soxers' Gallup." 13 Aug. 1956. http://www.time.com/time/magazine/article/0,9171,865481,00.html.

———. "Cinema: Shock Around the Clock." Review of *I Was a Teenage Werewolf,* directed by Gene Fowler. 9 Sept. 1957. http://www.time.com/time/magazine/article/0,9171,893673,00.html.

———. "The Manicured Fistful." 25 July 1955. http://www.time.com/time/magazine/article/0,9171,891500,00.html.

———. "Power to the Peebles." 16 Aug. 1971. http://www.time.com/time/magazine/article/0,9171,877217,00.html.

———. Review of *Angels with Dirty Faces,* directed by Michael Curtiz. 5 Dec. 1938. http://www.time.com/time/magazine/article/0,9171,760398,00.html.

———. Review of *Dead End,* directed by William Wyler. 6 Sept. 1937. http://www.time.com/time/magazine/article/0,9171,758163,00.html.

———. "Rock 'n' Roll." 23 July 1956. http://www.time.com/time/magazine/article/0,9171,865369,00.html.

————. "Yeh-Heh-Heh-Hes, Baby." 18 June 1956. http://www.time.com/time/magazine/article/0,9171,862239,00.html.

Toumarkine, Doris. "'Homeboys' Release Pushed Back to Oct." *Hollywood Reporter*, 22 July 1991.

Travers, Mary Ann. Letter to the editor ("Troubled Fan"). *Dig!*, 1960, 24.

Tropiano, Stephen. *Rebels and Chicks: A History of the Hollywood Teen Movie*. New York: Back Stage, 2006.

T.S. Review of *Pride of the Bowery*, directed by Joseph H. Lewis. *New York Times*, 24 Jan. 1941.

Tubbs, Darlene. Letter to the editor ("That Car of Yours"). *Dig!* Nov. 1956, 23.

Tudor, Andrew. "Genre." In Grant, *Film Genre Reader III*, 3–11.

————. *Theories of Film*. London: Secker and Warburg, 1974.

Turnquist, Kristi. "Violent Film Moved." *Portland Oregonian*, 26 May 1993.

2 Live Crew. *As Nasty as They Wanna Be*. Luke Records, 1989. Audiocassette.

Upski. "We Use Words like 'Mackadocious' (and Other Progress from the Front Lines of the White Struggle." *Source*, May 1993, 64–66.

USMagazine.com. "Jessica Simpson Movie Going Straight to DVD." 31 Oct. 2008. Available at http://www.huffingtonpost.com/2008/10/31/jessica-simpson-movie-goi_n_139592.html.

Vieira, Mark. *Sin in Soft Focus: Pre-Code Hollywood*. New York: Abrams, 1999.

Wallace, Michelle. "*Boyz N the Hood* and *Jungle Fever*." In *Black Popular Culture*, edited by Gina Dent, 123–131. Seattle: Bay Press, 1992.

Ward, Francis. *"Super Fly": A Political and Cultural Condemnation by the Kuumba Workshop*. Edited by Don Lee and Sterling D. Plumpp. Chicago: Institute of Positive Education, 1972.

Warshow, Robert. "The Gangster as Tragic Hero." In *The Immediate Experience: Movies, Comics, Theatre, and Other Aspects of Popular Culture*, 127–134. New York: Atheneum, 1974.

Watkins, S. Craig. "Ghetto Reelness: Hollywood Film Production, Black Popular Culture, and the Ghetto Action Film Cycle." In *Genre and Contemporary Hollywood*, edited by Steve Neale, 236–250. London: British Film Institute, 2002.

————. *Representing: Hip Hop Culture and the Production of Black Cinema*. Chicago: Univ. of Chicago Press, 1998.

Watson, Paul. "There's No Accounting for Taste: Exploitation Cinema and the Limits of Film Theory." In *Trash Aesthetics: Popular Culture and Its Audience*, edited by Deborah Cartmell, I. Q. Hunter, Heidi Kaye, and Imelda Whelehan, 66–83. London: Pluto, 1997.

Watts, Eric K. "An Exploration of Spectacular Consumption: Gangsta Rap as Cultural Commodity." In Forman and Neal, *That's the Joint!* 593–609.

Watts, Eric K., and Mark P. Orbe. "The Spectacular Consumption of 'True' African American Culture: 'Whassup' with the Budweiser Guys?" In *Channeling Blackness: Studies on Television and Race in America*, edited by Darnell M Hunt, 225–242. New York: Oxford Univ. Press, 2005.

Wayans, Shawn, and Marlon Wayans. Interview by Cynthia Fuchs. Pop Matters.

Accessed 12 Dec. 2005. http://www.popmatters.com/film/interviews/wayans .shtml.

Weinzierl, Rupert, and David Muggleton. "What is 'Post-Subcultural Studies' Anyway?" In *The Post-Subcultures Reader*, edited by David Muggleton and Rupert Weinzierl, 3–26. Oxford: Berg, 2003.

Wheels, Tail Fins, and Drive-Ins. No director listed. Unapix, 1996. DVD.

White, Armond. "Hollywood Fades to Black." *Essence*, July 1991.

Williams, Linda. "Melodrama Revised." In *Refiguring American Film Genres: Theory and History*, edited by Nick Browne, 42–88. Berkeley and Los Angeles: Univ. of California Press, 1998.

———. *Playing the Race Card: Melodramas of Black and White from Uncle Tom to O.J. Simpson*. Princeton, N.J.: Princeton Univ. Press, 2001.

———. *Screening Sex*. Durham, N.C.: Duke Univ. Press, 2008.

Williams, Linda Ruth. *The Erotic Thriller in Contemporary Cinema*. Bloomington: Indiana Univ. Press, 2005.

Within Our Gates. Directed by Oscar Micheaux. With Evelyn Preer and James D. Ruffin. 1920. Grapevine Video, 2007. DVD.

Wood, Robin. *Hollywood from Vietnam to Reagan*. New York: Columbia Univ. Press, 1986.

Wright, Judith Hess. "Genre Films and the Status Quo." In Grant, *Film Genre Reader III*, 42–50.

Wright, Will. *Sixguns and Society: A Structural Study of the Western*. Berkeley and Los Angeles: Univ. of California Press, 1975.

Yaquinto, Marilyn. *Pump 'Em Full of Lead: A Look at Gangsters on Film*. New York: Twayne, 1998.

Young MC. "Wild Thing." Vocal performance by Tone Lōc. *Lōc'ed After Dark*. Delicious Vinyl, 1988. Audiocassette.

YouTube. "*Menace II Society* Theatrical Trailer." 18 Feb. 2007. http://www .youtube.com/watch?v=CD2pjnGy8Fk&feature=related.

Zavattini, Cesare. "Some Ideas on the Cinema." In *Vittorio De Sica: Contemporary Perspectives*, edited by Howard Curle and Stephen Snyder, 50–61. Toronto: Univ. of Toronto Press, 2000.

Page numbers in *italics* indicate photos.

243